RECLAIMING BHARAT

ASHUTOSH

RECLAIMING BHARAT

WHAT CHANGED IN 2024 AND WHAT LIES AHEAD

WESTLAND
NON·FICTION

WESTLAND
NON·FICTION

Published by Westland Non-Fiction, an imprint of Westland Books, a division of Nasadiya Technologies Private Limited, in 2025

No. 269/2B, First Floor, 'Irai Arul', Vimalraj Street, Nethaji Nagar, Alapakkam Main Road, Maduravoyal, Chennai 600095

ISBN: 9789360451554

10 9 8 7 6 5 4 3 2 1

Typeset by Mukul

Printed at Thomson Press (India) Ltd

For Mogu/ Motu/Poco Loco ...

An angel who came to bless us for eighteen and a half years.

The purest soul ever.

Contents

Contents

Introduction

THE 2024 PARLIAMENTARY ELECTIONS WERE NO ORDINARY elections. They were probably the most important elections that the country has seen since 1977. They were exceptional because the results went on to allay fears that our democracy was in danger and that an amended Constitution would take us back to a medieval sensitivity. In many ways, these elections were about the battle to preserve the basic ethos of the Constitution and ensure that, come what may, the rights of the citizens would not be mortgaged to the unbridled power of the state. They were also about fighting to save the soul of an ancient civilisation in danger of losing the grandeur of its cultural diversity. Finally, this was an election to save elections and electoral democracy.

The results of the 2024 elections show that the people's concerns were genuine, and serious introspection is needed by the present dispensation and all those who control the levers of power. It is true that the 'will of the people' has not expressed itself in clear terms; it has not given a clear mandate to one particular group. In fact, the verdict is split; it is a kind of no-confidence motion against the entire political class. If the

Bharatiya Janata Party (BJP) has not won the election, then the opposition led by the Congress has not lost it either. Neither BJP nor Congress is in a position to form the government on its own. The people's mandate is simple: collaboration and partnership should be the rule of thumb if we want to sustain and strengthen democracy. No one group or ideology should be in a position to dictate terms to others. The message is simple: Narendra Modi can be the prime minister, but he has to change his style of governance; he has to take everyone along; and he has to listen to other stakeholders. His dictum of 'my way or the highway' cannot be allowed to prevail. The voters have dictated that the equilibrium of Indian democracy, which had shifted to the right, should return to the Centre. There is also a message for the opposition that they must reinvent themselves; the old style of politics, laden with corruption and entitlement, must go. People-centric politics is the need of the hour. Rahul Gandhi cannot claim to be the natural inheritor of the opposition space; he has to fight; he has to face the government's wrath and earn the people's goodwill.

It was an important election for the nation, but people like me, who have faith in the civilisational ethos of the country and its democratic moorings, were not surprised by the results at all. From day one, I was of the opinion—and I said it often, categorically and unhesitatingly—that it would not be easy for BJP and Modi to win a majority for the third consecutive term. In television debates during the elections, when I said that BJP would struggle to get a simple majority, I was mocked by opponents and ridiculed by colleagues. They would point out that after the consecration of the Ram Temple in Ayodhya, the opposition was left with no chance of a win. In fact, a senior election analyst told me that Congress would be lucky to retain 52 seats. He believed Congress might end up with its worst-ever performance. A few predicted less than forty seats for the grand old party.

Of course, this was the time when the Congress-led Indian Nationalist Developmental Inclusive Alliance (INDIA) was in total disarray. There was no strategy, leadership or coordination among the alliance partners. Despite tall claims in the three joint opposition meetings held prior to the assembly elections in five states in December 2023, no joint rally could be organised, and no common agenda for governance could be presented before the people to counter Modi's national vision. But I could sense a strong anti-incumbency against the Modi government. Unemployment and price rise were huge issues. People were genuinely upset. A sense of disillusionment with the government's delivery was discernible. Modi's magic was fading. But thanks to the ruling party's strong propaganda, a few political analysts strongly pushed BJP's theory of the invincibility of Modi. Guided by hubris, BJP took its victory for granted. Consequently, leaders in the opposition appeared demoralised.

Within Congress, there was talk that Rahul Gandhi was not interested in the 2024 battle; rather, he was preparing for 2029. His second Bharat Jodo Yatra was seen from this perspective. Around this time, I had a chat with a Samajwadi Party leader, who told me that the party could not win more than half a dozen seats in Uttar Pradesh (UP), and it had decided to identify two dozen seats and pool all its resources and energy there, as there was no point in wasting money contesting all 80 seats. However, the situation changed as the campaign for the first phase of polling neared. One could tell that Modi's rhetoric was not enthusing people anymore. Indifference and lack of enthusiasm among BJP voters shook the party, and they realised that their party might be on a sticky wicket. The slogan 'Abki baar 400 paar' was a defensive strategy. The brazen communalisation of the election campaign by the prime minister himself also pointed towards BJP having sensed defeat. From the first phase of polling onwards, BJP's endeavour was to save itself from a surprise humiliation on 4 June 2024.

But BJP, led by Modi, could not face defeat. That would have been apocalyptic for the Rashtriya Swayamsevak Sangh (RSS) agenda. A defeat at the Centre would halt what I've called in my book *Hindu Rashtra* the 'march of the Ideological State' that the Sangh Parivar had put in motion since 2014, after winning a majority in Parliament. Political analysts often make the mistake of assuming that BJP is just like any other party. Unlike Congress and the old socialist parties, BJP is an ideological party with a clear plan for the future, and its concept of the nation and of Indian society is diametrically opposite to the vision of Mahatma Gandhi and Jawaharlal Nehru. Their idea is to radically redesign Indian civilisation; it is to re-engineer the Indian nation; to change the basic contours of Indian polity, and create a new consciousness, which they proudly call 'Hindu consciousness'. It intends to create a Hindu Rashtra in which Hindus will have primacy and members of other faiths will have a secondary role. This is why the regime change in 2014 was no ordinary transfer of power.

With the appointment of Modi as the prime minister and his cabinet in 2014, the basic nature of the government changed. This was akin to what happened on 15 August 1947. What happened at the time of Independence was not a simple transfer of power between the two regimes, or simply a change of the government. With the transfer of power from the British to Indians, the basic nature of the government changed. What also changed was the nature of the relationship between the government and the people. It was no longer a relationship of master and slave. Now, India came to be governed by Indians and we became masters of our own destiny. Once the Constitution was adopted, the people became sovereign. Despite the civilisational inequality ingrained in our culture, equality before the law became the defining principle of the society and polity. From then on, every individual, irrespective of their placement in the caste hierarchy, was equal in the eyes of the law. People now had the power to choose their rulers and the power to change them. India was a democracy, and its rulers were not nominated by the Crown of England but elected by the people.

I know my left-liberal friends will lynch me for saying this, but there is no denying the fact that what the country witnessed in May 2014, when Modi was sworn in as the prime minister, was not a routine affair. It was nothing less than a revolution. A revolution has three distinct characteristics: it is defined by 'disconnectedness' from the past, 'disruption' in the present and 'de-construction' of the future. A revolution is a transformative change, catalysed by an ideology or a thought process with a promise of paradise (of a better and safer future), of relieving the people from the trauma and tribulations of the past, and scourge of the present. The construction of utopia is the driving force behind the whole process. This is why I say that, with the regime change in 2014, a revolution unfolded. Since then, one can easily see how a concerted attempt has been made to delink the present regime from the immediate past. It has made every effort to distance itself from the Nehruvian consensus, which was the hallmark of India since gaining independence. Steps were taken to discredit and malign Nehru and Congress, painting them as villains of history. Every attempt was made to colour them responsible for every malaise in the country. Disruption was the order of the day. One may not say it, but disruption in the present times can be felt in every walk of life. The relationship between different communities and faiths has transformed. One can see a qualitative change in the response of the constitutional institutions. Even fiercely independent institutions, like the media and the judiciary, have been accused of collaborating with the government. Highly exaggerated national security concerns have hijacked human and individual rights. And all this is done to chase their version of utopia, to make India in the future a Hindu Rashtra, a Vishwa Guru.

Every revolution has its self-styled vanguards who lead and promise to take the transformation to its logical conclusion. The communist party of the USSR evolved the concept of 'dictatorship of the proletariat'; the Iranian revolution created the 'council of clerics' who monitor, supervise and lead the transformation; and in the Indian context, the idea of transformation was engineered, propagated and powered by an organisation founded in 1925, led by K.B. Hedgewar. The organisation is called the Rashtriya Swayamsevak Sangh, and its perseverance and that of its leaders has shaped and galvanised the thought process of Hindutva through several audacious initiatives, creating a political machine that captured power in 2014. This machine, led by Narendra Modi, is called the Bhartiya Janata Party.

15 August 1947 marked a radical change in the nature of politics in India. If politics before that date was to free the country from the colonial power, then in post-Independence India politics was defined by the ethos of nation-building and its processes. Gandhi's genius lay in making politics a mass movement, taking every section of society along and minimising the fissures created by caste and religion. Gandhi was heavily criticised at one end of the spectrum by Babasaheb Ambedkar and at the other by merchants of religious politics. Both Muslim League, led by Mohammad Ali Jinnah, and Hindu Mahasabha, led by V.D. Savarkar, were opposed to Gandhi's idea of India

being a composite nation. They advocated the 'two-nation theory'. The RSS, though not very powerful at that time, differed from Gandhi on the 'Muslim question'. Despite being a loyal Congressman and an admirer of Gandhi, Hedgewar was opposed to giving any concessions to Muslims. He believed that 'the day Muslims will realise that Hindus are more united and are capable of attaining freedom, they [Muslims] will join the mainstream.'[1]

While India gained independence, it paid a heavy price for communal politics. Along with independence came the partition. Gandhi's politics was endowed with ethical boundaries. He fought with the British but did not hate them. He did not agree with Ambedkar and Syama Prasad Mookerjee but asked Nehru to induct them into his cabinet. After Independence, India evolved a national consensus. The Constitution was the product of that consensus. But the RSS and its political wing, Jan Sangh, and later BJP, had differing views. They were, and are, armed with a well-structured ideology. Their guiding principle is 'Hindutva', propounded by Savarkar, whose sociopolitical contours were defined by M.S. Golwalkar, the second chief of the RSS. According to them, India is a Hindu nation, and everyone who lives here is a Hindu, irrespective of their religion. They claim that Hindus were ruled by Islam and Christianity for 1,200 years because they were not united. Rashtriya Swayamsevak Sangh has taken up the task of uniting Hindus and creating a Hindu Rashtra, in which members of other faiths will live at the mercy of the majority of Hindus.

Within the framework of Hindutva, the Constitution-makers were influenced by Western thoughts. Therefore, there was nothing 'Bhartiya' in the Constitution. Rashtriya Swayamsevak Sangh pracharak, Jan Sangh leader and their ideologue Deendayal Upadhyay developed the doctrine of 'Integral

Humanism', which was nothing but a politico-economic document of Hindutva. This was an attempt to build an alternate vision of the constitutional consensus in the political sphere. This vision seriously challenged the Constitution's basic features and questioned the fundamentals of 'democracy'. Upadhyay even rubbished the concepts of secularism and federalism, propagating instead the idea of 'Dharma Rajya'. While explaining the doctrine of Integral Humanism, he said, 'Nowadays, the word "Secular state" is being used as opposed to a theocratic state. The adoption of this word is a mere imitation of the Western thought pattern. We had no need to import it . . . The state can only be Dharma Rajya and nothing else. Any other definition will go against the very raison d'etre of the state.'[2]

Upadhyay tried to redefine the very idea of democracy. He did not believe in the concept of 'majority' or 'government of the people'. For him, dharma was supreme, and if even one person was on the side of dharma, then the view of that person should prevail, not the majority opinion. That way, even the Parliament would be subordinate to dharma. He said, 'Let us understand very clearly that Dharma is not necessarily with the majority or with the people. Dharma is eternal. Therefore, it is not enough to say, while defining democracy, that it is the government of the people. It has to be the government for the good of the people. What constitutes the good of the people? It is Dharma alone which can decide.'[3]

In 1984, BJP moved away from its ideological doctrine of Gandhian Socialism and adopted Integral Humanism as its guiding principle. Even after forming the government in 1996, 1998, 1999, 2014, 2019 and 2024, it has not disowned the doctrine. This means that though its government swears by the Constitution, it does not believe in it. It is no accident then that 'change the constitution' became one of the defining issues in this election. But BJP had to pay a heavy price for the claims made by its leaders that if the BJP won 400 or more seats, then it would change the Constitution. Rahul Gandhi took the campaign to the last strata of society to educate voters on how BJP was intent on replacing the present Constitution created by Dr Babasaheb Ambedkar, which had given a voice to the most vulnerable sections of society—the Shudras, the Dalits, the Adivasis and the backward castes.

While RSS and BJP talk about the ongoing war with Islam, they keep strategic silence on the issue of inhumane oppression inflicted by the majority community (that is, the upper caste) on the minority communities (Dalits and OBCs) among Hindus. Their literature is witness to the fact that RSS has gone to the extent of justifying the oppressive caste structure and propagated that the Manusmriti should be the guiding light of the Indian society instead of the allegedly foreign-owned Constitution. In an article published in *The Indian Express* on 14 November 1993, the fourth chief of RSS Professor Rajendra Singh advocated for a change in the Constitution. He wrote, 'In a very fundamental sense, this country has a unique cultural oneness. No country, if it has to survive, can have compartments. All this shows that changes are needed in the constitution. A constitution that is more suited to the ethos and genius of this country should be adopted in the future.'[4] As K.S. Sudarshan, the RSS chief said, 'The constitution should be scrapped.'[5]

During the 2024 election campaign, BJP leaders, including Prime Minister Modi, tried to allay the resulting fear, promising that the Constitution would not be touched. However, a large section of the oppressed classes did not buy into their argument. Along with the 'Change the Constitution' campaign came the issue of reservation. To counter Congress's promise of breaking the reservation limit of 50 per cent and giving reservations to

Dalits, Adivasis and OBCs in the private sector, BJP accused Congress and the INDIA of angling to remove reservations for Dalits, Adivasis and OBCs to give them to Muslims instead. Given BJP's past track record, a large section of the aforementioned groups did not listen to them and decided to vote against the party.

In the last few years, BJP has strategically moved to integrate this section of the society into their Hindutva fold. This was the main reason BJP could get 71 seats out of 80 in the 2014 elections and 62 in 2019 in a state like UP, where the party had struggled for almost two decades. However, the 2024 elections proved to be catastrophic for the party. A revolt by a section of Dalits and by the OBCs reduced the party's seats to 33 in UP, which became one of the reasons for Modi's failure to get a majority in the Lok Sabha. This leads to a new question: Have the underdogs of the society seen through the deception of Hindutva and reached the conclusion that the Sangh Parivar wants their votes but does not want to operate their agenda of social justice? If this realisation is cemented in the future, then RSS will be in deep trouble and their Hindu Unity Project will be in jeopardy.

If the adoption of the Constitution had unleashed a democratic revolution in a hierarchical society, then the late 1980s and early 1990s were witness to the initiation of three mini revolutions: the Hindutva movement led by the RSS/BJP, the Mandal movement with the implementation of 27 per cent reservation for OBCs and the economic reforms initiated by the Congress government led by Narasimha Rao. These three events designed a new sociopolitical order in India. The Congress party, which had ruled till then, except from 1977 to 1980, lost its hegemony to BJP, which, for the first time, formed the government in 1996 for thirteen days under the leadership of Atal Bihari

Vajpayee. Due to its inability to take a firm stand on the Mandal Commission and the Ram Mandir movement, Congress was left behind and struggled to survive despite having a government for ten years from 2004 to 2014.

All three movements infused new energy into three different social groups. If the Ram Mandir movement re-energised the upper caste, which became the main social base for BJP, then the Mandal Commission unleashed the latent energy of the subaltern class that suddenly became very ambitious and power-conscious. People like Kanshi Ram, Mayawati, Mulayam Singh Yadav, Lalu Prasad Yadav, Nitish Kumar and Ram Vilas Paswan emerged as new leaders who refused to piggyback on the upper caste. Economic reforms created a new middle class that aspired for upward mobility. With the media explosion, all three social groups competed with each other to have a share in the power structure.

Under the leadership of Narendra Modi, BJP lured all three social groups. If the upper caste saw a civilisational saviour in Modi, then a section of the subaltern class decided to test him on his commitment to equitable justice. The Gujarat economic development model seduced the middle class. This troika of support brought Modi back with an increased vote percentage in 2019, but as the disillusionment set in due to the huge gap between the promise and delivery, the Mandal social group and middle class started rethinking their support. Uttar Pradesh became the real battleground. Mandal politics had overshadowed the politics of Hindutva for almost two decades in UP till the Modi-led BJP broke the shackles in 2014. The results of 2024 indicate that the power balance is once again changing in UP. Bharatiya Janata Party has to reinvent itself and redesign its electoral strategy, and RSS has to re-engineer its ideological architecture.

The debacle in UP is extremely significant because the state was considered to be the next laboratory for Hindutva after Gujarat. Without substantial success in UP, BJP will always find it difficult to form government at the Centre on its own. Three temples which are significant to the Hindu sentiment—the Ram Mandir in Ayodhya, the Kashi Vishwanath temple in Varanasi and the Krishna Janmabhoomi Mandir in Mathura—are situated in UP. Bharatiya Janata Party and RSS planned to use these to polarise Hindus during elections for votes, by vowing revenge on Muslims for the past. After the demolition of Babri Masjid, BJP and RSS had been pompously saying, '*Ayodhya to jhanki hai, Mathura Kashi Baki hai* (Ayodhya is only a trailer, Mathura Kashi will follow)'. Litigations for both the temples are in the advanced stage in the courts, and Hindutvavadi forces are confident that, like the Supreme Court's verdict on Ram Janmabhoomi, favourable judgment will be delivered in these two cases too. Additionally, the two biggest icons of Hindutva in contemporary history, Narendra Modi and Yogi Adityanath, are associated with UP. If Modi has adopted Varanasi as his second home after Gujarat and contests elections from there, then Yogi has made Gorakhpur his religious and electoral abode. The religious significance of Varanasi is globally known, and Gorakhpur is the spiritual seat of Mahant Gorakhnath, one of the greatest spiritual saints within the Hindu fold. Yet, both the Hindutva icons failed miserably in UP. Most surprisingly, Modi's victory margin in Varanasi declined against the previous two elections, and he won merely by a little over 1.5 lakh votes as against the tall claims of winning by more than ten lakh votes. And to rub salt on the wounds, the party also lost in Ayodhya, in the Faizabad Lok Sabha constituency where Ram Mandir is situated. This electoral debacle came within four months of Ram Mandir Pran Pratishtha. If Modi's Midas touch, Yogi's masculine bulldozers and the Ram Mandir consecration could not save UP for BJP, then it can't be considered an ordinary event. Clearly, there are deeper reasons for BJP's defeat, which require serious study.

Let's not forget, UP was the ground for Mandal and Dalit politics since the 1990s, for the liberation of civilisational victims from inhuman caste atrocities; it was a fight for the dignity of human life. It was the place where Kanshi Ram successfully installed the first Dalit chief minister, not once but four times. Mulayam Singh Yadav epitomised social justice movement in the state. Together, these two stalled Hindutva's robust march in UP for almost two decades. Mayawati might have disappointed her community with her opportunistic and timid politics but a Dalit movement of a different kind has surged in this election which proves the point that a 'new' aspirational class has emerged among Dalits, one that is independent of Mayawati. For this new class, the Constitution is sacrosanct because it has given them a 'new' social identity, empowering them politically. The 'Change the Constitution' campaign became a matter of life and death for them.

In the election of 2024, Rahul Gandhi emerged as the new leader of Mandal politics. The Congress Manifesto is a revolutionary document that has positioned Congress as the new champion of social justice. Caste Census became Gandhi's calling card. Social justice has never been the Congress's plank, which was the main reason for its downfall from the pinnacle of power. Through the social justice plank, Rahul Gandhi has cleverly built a parallel narrative to BJP's politics of Hindutva.

It is important to note that senior journalists with whom the author was working during the elections have consistently reported these changes and had claimed that UP would be an electoral graveyard for BJP long before the results were declared, as opposed to the predictions of opinion and exit polls commissioned by TV channels. They had maintained that BJP was in crisis in UP and would be lucky if it could retain half the seats it won in the 2019 elections. Therefore, this book especially focuses on UP to understand the fast-emerging new politics.

In the end, the most important question is whether, in the busy streets of UP, an antidote has been found to neutralise the virus of fascism that has been posing the greatest threat to India. Jason Stanley has brilliantly summed up the reason for the threat. 'Historically, fascist leaders have often come to power through democratic elections. However, the commitment to freedom, such as the freedom inherent in the right to vote, tends to end with that victory.'[6]

Fortunately, it seems that India is far from that stage, for the time being. We may have dodged a bullet but the struggle for democracy is not over. In the words of Francis Fukuyama, 'The rise of identity politics in modern liberal democracies is one of the chief threats that they face, and unless we can work our way back to a more universal understanding of human dignity, we will doom ourselves to continuing conflicts.'[7]

1

Indian Politics and the Hindu Right

As independent India's first prime minister, Jawaharlal Nehru had the Herculean task of rebuilding a country at a time when the historians of that era refused to even believe that India was a nation. India had just won its independence after centuries of being ruled by foreign powers, first by the invaders from Central Asia and later by the British. It was one of the poorest countries in the world then, with abysmal literacy rates and a society that was divided by castes and sub-castes. It was also multilingual and had so much diversity that Western authors talked of it as being many countries rolled into one. It was predicted that India would not survive as a nation once the British left. Winston Churchill had already prophesied that the country would disintegrate within a few years.

The great leaders of India's freedom movement had revelled in agitational politics. They had withstood the brutalities of the British Empire with great courage and fortitude. However, they had no experience of democracy as a governing principle. With freedom came the great challenge of governing a country as diverse as India.

There is no doubt that India was blessed with a galaxy of visionary leaders, people with an infinite appetite for scholarship and a deep understanding of India's culture and tradition. They were aware of India's great history and rich philosophical pursuits. Most importantly, they had not joined the political arena for power or position but to selflessly serve the people with great devotion to the motherland.

They were idealists and dreamers. Their foray into politics at a time when India was fighting the colonial power came with a strong possibility of spending a lifetime in jail. These leaders had so much devotion, conviction and honesty of purpose that when Gandhi, ignoring the proposal of the party organisation to make Sardar Patel the leader, decided to make Nehru his successor and finally the prime minister, everybody, including Patel, accepted Bapu's choice.

While there were differences of opinion amongst them, they were resolved with dignity and mutual respect. But all said and done, governance was an unknown entity for them. Gandhi knew the trickery and complexity of governance, so he invented the first principle of free India: consensus building. It was magical. In one stroke of genius, Gandhi created a recipe that united India. If India were to remain a democracy, then no one idea or ideology should bulldoze others; and consensus-building could be the only path to arriving at decisions. The key to success as an independent nation was to celebrate diversity and resolve any differences harmoniously.

It was Gandhi's suggestion that the first government after the British should be a national government. He insisted that leaders from other parties ought to be included in the council of ministers. Gandhi's harshest critic, Babasaheb Ambedkar, was not only made the law minister in Nehru's cabinet but was also entrusted with the responsibility of drafting the Constitution.

Syama Prasad Mookerjee of the Hindu Mahasabha, a bitter critic of Congress and Gandhi, was also drafted into the cabinet. It is a different matter that both the leaders resigned later. Ambedkar left on the issue of the Hindu Code Bill and Mookerjee resigned when the Liaquat–Nehru Pact was signed between India and Pakistan to find a solution to the problem of the treatment of minorities in their respective countries. But by then, a solid foundation for democracy had been laid and a minimum consensus was reached among the leaders as to which direction the country should be taken in.

The difference with Pakistan was stark. Pakistan had been created at the same time, but unlike India, it could not decide on its Constitution for more than a decade and could not remain a democracy for long. Religion became the determining factor in its polity.

As a prime minister, Nehru had serious issues with some of his colleagues, including Sardar Patel and independent India's first president Dr Rajendra Prasad. But these differences never took an ugly turn. There were also instances of Nehru being very upset with a section of Congress that wanted to give the party a Hindutva turn.

Nehru was a modern man; secularism was his creed and he firmly believed that India could only survive if it respected pluralism and embraced its diversity as its first nature. He knew that India was a Hindu majority nation but it could not be imagined without the active participation of Muslims, Christians and other minorities in every walk of life. He had envisioned the dangers of Hindu majoritarian politics and it is no coincidence that he turned the first election (1951-52) into a referendum on Hindu communal politics. Rashtriya Swayamsevak Sangh was active then and had developed deep roots in many pockets of the country due to the partition and subsequent bloodbath. On the eve of the first election, Mookerjee, once Nehru's colleague, created Jan Sangh, a political party, at the behest of the RSS.

To fight the menace of communalism, Nehru did not resort to coercive means but used the instruments of democracy. He did not use the power of the State to weaken his political opponents, nor did he muzzle the voices of dissent. For him, the Parliament was not just made of brick and mortar, it was a temple of democracy. It was with this spirit of governance that Nehru led the country for seventeen years and won three consecutive elections with two-thirds majority. After his demise, the edifice of Congress did not crumble; it continued to have a majority in the lower house of Parliament, uninterrupted till 1977.

The present dispensation might rejoice that it has won three consecutive parliamentary elections and paralleled Nehru's record, but chinks are already visible in their armour. Modi is facing a peculiar problem: he has to battle himself. The Modi of 2014 is asking the Modi of 2024 some tough questions. When he campaigned for the prime minister's chair in 2014, Modi raised the hopes of the people. He smartly packaged himself as a one-window solution to all the problems of the country; he was a breath of fresh air after the catastrophic charges of corruption against the Manmohan Singh government. Unlike Singh, Modi was a master communicator. He tried to establish a direct connect with every voter. He convinced people, especially in the Hindi-speaking regions, that he was the messiah the country had been waiting for ever so long. Once he became the prime minister, this image was magnified manyfold by the mainstream media.

This was similar to how at the time of Independence, the aspirations of people had soared sky high. The common man had believed that since the country had attained freedom from foreigners and was now ruled by one of them, mundane problems of daily life would disappear into thin air. That, in no time, rivers of honey and milk that they had heard about from their forefathers or read about in mythology would flow again. That there wouldn't be injustice and everyone would be treated equally. That the rich and the poor would have the power of one vote. That everyone who needed a job would have one, and no one would have to sleep on an empty stomach. No leader on earth, however mighty and visionary, can solve all the problems of a country of India's magnitude and satisfy aspirations of such high intensity. Truthfulness and forthrightness in communication with the citizens are the only solutions.

Nehru knew from the beginning that he was no superhero, that he did not have a magic wand. He knew that patience and perseverance were the only armour to win people's confidence, and education and training were the only ways forward. He avoided making unrealistic promises. In contrast, Modi lives with hyperbole, making tall promises and weaving narratives around them is a part of his political communication strategy. Ever since he was declared the prime ministerial candidate in 2013, he has presented himself as God-sent. If in 2013-14 this evocation was subtle and nuanced, in 2024, it is unapologetic and unabashed in declaring divinity in him.

In 2014, in Varanasi, I saw huge posters proclaiming, '*Maa Ganga ne bulaya hai* [Mother Ganges has called]'. River Ganges is considered the most sacred of rivers among the Hindus and it is believed that taking a dip in its waters washes away the sins of devotees.[1] The legend goes that Ganga is a celestial river which landed on this planet, and because the force of it would have caused damage to the world, Shiva took it on his head and let it flow through his hair gently down the Himalayan slopes.

During the 2024 elections, in an interview with the news channel Times Now, Modi got emotional while talking about his connection with the river and with Varanasi, which he fondly referred to as Kashi. He said, 'When I went to Kashi in 2014, my candidature was decided at the last moment, so after the nomination procedure, when the people from the media spoke to me, I casually said, I admit that at that time, I was not prepared. I said that I didn't come here, no one sent me here, I am here because Maa Ganga asked me to come. Today after 10 years, I can say that Maa Ganga has adopted me.'[2] Modi then went on to elaborate on his relationship with Kashi, which is not only one of the oldest cities in the world but also the holiest of all in Hindu religion. He said, 'In the last ten years, I have been so connected with Kashi that whenever I speak, I say that it's my Kashi. It's like a relationship between a mother and a son. That's the relationship I share with Kashi.'[3]

In 2014, Modi, who is from Gujarat, contested from both Baroda and Varanasi. He won from both the constituencies and chose to retain Varanasi. In his earlier avatar as the chief minister of Gujarat, he had projected himself as a Gujarati, as the saviour of Gujarat who would protect and fight for the Gujarati identity. He still carries that image but now it has transformed into a meta identity that is 'Bharat', and in his idea of 'Bharat', Hindu-ness is one of the markers. Before becoming the prime minister, Modi was hailed by many as a great Hindu leader who had taught the Muslims in Gujarat a lesson. But after taking on the mantle of prime minister, he deliberately worked to transform himself into a protector of all Hindus across the country and abroad, and to connect with them he used religious symbols. In this pursuit, Kashi and Ganga were the natural choice.

If Modi invokes his divinity in the Ganga, for Nehru, the Ganga was a symbol of India's great culture. Nehru beautifully writes in his will, 'The Ganga, especially, is the river of India, beloved of her people, round which are intertwined her memories, her hopes and fears, her songs of triumph, her victories and her defeats. She has been a symbol of India's age-long culture and civilisation, ever changing, ever flowing, and yet ever the same Ganga.'[4] Nehru was not an overtly religious person nor did he use religion to further his politics. For him, religion was deeply private; a personal matter. For him, the Ganga was not divine; it was a living history. He writes, 'The Ganga has been to me a symbol and a memory of the past of India, running into the present, and flowing on to the great ocean of the future.'[5]

One can understand Modi's psyche. When he became the chief minister of Gujarat and later the prime minister, he was no colossus. He was a pracharak of RSS and had spent many years in the organisation before he was loaned to BJP in the mid-1980s. When he was asked to go to Gujarat, nobody had high hopes for him or thought that one day he would emerge as the supreme leader of BJP with a mega following. So, he needed to present himself as exceptional. The selection of Kashi as the political battleground and invocation of a divine connection with the Ganga propelled him into the orbit of leadership. Nehru didn't need to do this, as even before he became the prime minister, he was a mass leader and hugely popular within the party. Even before Gandhi declared him his political heir, Nehru was seen as his natural successor.

Despite being born and brought up in an aristocratic environment, Nehru had a natural affinity for the poor and marginalised; he had fought for the farmers' cause and was sent to jail by the British government. Even abroad, he was seen as one of the shining stars of India's freedom struggle and was respected for his intelligence and understanding of world politics. Gandhi chose him as his successor because he knew that only Nehru had the talent to imbibe the best of the

East and the West, and deal with world leaders on an equal footing.

In contrast, Modi doesn't have the statesman quality. At best, he is a political leader and a Hindu icon. Many in the Western media too view him as a divisive figure. Hence, I was not surprised when in 2024 Modi struggled to win his election from Varanasi, despite half a dozen cabinet ministers being deputed in Varanasi and Amit Shah deciding to station himself there before the day of polling. When compared with a statesman, a leader is always vulnerable.

During Nehru's lifetime, Congress never lost a general election and always had more than two-third seats in the lower house of Parliament. In 1952, the party won 346 out of 489 seats with 45 per cent votes. In 1957, it bettered its record with 371 seats out of 494 with 47 per cent votes, and in 1962, it again won 361 seats with 44.7 per cent votes. Modi's electoral victories are great in contemporary politics but pale in comparison to Nehru's electoral achievements. Under Modi's leadership, BJP has not managed to cross 40 per cent vote share. In 2014, BJP won 282 out of 543 seats with a meagre 31 per cent vote share. In 2019, the party bettered its own record with 303 seats and 37 per cent vote share, but 2024 brought disappointment when it could not get a majority in the lower house of Parliament. Despite humongous claims of winning 370 seats in the 2024 election, Modi had to struggle for his own victory and the party could get only 36 per cent votes.

The idea here is not to belittle Modi's electoral accomplishments but to put things in historical perspective. History is dispassionate and brutal, and no leader or statesman is above the scrutiny of history's rigours. Modi and Nehru are no exceptions.

In February 2024, there was unanimity among a majority of political experts, senior journalists and pollsters that BJP would return to power, winning at least as many seats as it had in the 2019 elections. One of the most prestigious media houses in India, The India Today Group, surveys the popularity of the government every six months in its Mood of the Nation (MOTN) survey, conducted by the prestigious opinion poll agency CVoter. It had predicted the return of the BJP government with more than the majority number. The MOTN results were published by *India Today* in the first week of February, almost a month and a half before the election was announced by the Election Commission of India.

According to the MOTN survey, BJP was expected to win 304 seats, one seat more than it had in 2019 general election.[6] The National Democratic Alliance (NDA), which includes BJP and its allies, was slated to win 335 seats in the lower house of Parliament. It was predicted that the opposition, led by Congress, was nowhere close to stopping BJP from getting the magic number of 272. Despite Rahul Gandhi's bravado, Congress was not seen to be anywhere close to its political revival. According to the MOTN survey, the party was expected to win 71 seats, a meagre 19 more than it had in 2019, and the INDIA was expected to win 166 seats in all.[7]

Just a few days earlier, Modi himself had boldly proclaimed that the INDIA bloc would be relegated to the opposition seats after the parliamentary elections, as BJP was going to win 370 seats and the NDA would win 405 seats. He was being rhetorical and engaging in psychological warfare with his opponents. But the MOTN survey too was endorsing the prime minister's take on the election result.

According to the survey, when asked who was best suited to be the next prime minister of India, 55 per cent of the respondents were in favour of Narendra Modi and only 14 per cent named Rahul Gandhi.[8] With a rating of 44 per cent, not only was Modi rated the best prime minister the country had ever had, he also surpassed stalwarts like Jawaharlal Nehru, Indira Gandhi and Atal Bihari Vajpayee. Vajpayee came a distant second at 15 per cent. Even though Modi's recall value was bound to be higher than his predecessors as he is the current prime minister, his numbers were still quite astronomical. Especially, as one would normally expect an anti-incumbency sentiment in the case of someone who has been spearheading the government for the last ten years. When asked how they would rate Modi's performance as prime minister, 42 per cent of respondents said 'outstanding', 19 per cent voted 'good' and 12 per cent 'average'; only 24 per cent rated his performance as 'poor' or 'very poor'. In terms of his government's performance, 56 per cent of respondents voted for 'satisfactory' or 'very satisfactory', and only 17 per cent were 'unsatisfied' or 'very unsatisfied'.[9] Despite these favourable ratings, 26 per cent mentioned unemployment and 19 per cent mentioned price rise as the biggest issues faced by the country.

During the 2019 general election too, these two issues had been troubling our country. In fact, at that time, the rate of unemployment was reported as the highest ever in the last forty-five years. Though the Modi government did not acknowledge its existence during the elections, a day after the government led by Modi was sworn in, the Ministry of Statistics and Programme Implementation admitted that the rate of unemployment rose to 6.1 per cent in the fiscal year 2017-18.[10]

Ahead of the 2024 general election, the government was not worried on this count. It was confident that, like 2019, unemployment would not spoil its chances in 2024 either. The government's confidence was largely shared by intellectuals, mediapersons and political analysts for three reasons.

First, December 2023 was very important for both BJP and the opposition. The results of five assembly elections were impending. These were the last state elections that were to be held before the parliamentary elections. Among the five states, three—Rajasthan, Madhya Pradesh and Chhattisgarh—belonged to the Hindi-speaking region, which was supposed to be BJP's stronghold and where Prime Minister Modi commanded more than 50 per cent vote share in the 2019 parliamentary elections. The other two were Telangana and Mizoram. In the last assembly elections held in 2018, Congress had won all three former states. In Telangana, the regional party called Telangana Rashtra Samiti (TRS)—which later changed its name to Bhartiya Rashtra Samiti (BRS)—had formed the government, and in Mizoram, another regional party, Mizo National Front, had won. For BJP led by Modi, these elections were very important as they would indicate that BJP was still popular. A victory in these elections would successfully create a narrative that Modi was unassailable and there was no challenge to his leadership.

In 2018, Congress had surprised everyone by defeating BJP in all three Hindi-speaking states, which had created an uncertainty about the results of the 2019 national elections for BJP. In Madhya Pradesh, BJP staged a coup and installed its own government by luring over a dozen MLAs, under the leadership of Congress's heavyweight leader Jyotiraditya Scindia, to defect to BJP. But in Chhattisgarh and Rajasthan, Congress governments, under the leadership of Ashok Gehlot and Bhupesh Baghel respectively, were comfortably in the saddle. It was widely believed during the elections that BJP could snatch Rajasthan from Congress, but it might lose Madhya Pradesh and Chhattisgarh. In Telangana, BJP was very hopeful of improving its tally and emerging as the main opposition party to BRS. Six months before the election, nobody was willing to bet on Congress. Many believed that Congress could be wiped out in yet another state.

But as the campaign gained momentum, opinion polls predicted good news for Congress. They were of the opinion that in the best case, Congress might win in Madhya Pradesh, Chhattisgarh and Telangana, and Rajasthan could go to BJP. In the worst-case scenario, Congress would retain Chhattisgarh and win back Madhya Pradesh, but lose Rajasthan and Telangana. Congress was of the opinion that if it could win in even two states, then it could weave a narrative that the people were unhappy with Modi and his leadership, and in the general elections of 2024, BJP might be on its way out. But to the Congress's dismay, the party lost all three states—Rajasthan, Madhya Pradesh and Chhattisgarh.

The results in Madhya Pradesh and Chhattisgarh, the latter even more than the former, came as a shock to the party. Off the camera, even BJP leaders used to say that the there was no fight in Chhattisgarh and Congress would win easily. But in a reversal of fate, BJP won 54 seats and Congress could manage only 35 out of a total of 90 assembly seats. In Madhya Pradesh too, the party was expecting an easy win but faced a humiliating defeat. Bharatiya Janata Party's victory was stupendous as it had won 163 seats, which was two-third of the total 230 seats, leaving Congress with only 66 seats. In Rajasthan, Congress expectedly lost, but after putting up a good fight. Bharatiya Janata Party had 115 seats while Congress ended up with 69 out of 199 assembly seats. Congress president Mallikarjun Kharge is reported to have said that Congress's performance in Madhya Pradesh, Chhattisgarh and Rajasthan assembly polls was disappointing, and that it will overcome the temporary setback and prepare fully for Lok Sabha polls along with its alliance partners.[11] Congress had a consolation prize in Telangana where it unexpectedly decimated BRS and relegated BJP to the third position. Here, Congress won 64 seats, BRS was reduced to 39 and BJP could get only 8 out of 119 assembly seats. In Mizoram, both the national parties had to contend with a marginal presence: BJP won 2 seats and Congress 1 seat. The regional party Zoram People's Movement (ZPM) swept the elections with 27 seats out of 40. Mizo National Front (MNF) could win only 10.

Professor Sanjay Kumar, one of India's leading and most respected psephologists, aptly analysed the assembly election results. He said, 'The results send out a few important messages. First and foremost is that the Modi magic is still working. Prime Minister Narendra Modi's campaign played an important role in the BJP's victory in the three states it won. The results also reinforce the Congress's inability to take on the BJP in Hindi heartland states in a direct contest. However, the party still has a presence in the southern states. [. . .] A careful analysis of the results indicates that there was no anti-Congress wave, rather it was pro-BJP wave. That much is clear from the vote share of the Congress and the BJP in the three states in which the Congress lost to the BJP.'[12] Sanjay Kumar's emphasis on the 'Modi magic' and 'pro-BJP wave' in the Hindi heartland meant that Modi would again have a cakewalk in the most important geographical area in parliamentary election, like it had in 2014 and 2019.

Second, in post-Independence India, three incidents have defined and redesigned India's politics: the imposition of Emergency by the then prime minister Indira Gandhi, the implementation of the Mandal Commission Report to give 27 per cent reservation to Other Backward Classes (OBCs), and the Ayodhya movement for the construction of Ram Mandir in Ayodhya.

The Emergency conveyed to the people of India that democracy was not safe if there was an authoritarian leader; it could be manipulated for a one-person rule if the party they were heading was subservient to their dictatorial instinct. The people and the opposition, therefore, had to be vigilant while choosing the prime minister.

The implementation of 27 per cent reservation by the then prime minister V.P. Singh in 1990 unleashed such latent energy in India's electoral politics and inflicted such wounds to Congress that the party, which was once a colossus, could not regain half of its original strength. India's politics, once led by the hegemonic upper castes, now had to allow backward castes to rule in major Hindi-speaking states like UP and Bihar. In other states too, it became impossible to ignore claims of these castes that comprise almost 50 per cent of the population. Even a party like BJP, which was once known as the Brahmin–Bania party, had to do social engineering across the country to get their votes.

Equally important was the Ayodhya movement led by BJP. This movement was started by the Vishva Hindu Parishad (VHP) in the early 1980s, at the prompting of its mother organisation, RSS. Before this movement, BJP was a fringe player in Indian politics. The Rath Yatra in 1990 by BJP's then president Lal Krishna Advani changed the texture of politics and helped BJP attain the pole position in 2014. If Advani is to be credited for bringing Hindutva through the Ayodhya movement to the front row of Indian politics, then Modi should be credited for fundamentally transforming the DNA of India's politics. He broke the Nehruvian consensus derived from the great tradition of the freedom movement and made Hindutva the livewire of new politics.

Modi is the only politician in BJP who recognised the 'full' potential of Hindutva as an instrument of politics. He first experimented successfully in his home state, Gujarat, and then superimposed that model on Delhi after becoming the prime minister. When BJP announced that the Ram Mandir Pran Pratishtha (consecration) would be held on 22 January 2024, two months before the national elections, it was assumed that Modi had played his masterstroke and BJP would have an easy run in the elections, ensuring a third term for him. Congress had declined the invitation for the consecration, potentially costing the party dearly.

Swapan Das Gupta, a leading intellectual from the Hindutva fold, wrote in *The Times of India*, 'If the inauguration of the Ram Temple in Ayodhya is viewed by Hindu India as a one-off spectacle that will, at best, bolster religious tourism, the Congress boycott is unlikely to have negative consequences.' But he also wrote, 'However, if the Ram Temple creates an emotional upsurge among Hindus and is seen to signal a turning point after thousand years of submission, its political manifestation will be deeply unsettling to a Congress which is proceeding on the belief that Ram Lehar will pass, leaving the India Alliance unaffected.'[13]

Congress had undoubtedly taken a huge risk by declining the invitation. A large section of the society viewed this as a mistake because, after all, it was the Ram Mandir movement that had carved a distinct and powerful political identity for BJP and propelled it to the centre stage of Indian politics. Till 1984, BJP was a failed political project of RSS. It was constituted in 1951 as a political party named Jan Sangh on the eve of the first national elections. Till 1984, it could not get more than 10 per cent votes and 50 seats in any Lok Sabha elections despite stalwarts like Atal Bihari Vajpayee and L.K. Advani in its ranks. In 1989, it crossed the 10 per cent vote benchmark for the first time. Even then, it had a seat adjustment with Janta Dal, led by V.P. Singh, who became the prime minister after the elections, supported by BJP from outside. In 1989, as a part of a larger opposition, BJP managed 11.36 per cent votes and 85 seats. Till then it had also failed to win any state elections. For the first time, BJP formed a state government in March 1990 in Rajasthan, with Bhairon Singh Shekhawat as the chief minister. Subsequently, it formed governments in UP, Madhya Pradesh and Himachal Pradesh. All four governments were sacked in the aftermath of the demolition of Babri Masjid in December 1992.

If BJP has touched the pinnacle of its political power, it is only due to the Ram Janmabhoomi movement. The movement was woven around the narrative that in 1528, Mir Baqi, a Mughal commander under the reign of Emperor Babur, demolished a Ram Temple and built the Babri Masjid in its place. Rashtriya Swayamsevak Sangh launched the movement to free the Ram Temple from the relics of the past. A new grand temple was to be constructed where the mosque had stood for centuries. After several attempts, a mob led by VHP, RSS and BJP leaders demolished the mosque on 6 December 1992. The demolition was termed illegal by the Supreme Court of India, but surprisingly, none of the organisations behind the demolition ever admitted their role in it. In fact, Advani went so far as to say that the demolition day was the saddest day of his life. The matter was heard in court. While many BJP leaders were accused of hatching a conspiracy to demolish the mosque, no one was ever convicted for lack of evidence.

Lord Ram, the king of Ayodhya, has been integral to the imagination of Hindus for thousands of years. It is not uncommon for the Ramayana, originally told by sage Valmiki in Sanskrit, to be narrated in Hindu households. 'For many Hindus, the Ramayana is simply the divine truth revealed to Valmiki.'[14] It is a myth that Ram's story is only popular in north India, and not in east and south India. The truth is different.

Ram's story has been told in many ways, in almost every Indian language. The story was so popular that it became a part of Buddhism and Jainism too. 'Renderings of the Ramayana have varied by region, shifted emphasis depending on the bard or storyteller. While Tulsidas wrote the Ramcharitmanas that north Indians know, versions by Krittibas, Kampan and Ezhuthachan are the primary texts in east and south India. The Ramayana has been rendered into all languages in south India, starting with the highly devotional Iramavataram by Kampan in the 12th century.'[15] Professor N. Ganesh, the chair of Kerala Council for Historical Research, told *The Times of India*, 'The art form of Ramayana Koothu has been practiced in temples since the times of the zamorin in Malabar. The story of Ram is very popular in south India but it has not translated into mass worship.'[16]

Till VHP actively took up the cause of Ram Janmabhoomi in the early 1980s, BJP was oblivious to the issue. Upon witnessing the response of Hindus in north India to the Ram Janmabhoomi movement, the political party joined the issue with VHP in the mid-1980s. It passed a resolution in its Palampur session in 1998 that 'Ram is the matter of faith and courts can't decide its fate'. When V.P. Singh announced the implementation of the Mandal Commission report, Advani embarked on a Rath Yatra from Somnath Temple to Ayodhya to counter its impact. Bharatiya Janata Party was overwhelmed with the response of Hindus during the Yatra. It had stumbled upon the key to succeed in electoral politics. Advani was an astute politician, and he used the Ram Mandir issue to attack the liberal order built around Nehruvian consensus since Independence.

The Nehruvian consensus was built around secularism, constitutionalism, scientific temper, socialistic thinking and mixed economy. Mixing of religion in politics was an anathema. Advani's attack on secularism was so fierce that it set off a new debate in Indian politics: Was the secularism practised by Congress and other parties based on the negation of the Hindu religion? Advani and BJP accused Congress of appeasement of Muslims for votes. Advani called Congress pseudo-secular. It is a matter of academic debate and research whether it was coincidental that his claim gained currency at a time when the credibility of the liberal order itself was under pressure. This was when the Soviet Empire, along with its east European communist bloc, was dramatically crumbling. People in communist countries had risen in revolt and the West had pronounced that communism had failed as an ideology.

In the Indian context, this was the time when the Congress government led by P.V. Narsimha Rao had started dismantling the socialist structure, permitting market forces to come into play. Rao was an old fox, and he was well-versed with the concept and legitimacy of the 'socialistic pattern of the society'. But by 1990, the Indian economy was in a mess and the only route to rehabilitate it was to walk on the capitalist road. Rao was astute enough to realise that the old liberal order that had been in operation since Independence had outlived its utility, and the times demanded the construction of a new one. In their own ways, both Congress and BJP were challenging the old liberal order, which helped stabilise the democratic polity in the country. If Advani was raising questions within the social framework, then Rao was unsettling the economic model. In his book *The Rise and Fall of the Neoliberal Order*, Gary Gerstle, while analysing the American system since the time of the First World War, writes, 'And yet, the success of a political order depends on its proficiency in shaping what broad majorities of elected officials and voters on both sides of the partisan divide regard as politically possible and desirable.'[17]

Paradoxically, the old order, invented by India's first prime minister, which talked about equality and liberty, advocated free society, free speech and freedom of religion, had imbibed socialism as one of the founding stones of the Indian republic, and yet was called a liberal order. By the 1980s, this liberal order had begun to show signs of failures. As Gerstle says, both sides of the 'partisan divide'—Congress and BJP—were hinting that the liberal order was no longer 'possible' and 'desirable'. Gerstle prophetically stated, 'By the same token, losing the capacity to exercise ideological hegemony signals a political order's decline. In these moments of decline, political ideas and programs formerly regarded as radical, heterodox, or unworkable, or dismissed as the product of the overheated imaginations of fringe groups on the right or left, are able to move from the margins in to the mainstream.'[18] In the American context, Gerstle writes, 'This happened in the 1970s, when the breakup of the New Deal order allowed long scorned Neo-liberal ideas for reorganising the economy to take root; it happened again in the 2010s, when the coming apart of the neoliberal order opened up space for Trump-style authoritarianism and Sanders-style socialism to flourish.'[19]

It is for historians to judge if it was the market that provided legitimacy to the politics of religion, or it was religion which dug up space for the market forces, or whether both needed each other and coincided to write the epithet of the old order. This beginning of the mainstreaming of the margin in the late 1980s and early 1990s was a defining moment in Indian politics. For the supporters of Hindutva politics, this is referred to as the Ayodhya moment. For them, it was a time for a new awakening. The senior journalist R. Jagannathan had welcomed Modi's arrival in 2014. On the occasion of the Ram Mandir's consecration in 2024, he wrote, 'Yesterday's Pran Pratishtha ceremony at Ram Mandir in Ayodhya marks a major milestone in the rediscovery of Bharat by Indians, and of Hinduism by Hindus.'[20] He further wrote, 'This reaffirmation of India's core Hindu identity goes beyond Ayodhya. Ram Mandir was preceded by Varanasi's Kashi Vishwanath corridor, Ujjain's Mahakal corridor, and initiation of plans for the corridor around Mathura's Sri Krishna Janmasthan. A major event outside the traditional Hindi belt was Odisha CM Naveen Patnaik's effort to rejuvenate areas around Puri's Lord Jagannath Temple with Shri Mandira Parikrama Prakalpa being inaugurated barely five days before Ayodhya's mega event. India's sacred spaces are being expanded and refurbished as part of a longer-term civilisational reawakening that has both political and non-political content and intent. This process did not begin in 2014.'[21]

One of the ironies of postcolonial history in India was that a conscious effort was made to relegate religion to a corner. Under the influence of the left philosophy, religion was seen as regressive, and those who embraced religion in public spaces were anything but secular. Jagannathan hints at how the march of this secular project was disrupted in the 1980s. He writes, 'Sparks of this revivalist trend were first seen during [the] 1980s Doordarshan telecast of Ramanand Sagar's *Ramayana*, which millions watched in groups of extended families that often included neighbours without TVs. It was a moment when the embedded knowledge of Hindu heritage was passed from one generation to another – a process that had been interrupted by the "secularism" project adopted after independence.'[22]

Time and again, Modi has used Hindu optics to his advantage. He hasn't missed an opportunity to visit a Hindu temple and perform religious rituals, in full TV glory, attired like a Hindu sage. The Pran Pratishtha of Ram Mandir was a seminal event that had been orchestrated to showcase Modi as the protector and redeemer of the Hindu religion. The construction of the temple was packaged as Modi's great achievement, though the road for its construction was only made possible by the verdict of the Supreme Court.

The consecration ceremony was used as a platform to make Hindus believe that Modi was the miracle man who had freed Ram from the shackles of a traumatic past. It was used to convey that the equilibrium of the Hindu civilisation, which had been destabilised by the onslaughts of Islam and Christianity, had been brought back to the centre, and this had been possible only because of the prime minister. His visuals while entering the temple were shown live on all TV channels, wherein he walked in, all by himself, holding prayer material in his hands. It was pure magnetism; seemingly a moment in which the civilisation was taking a new turn.

Modi spoke for thirty-six minutes. He is a good orator, but on this day his speech was historic for its messaging. He said, 'January 22, 2024 is not just a date on the calendar. It marks the beginning of a new cycle of time. Today, we have been rewarded for centuries of patience. Rising above the mentality of slavery and taking courage from every challenge of the past, the nation is creating the genesis of a new history. Even a thousand years from now, people will discuss this date, this moment. It is a great blessing of Lord Ram that we are witnessing it happen . . . These are indelible memory lines inscribed on the wheel of time with eternal ink.'[23] His speech was imbued with a great sense of history. He knew that with this one event he had engraved his name in history, but to imagine that he was not being political would be underestimating his political being.

An integral part of his character is that he never misses a single moment to attack his political opponents. Even at this historic moment, he took a dig at his opponents. 'There was a time when some people said if the Ram Mandir is built, the country will go up in flames. Such people fail to understand the purity of Indian society's sentiments. This temple is a symbol of peace, patience, harmony, and coordination. This construction has not ignited any fire, it is giving birth to positive energy. Today, I call upon those people to rethink their perspective. Ram is not fire, Ram is energy. Ram is not conflict, Ram is resolution.'[24]

Through his speech, Modi was constructing a new theoretical paradigm, which many found disturbing. He unhesitatingly said, 'Extend your consciousness from "Dev se Desh, Ram se Rashtra" [from deity to country, from Ram to nation]',[25] which was clearly blurring the lines between religion and politics. Nilanjan Mukhopadhyay, a foremost expert on the politics of Hindutva and author of Modi's biography, says, 'Significantly, the event was conspicuous by erasing the lines between religion and the Indian state. This marked a big stride from the blurring of lines between religion and politics per se.'[26] Mukhopadhyay has no hesitation in penning down, 'It is true that on January 22, Mr Modi resembled to the core the high priest of Sanatan Hinduism. However, it must be noted that the scale of the event and the nature of the Ayodhya ceremony was more grandiose and significant.'[27]

Mukhopadhyay firmly believes that the event had a political motive. He writes, 'The *"pran pratistha"* ceremony at the Ram Mandir in Ayodhya on January 22 had little to do with religiosity and was essentially an audio-visual spectacle.'[28] Even *The Times of India* has hinted that through this spectacle BJP was hoping to reap electoral benefits. 'Economic realities matter in an election. BJP hopes Ayodhya will pay electoral dividends.

In northern states that's likely to happen.'[29] Aniruddha Dhar wrote for *Hindustan Times*, 'Political analysts and critics see Monday's ceremony as the beginning of the election campaign for Modi. . . . The grand Ram Temple in Ayodhya is expected to embolden Modi's chances of returning to power by drawing on the religious sentiments of Hindus, who make up 80% of India's population.'[30]

There is no denying the fact that Modi had a political reason for the Ram Mandir consecration, but the big question was, would it help the BJP win the election? The party had milked the issue for over three decades, but once the temple was constructed, would it still be the prime mover for its electoral success? Many political observers were sceptical. Professor Hilal Ahmed wrote, 'No one can deny that BJP will highlight Ayodhya Temple as an important political achievement in the upcoming elections. However, it is difficult to predict the specific location of Ram Temple in BJP's future electoral packages. BJP establishment, it seems, is aware of the possible limitation of Ram Temple issue in 2024 elections.'[31] In retrospect, Hilal's analysis was right. The Ram Mandir consecration failed BJP where it should have mattered the most.

Third, if BJP was overconfident about forming its own government post-consecration of the Ram Mandir, then the blame lies with the opposition. In August 2022, Nitish Kumar moved towards Rashtriya Janta Dal (RJD) after breaking his alliance with BJP, generating the first ray of hope in the opposition camp. It was believed that BJP would find it difficult to repeat its 2019 general elections performance in Bihar, when it, along with Janata Dal (United) [JD(U)], had won 39 out of 40 parliamentary seats. Rashtriya Janata Dal had drawn a blank that year. Such was the dominance of the BJP–JDU alliance, catalysed by the charisma of Modi. In

Bihar, if two out of three political forces are aligned with each other, the third one finds it difficult to win substantial seats in the assembly and parliamentary elections. Therefore, Nitish Kumar walking away from the NDA to RJD was an enormous setback for BJP.

Nitish Kumar is a wily politician who harbours ambitions of one day being India's prime minister. His is a small party, but in India's strange game of coalition politics, he—or any other leader like him—could always emerge as a concessional candidate for prime minister, if the national parties are in no position to form the government. Nitish Kumar must have sensed that due to the pandemic and the bad economic situation, BJP would struggle to attain majority in Parliament on its own in the 2024 elections. He chose the right moment to switch parties, with a little more than a year and a half to prepare for the final kill. He was aware that Congress was in dire straits and was in no position to challenge the might of Modi. If he could be instrumental in bringing the anti-Modi forces under one umbrella, then he would have a chance to fulfil his ambition. Nitish Kumar publicly said that going back to BJP in 2017 'was a mistake, forget about it'.[32]

Nalin Verma wrote, 'There is every indication to suggest that Nitish's return to the Mahagathbandhan this time will be long-term. And in the process, opposition parties across the country will have a strong and articulate operator to take on the BJP in the 2024 Lok Sabha elections. Just ask former prime minister H.D. Deve Gowda, who said the developments in Bihar signal the possibility of a good alternative for the nation.'[33] Rajdeep Sardesai, who has spent over three decades in journalism, covering politics across the country, wrote for *India Today*, 'Nitish may now seek to revive his hope of being seen as a long-term rival to Prime Minister Narendra Modi nationally. There is also a theory of Nitish Kumar, once out of NDA, emerging as one of the prime ministerial candidates in 2024 if the Congress does not do well and state leaders somehow have the numbers to put together a "khichdi Sarkar".'[34]

After switching sides, Nitish Kumar started meeting leaders of the non-BJP parties to explore the possibility of creating an anti-BJP conglomerate in order to present a national alternative to Modi. Once the Karnataka assembly elections were over, a meeting of the leaders of sixteen opposition parties was organised in Patna on 23 June 2023. Patna is symbolic in history. It was here that Jay Prakash Narayan started the movement, famously known as the JP Movement, to oust Prime Minister Indira Gandhi in 1974. The meeting was deemed a great success as parties who had had a frosty relationship in the past agreed to share the dais and Nitish Kumar was, undoubtedly, the master of the ceremony. 'The highlight of the meeting was the coming together of the Trinamool Congress (TMC), Samajwadi Party and Congress. Both TMC and SP have, for long, expressed their reservations over sharing a stage with the Congress party.'[35]

Buoyed by the success of the Patna conclave, another meeting was planned in Bengaluru for 17–18 July 2023. Congress had won back Karnataka, defeating BJP handsomely in the recent assembly elections. The victory in Karnataka, despite a fierce personalised campaign by Modi, had boosted the morale of the opposition. The opposition leaders were convinced that with a cogent strategy and a smart campaign, a united front could pose a serious challenge to the Modi-led BJP in the national elections in 2024. In Bengaluru's two-day conclave, the number of parties increased to twenty-six, and a name was given to the united opposition—Indian Nationalist Developmental Inclusive Alliance, in short, INDIA. They decided to create an eleven-member coordination committee and a common secretariat. However, Nitish Kumar left the meeting early, leading to speculation that he was unhappy for not being made the convenor of the alliance.

The momentum that the opposition had gained after the Patna conclave made BJP nervous. The tension in the BJP camp was palpable. Bharatiya Janata Party under Modi, which had never bothered to have a formal meeting with its alliance partners under the banner of NDA, suddenly cobbled together a meeting of thirty-eight parties on 17 July in Delhi. The date coincided with the opposition's meet in Bengaluru. It was apparent that BJP was desperate to kill the perception that the united opposition had more support than them. The party's desperation could be gauged from the fact that out of the thirty-eight parties which had gathered in Delhi at BJP's invitation, twenty-four had no members of parliament (MPs), seven had only one MP each and two had two MPs each. The prime minister admitted that he could not meet many of the alliance partners in the last nine years.[36]

Bharatiya Janata Party was also disturbed by the name of the opposition alliance—INDIA. Addressing this, I wrote in *The Diplomat*, 'Speculation is rife that Modi is rattled by the opposition unity and that he is especially taken aback by the acronym INDIA of the opposition alliance . . . INDIA is not simply a political response but a serious ideological argument that challenges the fundamentals of his ideology, Hindutva.'[37] The reason was easy to decipher. I explained BJP's concern. 'The acronym INDIA has been deliberately created. It has lot of symbolism. It is a bold announcement that BJP/RSS can't claim India as their own as they are opposed to the very idea itself. In the last few years, Hindutva forces have claimed ownership of India as a praxis, and in their opinion, the opposition stood for everything that is not India. It was fashionable for the ruling dispensation to call their critics anti-India or supporters of Pakistan. Can they call INDIA, anti India? If they do, it will look bizarre and boomerang.'[38] As a counter, BJP decided to call the INDIA INDI alliance. Modi himself equated the alliance with Indian Mujahideen, a terrorist organisation.

This time, the opposition was ahead in psychological warfare. Unlike earlier, they were the ones setting the agenda, and BJP was only reacting.

The opposition's next destination was Mumbai, where meetings were held over two days—31 August and 1 September 2023. The number of opposition parties increased to twenty-eight. It was unanimously resolved that in order to defeat Modi, the opposition parties had to come together to contest elections, and sooner rather than later the seat distribution will have to be decided. The opposition was undoubtedly moving in the right direction. Nonetheless there was plenty ground yet to be covered. The INDIA's strategy was to engage BJP in a 'one to one' contest on more than 400 seats. It was not an easy task. There were several internal contradictions and Congress was the biggest of them all. It was the only national party that had always contested more than 400 seats on its own. Therefore, for it to share seats with allies meant that it had to compromise on its demand for seats. Mamata Banerjee was in no mood to have an alliance with Congress and Left parties in West Bengal. Aam Aadmi Party's (AAP) relationship with Congress was complicated, and they had to figure out how they would work together in Delhi, Gujarat, Haryana and, of course, in Punjab, where they were engaged in a bitter fight with each other. Samajwadi Party, too, was not happy with the attitude of Congress leaders in UP.

Moreover, a consensus had to be reached on a common minimum programme that would present an alternate vision before the people of India. This vision had to be strong enough to counter that of the Modi government. Till now, their raison d'être had been anti-Modi-ism. The manner in which the Modi government had weaponised government investigating agencies had created a crisis of monumental proportions for every opposition party. *The Indian Express* aptly summed up the political scene in its editorial: 'The sense that emerges from Mumbai, as it did from Patna and Bengaluru, is that the alliance is looking to frame its campaign in negative terms. It is asking the electorate to vote against Narendra Modi's BJP. Its articulation of what is at stake in 2024 follows from this negative pitch and it is apocalyptic—it paints a picture of endangered secularism, democracy, federalism and fundamental rights. What is missing still is a big affirmative idea that is being offered by the opposition alliance.'[39] It was a huge endeavour. Four committees were formed to deal with different tasks and there were promises made to work in coordination.

At this time, there was apprehension that with the opposition gaining momentum, BJP might try to hold the elections in December 2023, along with the assembly elections in five states. Amongst the five states that were slated to go to polls, BJP was unsure of its success in at least two Hindi-speaking states—Madhya Pradesh and Chhattisgarh. In Rajasthan, the party expected to sail through. It was worried that if Congress won two Hindi-speaking states, then the INDIA would be able to set a believable narrative that BJP was losing the support of the people even in the Hindi belt, which had always been its stronghold. Analysis showed that with the increased opposition unity index, unlike in 2014 and 2019, coupled with ten years of anti-incumbency against the Modi government, the electoral balance might tilt in favour of the INDIA.

The next conclave was to happen in Delhi, which could take place only on 19 December 2023, after the assembly elections.

Congress faced a humiliating defeat in these elections, and the alliance, too, lost its momentum by then. From 2 September to 18 December, no meaningful initiative was taken by the INDIA bloc. No meetings took place, no joint rallies were organised, no seat-sharing formula could be clinched. Congress was partly to blame for this, but other allies could not be absolved either. While Congress was busy with elections, none of the partners took initiative. Congress was one of the main parties in at least four states—Rajasthan, Madhya Pradesh, Chhattisgarh and Telangana—and could not afford to not pay attention there. But it was also true that Congress tried to play smart. The party was overconfident that if it could win three states, or even two, in the Hindi belt, then it could negotiate for more seats from its alliance partners. Unfortunately, it lost all the states in the Hindi belt, managing to win only Telangana. Meanwhile, they lost precious time, and by the time the Delhi meeting was organised, the INDIA was in total disarray. Instead of regrouping, the alliance partners were snapping at each other. Rahul Gandhi unilaterally planned his Nyay Yatra from Manipur to Mumbai. He was accused of ignoring allies. Mamata Banerjee was so upset with Congress, she publicly said that Congress would not win even 40 seats in Lok Sabha polls.[40]

By the end of December 2023, it was apparent that the opposition parties' alliance had squandered its chances and lost the will to fight elections. The last nail in the coffin was hammered in by Nitish Kumar. He had given enough hints that he was not happy with the way things were happening in the INDIA bloc. It was widely rumoured that he might desert the alliance and go back to BJP, because he was neither made the convenor nor presented as the face of the alliance. On 28 January 2024, Nitish Kumar finally said goodbye to the alliance. This was the same Nitish Kumar who, while leaving BJP a year and a half earlier, had said, 'I'd rather die than tie up with them [BJP].'[41] What an irony! The man who was to lead the opposition had backstabbed it at the most inopportune moment. Nothing could have been more fatal. The wound was deep and the INDIA had lost all hope. Modi and Shah were smiling. They were confident that Modi was destined to match Nehru's record of winning three consecutive national elections, with a majority of their own in the Lok Sabha. Of course, we know this was not to be.

2

The Constitution Debate

'. . . However good a Constitution may be, it is sure to turn out bad because those who are called to work it, happen to be a bad lot. However bad a Constitution may be, it may turn out to be good if those who are called to work it, happen to be a good lot.'

—Babasaheb Bhim Rao Ambedkar,
chairman of the drafting committee
of the Constitution

'The Constitution can provide only the organs of State such as the Legislature, the Executive and the Judiciary. The factors on which the working of those organs of the State depends are the people and the political parties they will set up as their instruments to carry out their wishes and their politics.'

—Babasaheb Bhim Rao Ambedkar,
chairman of the drafting committee
of the Constitution

The Constitution is a living document, not a dead letter that is enshrined in dungeons of the past. When the framers of the Constitution of India put the final seal on the written document, which was supposed to lead a country with infinite diversity, they were of the consensus that no man or woman, however charismatic and powerful, would be free to run the country the way they wanted to; they would be creatively fettered by the pages of the Constitution. It would not be their free will which would guide the emerging nation, but the collective free will of the population, reflected in the Constitution.

Babasaheb had apprehensions even then that there would come a time when a powerful leader would try to usurp the powers of the common person, one who would believe and behave like a sovereign and take the country to the dark ages. In his last speech, he said, 'There is nothing wrong in being grateful to great men who have rendered lifelong services to the country. But there are limits to gratefulness. As has been well said by the Irish Patriot Daniel O'Connell, no man can be grateful at the cost of his honour, no woman can be grateful at the cost of her chastity and no nation can be grateful at the cost of its liberty.'[1]

Ambedkar came from a very humble background and was well-versed in the social reality of the country, where he was born and had risen to the greatest of heights and yet was subjected to the worst kind of social treatment. He knew how easily common folks, out of simplicity and naivety, could put any person on a pedestal and believe that they would be their saviour. Subject to this Indian reality, he said, 'This caution is far more necessary in the case of India than in the case of any other country. For in India, Bhakti, or what may be called the path of devotion or hero-worship, plays a part in its politics, unequalled in magnitude by the part it plays in the politics of any other country in the world. Bhakti in religion may be a road to the salvation of the soul. But in politics, Bhakti or hero-worship is a sure road to degradation and to eventual dictatorship.'[2] Many years later, his words are proving to be prophetic.

Since 2014, the words 'bhakti' (worship) and 'bhakt-gan' (worshipper) have become part of the popular political parlance—mostly as a slang to ridicule the blind supporters of Prime Minister Narendra Modi. These staunch supporters cannot take any criticism of the prime minister, and they viciously troll his critics. In the twentieth century, India had many political leaders who provided leadership to the country at a critical juncture and helped the common person navigate through choppy waters. But I don't know of there being such violent support for any political leader. This blindness of support, which has provided legitimacy to the cult of Modi's followers, seems to be industrially produced and is called 'Moditva'.

I knew Narendra Modi when he was BJP's general secretary and lived in a single room in the backyard of the party's headquarters at 10, Ashoka Road. He was always friendly with journalists and had an opinion on every subject. He was not fixated on the past, very firm in his thought process and unwilling to change at the behest of others. After becoming the chief minister of Gujarat, the man stunned everyone, not only with his political genius but also with his administrative acumen. The man, who had not contested a single election before becoming the chief minister, surprised his critics by winning three back-to-back state elections. He was a mass leader even then. He was controversial, polarising and also a centralising figure. But when he came to Delhi, the cult around him made a new addition to his personality. If in Gujarat he transformed himself from being a party bureaucrat to a powerful political leader, in Delhi he evolved into a demigod who makes no mistakes and is accountable to none. Modi became exceptional, extraordinary and incomparable, beyond the reproach of his contemporaries, and over the years his image-makers have tried to sculpt him with a touch of divinity. The divine is always perfect, unchained by the shackles of laws, institutions or the Constitution.

During his ten-year tenure as prime minister, Modi reinforced his followers' belief that he is a leader who can resurrect the Hindu religion from the curse of the past, rebuild its present and construct a magnificent future. His critics were convinced that, in his narcissism, he was frittering away the gains of democracy, and India was turning into an authoritarian regime in which Modi is the government, the parliament and even the law. It is this understanding that created a fear in the minds of the vast majority of the country that the 2024 elections might be the last democratic elections in India. It was widely believed that if Modi were to come back with a large majority, then the Constitution and democracy wouldn't be safe, and India would turn into a Hindu Rashtra.

I was not surprised when a friend of mine confided that he was feeling relieved after the election results. That he believed the nation was safe. I wrote about it in my column for *The Free Press Journal*, published from Mumbai. '"The country is saved" is how an elderly friend reacted when I called him up after the election results. I can't call him a left liberal but he is a hardcore political person for whom "country first" has been the leitmotif for life. I have known him for a very long time and can vouch for the honesty of his conviction. He was a worried man. We had many discussions over the years since the Bharatiya Janata Party formed the government in 2014. As elections neared this time, he told me in one of his friendly but very enlightened chats that if the BJP were to get more than 300 seats, then the country would not be the same again; the Constitution would be changed, parliamentary democracy would be consigned to the dustbin of history; parliament and the constitutional institutions would have no meaning and the country would be proclaimed a Hindu Rashtra. He said this even before BJP called for "Iss baar, 400 paar" and before the opposition accused the Modi government of having intentions of changing the Constitution if it managed to get 400 seats.'[3]

My friend was not alone in feeling relieved after the elections. Pratap Bhanu Mehta, one of the foremost political thinkers of our time, wrote in his column in *The Indian Express*, 'The general election of 2024 is a wondrous moment. The air of despondency, the suffocating shadow of authoritarianism, and the nauseous winds of communalism have, at least for the moment, lifted.'[4]

Similarly, Professor Ashutosh Varshney also wrote, 'In short, at least in UP, and perhaps elsewhere, we are witnessing a re-birth of the idea of India, heavily suppressed for the last several years. What is even clearer is that if the BJP had returned to power with a majority of its own, the constitutionally enshrined idea of India would have been subjected to a vigorous assault, leading to its decimation.'[5] While he lives in the USA, Professor Varshney makes it a point to visit India during elections and goes to the hinterlands of electoral politics to talk to common voters of different communities in villages and cities. This time, too, he journeyed through UP and other places.

Bharatiya Janata Party was not unaware of these accusations, but they refused to admit that these concerns had any merit, and that the party and the government needed to mitigate this perception. Rather, they resorted to brinkmanship and moral grandstanding. They rubbished the concerns of the opposition and of dissenting voices as part of a bigger global conspiracy to discredit the Modi government, denigrate the rise of Hindutva, and devalue the assertion that India is an emerging global power.

The party believed that this was done with the connivance of the international media.

Swapan Dasgupta, a brilliant journalist and a leading columnist, moved towards BJP much before it became a formidable force in Indian politics, and rose as one of the leading intellectuals of the party. He has been consistently writing, defending BJP, and evaluating the rise of Hindutva as a sociopolitical phenomenon. Responding to the negative writings in international media on the dangers to constitutionalism and democracy, he wrote, 'Much of the problem seems to be cultural. Accustomed to dealing with the cosmopolitan, Anglicised leadership of the Congress-dominated ancient regime, foreign correspondents today are politically and culturally detached from a BJP leadership that is more at home in an indigenous setting. The social makeover of the governing elite in the past decades has not been fully digested by the West's India watchers.'[6]

Rejecting these accusations, Dasgupta wrote, 'The wariness that democracy is incompatible with an assertion of cultural nationalism stems from the western notion that liberal democratic assumptions must shape the contours of nationhood.'[7] He further wrote, 'Modi has pitched these elections as a mandate to put an assertive and self-confident India in the comity of developed nations. The rise of such an India will unsettle the status quo. Hence the pre-emptive strike to question his very legitimacy. This is toolkit politics.'[8]

If BJP thought that these were simply the concerns of the Anglicised elite who were not comfortable with the subaltern nature of the Modi government, then the party was grossly mistaken. While the belief that there was a danger to the Constitution, democracy and the republic were only debated and discussed amongst a small group of academia and media, for the common person in the streets, this was a non-issue. For them, the real issues were roti, kapda aur makaan (food, clothing and shelter). The cacophony around '*Abki baar, 400 paar*' was met with a strange reaction on the ground. People had watched the erosion of democracy in the country silently for the past ten years and were now worried.

The '400 paar' debate was initiated by none other than the prime minister himself. Riding the self-assumed wave of Hindutva with the Ram Mandir consecration, emboldened by the switchover of Nitish Kumar to BJP in Bihar, and massive victories in assembly elections in December 2023, Prime Minister Modi triumphantly said so in the first week of February 2024, on the floor of the house in Parliament: 'Although I am not in the business of predicting numbers, BJP is definitely going to get more than 370 while NDA's total will cross 400.'[9] The prime minister exuded so much confidence about his third term, with improved majority, that he announced, 'We used our first term to fill up the ditches left by UPA. The second went towards fulfilling promises and pledges. We will use our third one to turn India into a developed country.'[10]

This was the prime minister's last speech in the Parliament before the country went to polls. A few BJP members confided in me that the party was very confident about its massive victory, and the opposition should instead make preparations for 2029. The prime minister was equally boastful in his public addresses. He said, 'For decades you [oppn] sat here [treasury benches], but now you have resolved to stay there [oppn benches] for several decades. People'll bless you and keep you there. You'll achieve greater heights and will be soon seen in the public galleries [of the House].'[11]

The prime minister's speech was a green signal to the entire brass of BJP to mock the opposition, mostly Congress, and boast that BJP was getting 400 seats. Amit Shah, the second most powerful leader after the prime minister, asked voters to bring the party 370 seats, with a twist. 'We have abrogated Article 370 [of the Constitution, which gave a special status to the erstwhile state of Jammu and Kashmir]. So we believe that the people of the country will bless the BJP with 370 seats and the NDA with over 400 seats.'[12]

Yogi Adityanath, another Hindutva icon and the chief minister of UP, repeated the prime minister's words. Speaking to the Times Now Navbharat TV channel, Yogi claimed that the BJP-led NDA would win more than 400 seats in the Lok Sabha elections and all 80 seats in UP.[13]

Bharatiya Janata Party has developed a system of communication and a very powerful propaganda machine—once a political line is decided at the top, it is repeated ad nauseam. In its communication laboratory, BJP has evolved a science to condition the minds of people; it is to train people to believe a particular narrative, to capture the mind space of citizens. Receivers are bombarded with information so many times, in so many ways, and at so many levels that the consumer, instead of feeling like a victim, becomes an accomplice and willing carrier. The technique is simple and modern technology has made it simpler.

The party has developed a pyramid-like structure with multiple verticals. Once information is curated at the top, it reaches its base in no time and the chorus begins. In every TV debate, in every language, across the country, all panellists representing the party, camouflaged as independent political analysts, verbalise the same line and even the same words, irrespective of the topic of the debate. The same technique is used more effectively on social media platforms. This kind of propaganda management creates a magnificent cacophony at a grand scale so much so that, after a point, sometimes even critics subconsciously start believing the messaging. The availability of modern communication technology and support of mainline media network has made this technique a thousand times more lethal. Those who are beyond the reach of this communication trajectory face the foot soldiers of BJP, RSS and other subsidiary organisations.

It was no wonder then that once the prime minister spoke his mind, the entire political system started buzzing with the noise that BJP would win 370 seats, maybe even more. I regularly participate in TV debates and also have my own debate show on my YouTube channel *SatyaHindi.com.* I have no hesitation in saying that many leading psephologists and political analysts of the country, who appeared in such debates, were taken in by BJP's narrative. They were heard saying that the party might find it difficult to reach 370 seats, but it would definitely better its 2019 number of 303 seats. Most of them were of the opinion that BJP would certainly improve its vote share; it could go beyond 40 per cent. And those like me, who dared to say that it was too early to predict such a massive victory for the party, were mocked in TV studios and on social media platforms.

In my opinion, ten years is an eternity in politics and anti-incumbency was bound to work against the Modi government. Many a time, I was told that my refusal to read the writing on the wall stemmed from my personal 'hatred' for the prime minister. One very reputed psephologist told me that Congress should feel lucky if it gets 40 seats nationally, pronouncing that the party was heading for its worst-ever performance. In his opinion, the debacle would mark the end of Rahul Gandhi's political career. That the same Rahul Gandhi is the leader of the opposition in the lower house of the Parliament tells another story.

With the '400 paar' slogan, BJP caught itself in a trap, and by the time it realised so, it was too late. The liberal section of Hindus had already been saying that if BJP got more than 300 seats, it would drastically change the Constitution. This got the Dalits, OBCs and tribals thinking. As the elections progressed, the elite debate turned into a mass argument. Anastasia Piliavasky and Vikramaditya Thakur wrote, 'In just six weeks the C word has been transformed from an obscure technical term into a buzzword of India's political common sense.'[14]

People's apprehensions about the Constitution changing were exacerbated when BJP's loudmouth leaders started saying that they needed 400 seats to change the Constitution. Anant Hegde, the party's member of parliament from Karnataka, was the first to say this publicly. On 10 March 2024, he said, 'You all must help BJP to win over 400 seats. Why does the BJP need 400+ seats? Congress leaders in the past made changes to the Constitution in a way that doesn't put Hinduism in front. We need to change it and save our religion. We already have a two-third majority in Lok Sabha, and we do not have that in Rajya Sabha to amend the Constitution. 400+ numbers will help us achieve that.'[15] He did not just stop at 400+ seats in the Lok Sabha. He laid out a blueprint. 'We need a two-thirds majority in Lok Sabha, Rajya Sabha and even in the state. All hurdles to rewrite the Constitution will then go away and help us to put Hinduism in the forefront.'[16]

After Hegde it was the turn of Jyoti Mirdha, BJP's candidate from Nagaur, Rajasthan. She said, 'Several tough decisions need to be taken in the country's interest and for that we have to make constitutional amendments. If we have to make amendments in the Constitution, many of you would know that we need the nod of both Houses of Parliament, the Lok Sabha and the Rajya Sabha.'[17]

Her remarks were immediately picked up by Hanuman Beniwal, who was contesting against her. He said, 'The statement makes it clear that the BJP is bent on finishing Babasaheb's Constitution.'[18] Mirdha tried to clarify that her statement had been blown out of proportion, but it was too late. Shashi Tharoor wrote on X, 'After Anant Hegde let the cat out of the bag, BJP leaders hastily stuffed it back in and dropped him from their candidate list. Now another BJP candidate openly says the BJP's aim is to change the Constitution.'[19]

This did not stop Arun Govil, BJP's candidate from Meerut, and Lallu Singh, the candidate from Faizabad, from repeating the same thing. In fact, Lallu Singh went on to put this out loud and clear: 'Govt can be formed with 272 MPs in Lok Sabha, but to make amendments to the Constitution, or to have a new Constitution, we need more than two-thirds majority.'[20]

Awadhesh Prasad, Samajwadi Party's candidate from Faizabad, reacted strongly. He said, 'Lallu Singh has revealed the hidden agenda of BJP, as they want to eliminate the democratic system of the country and put in place a dictatorial set-up.'[21] Apparently, the hidden agenda that Prasad was referring to had been exposed by his party president, Akhilesh Yadav.

Bharatiya Janata Party had made substantial inroads amongst OBCs and Dalits in UP in the last ten years, which had been one of the main reasons for the party's exponential growth in the state. Yadav gave a 'Mandal' twist to the Constitution debate, using it as an opportunity to instil fear in the minds of OBCs, Dalits and minorities. Launching a fierce and politically damaging attack on BJP, he said, 'PDA will defeat BJP, because BJP wants to end the reservation given to backward classes, Dalits and minorities by making a new Constitution. BJP wants to win not for the service or welfare of the people but to change the Constitution made by Babasaheb Bhimrao Ambedkar.'[22]

Aam Aadmi Party's Rajya Sabha MP Sanjay Singh was also quick to react in the same way. He wrote on X, 'The 85 per cent Dalits, backwards, deprived and exploited people of the country, beware. It is now clear that BJP will destroy the Constitution. The reservation will end. After Lallu Singh, Jyoti Mirdha, Anant Hegde and now even Arun Govil has said it. Arun Govil is directly Modiji's candidate.'

Akhilesh Yadav inherited Mandal politics from his father Mulayam Singh Yadav, who was on the forefront of Mandal politics when V.P. Singh announced the implementation of 27 per cent reservations for OBCs, as recommended by the Mandal Commission report. If Mulayam Singh Yadav was holding down the Mandal fort in UP in the 1990s and later, in Bihar, it was the RJD leader Lalu Prasad Yadav who was engaged in a fierce battle with the opponents of reservations for OBCs. Lalu Yadav warned BJP of dire consequences if it tried to play with the Constitution. He said, 'There is nervousness among BJP leaders and they have conceded defeat. The slogans they are giving, crossing 400 seats this time, are out of nervousness. Their leaders are continuously and openly talking about changing the Constitution. The Constitution was made by Babasaheb Bhimrao Ambedkar and not by any ordinary person. Whoever will make an attempt to change the Constitution, the poor backward and Dalits will gouge out their eyes.'[23] Familiar voices also rose from other states. Shiv Sena (Uddhav Balasaheb Thackeray) leader Uddhav Thackeray said, 'For them [BJP] the Constitution of India is like a burden. They think why should they follow the Constitution written by a Dalit? They want 400-plus seats so that they can change the Constitution written by Dr B R Ambedkar.'[24]

The opposition's scathing attack on BJP and the Mandal twist to the Constitution debate alerted the prime minister. To allay any fears about the Constitution being changed, Modi said that neither he nor BJP would consider attempting such an abomination.[25]

The Constitution debate has an emotional angle. For Dalits, any tinkering with the Constitution means tinkering with the memory of Babasaheb Ambedkar. Modi realised that this could cost his party votes. He emphatically said, 'The Constitution of the country is everything for the [BJP] government and even if Babasaheb himself comes, he cannot abolish the Constitution.'[26] To turn the direction of the debate, Modi accused Congress of tampering with the Constitution and reminded the opposition that it was the Congress government that had imposed Emergency in 1975.

Amit Shah, too, spoke on the issue. At a public rally in Akola, Maharashtra, he said, 'We want 400 paar, to implement bold reforms to transform the nation. BJP is committed to maintaining reservations for backward communities.'[27] The prime minister, in a two-page interview with *The Times of India*, explained why he coined the slogan '400 paar': 'One of the main reasons we want to win 400 seats is to protect the rights of SCs, STs and OBCs in our country. We want a thumping majority so that the evil designs of the opposition to take away their reservation and rights, and give them to their vote bank are foiled. ... It is ironic that people who have changed the Constitution the maximum number of times are saying that we will change the Constitution ...'[28]

But even these public proclamations by Modi and Shah didn't put an end to the debate. Reports from the ground suggested that the seeds of doubt that had been sown affected the electoral behaviour of voters, especially of Dalits and OBCs in states like UP, Bihar, Maharashtra and Rajasthan. For this, the opposition deserves some credit. In one of the most brilliant and creative moves by the opposition during these elections, Rahul Gandhi, who has been ridiculed to no end by BJP for his alleged political naivety, pulled out a copy of the Constitution, carried it to every election rally, waved it around during public speeches and reminded people on the ground that the BJP government was out to change Babasaheb's gift to the nation.

As Anastasia Piliavsky and Vikramaditya Thakur noted, 'Brandishing a copy in Bilaspur last month, Rahul Gandhi insisted that it is the solemn duty of Congress together with Dalits, tribals, minorities and the poor to rescue the Constitution from BJP.'[29] An astute observer, Professor Ashutosh Varshney said, 'Concerns about the Constitution have always been a matter of debate in elite circles—in English language media, in the seminar rooms of India International Centre, JNU, National Law Schools, Delhi School of Economics and Sociology, etc. But these concerns now entered mass politics, especially among educated Dalits and OBCs. A copy of the Constitution in Rahul Gandhi's hands, as he made campaign speeches with an approving Akhilesh Yadav on his side, signified how the opposition turned this "elite idea" into an election pitch.'[30] Professor Varshney visited UP extensively during the elections. His observation after talking to voters is revealing: 'Those who did field research during elections, including me, have noted that for the first time in India's electoral history, the voters were expressing concern about the Constitution, especially if the BJP won big. Of particular concern was the idea of 370 or 400 seats.'[31]

In this 'rescue' act, a mischief was also played out in the virtual world. Piliavsky and Thakur commented on a video planted in the digital space: 'A week before polls opened this year, a video suggesting plans were underway to replace the Constitution with another, based on Manusmriti, "which not even Babasaheb

Ambedkar himself could abolish," circulated on social media. The following day, on Ambedkar's 133th birthday, online media space filled with calls coming from all corners of opposition, from Congress to AAP, to rescue the Constitution. The video turned out to be fake, but its claim hasn't gone away.'[32]

Keeping aside the morality argument, the big picture in this election was that people, especially the marginalised sections of the society, were determined not to let their constitutional gains fritter away. The election was the right forum for them to signal to the forces of Hindutva to not take their support for granted. Gone were the days when they were dubbed a silent majority, this was time for pushback.

Bharatiya Janata Party failed to understand that Dalits, OBCs and other minorities might not know the meaning of the Constitution, but they definitely understood that the welfare benefits reaching them—the affirmative action in the form of reservations, which is now an integral part of their lives, and other constitutional facilities guaranteed to them—have been possible only because of the Constitution. And this became possible due to the long and torturous struggle of Ambedkar. Any change in the Constitution would mean the withdrawal of dignity, erosion of their identity, dilution of their existence and end of the welfare measures. A Dalit school teacher in Nandurbar summed it up rather well: 'Many historically subordinated groups especially women, Dalits, and Adivasis are now thinking, what is my problem, and how it can be addressed using the Constitution.'[33]

Since the early 1990s and until it ceded ground to the Hindutva ideology, UP was the laboratory of the Dalit movement led by Kanshi Ram and Mayawati. For mysterious reasons, Mayawati, the leader of Bahujan Samaj Party (BSP), has been passive since 2022, when the previous assembly elections were held in UP. With the rise of the '400 paar' slogan, Dalits were further disappointed that she did not show any inclination to counter BJP. Sheetal P. Singh, an experienced reporter who toured UP extensively during these elections, revealed to me that BSP supporters were seriously rethinking whether to vote for Mayawati. He was one of the first to gauge the mood of the Dalit voters in UP. In his opinion, 'A large section of Dalit voters was unhappy with Mayawati and was gravitating towards Samajwadi-Congress alliance in the state.'[34] A section of Dalits had already moved away from BSP in the last assembly elections. In this election, the shift became more pronounced, and Mayawati's vote share shrunk from 12.88 per cent to 9.39 per cent.

A post-poll survey conducted by the Centre for Studies for Developing Societies (CSDS) captured this shift. According to the survey, 56% non-Jatav Dalits voted for the INDIA, 29% voted for NDA and only 15% for BSP. Whereas in the 2019 parliamentary election, 38% non-Jatavs voted for BSP–SP alliance and 40.5% for NDA. This data clearly indicates that amongst the non-Jatavs whose first choice was BJP led NDA in 2019, 11.5% of them deserted the BJP-led NDA and chose the INDIA. Jatav voters, who had been the traditional backbone of BSP and had been overwhelmingly voting for BSP, had also shown disquiet with BSP. In 2019, 65.3% Jatavs voted for BSP–SP alliance due to Mayawati, but in 2024, only 44%, voted for BSP, a substantial drop of 21.3%. Whereas 25% Jatavs voted for the INDIA and 24% for NDA.[35]

Bharatiya Janata Party has gone through a massive caste churning under the leadership of Narendra Modi. Before his advent as the supreme leader, BJP was called the Brahmin Baniya party. The party had great support amongst the upper castes and upper class but was struggling to attract OBCs and Dalits. The upper castes are still overwhelmingly with BJP.

A survey conducted by CSDS in UP in June 2024 underlines that more than 79 per cent upper-caste voters had voted for BJP as against 77.2 per cent in the 2019 general election. Only 16 per cent voted for the SP–Congress alliance. This figure is staggering since there was speculation during the elections that the Thakurs were upset with BJP since Purushottam Rupala, the party's leader in Gujarat, had made unsavoury remarks about the Rajputs. However, BJP's remarkable success in UP was a result of the serious inroads that the party had made among OBCs and Dalits. Of the 80 seats in UP, the party had won 71 seats in 2014 and 62 in 2019. Rashtriya Swayamsevak Sangh, too, tried to reach out to OBCs and Dalits through its various programmes and used subsidiary organisations to build bridges with this section of society. When Amit Shah was made in-charge of UP in the run-up to the 2014 elections, he tried social engineering at an organisation level within the party. He promoted OBC and Dalit leadership at the grassroots level rather heavily. According to a CSDS survey conducted in 2019, other than Yadav OBC castes, Kurmi and Koeri decided to vote for BJP, amounting to 73.8 per cent votes. Even in 2024, when BJP's chips were down, these OBC castes did not desert the party. As much as 59 per cent non-Yadav OBCs still preferred BJP, which was a decline of only 7.7 per cent. The party also succeeded in attracting non-Jatav Dalits, with 40.5 per cent of that voter base choosing BJP in the 2019 election.[36]

The survey conducted by CSDS clearly hints that, despite Prime Minister Modi's assurance, a big section of Dalits and a section of OBCs other than Yadavs were not willing to take his words at face value on the issue of the Constitution and reservation. Based on the data of the 2019 and 2023 CSDS surveys, one finds that BJP received fewer votes from non-Jatav Dalits (29 per cent in 2024 as against 40.5 per cent in 2019) and non-Yadav OBCs (59 per cent in 2024 as against 66.7 per cent in 2019). This crisis of credibility was not delusional or a product of a false narrative created by the opposition and fake videos, but had its roots in the past and in BJP's ideology of Hindutva.

During the 2024 parliamentary elections, I wrote extensively on the subject. For the globally reputed online e-magazine *The Diplomat*, I wrote,

> In the last ten years, the BJP, and the Modi regime has consciously changed the national discourse. Minorities, especially Muslims, have been demonised, and it has been inculcated in the minds of a large section of Hindus that India is a Hindu *rashtra* [Hindu nation] and minorities have no other option but to accept this fact and live as second-class citizens.
>
> The opposition has been contesting this formulation but without much success. On the eve of national elections, its apprehensions have deepened as Modi has given enough hints that if he comes back as prime minister then 'his government will take big decisions.' Though he has not spelt out what those decisions will be, his statements that the BJP will get 370 seats, and along with alliance partners, the number will cross 400, is indicative of his intentions. . . .
>
> The Modi government has already taken a few steps to engineer fundamental changes in the Constitution. A committee was constituted under the chairmanship of the former president of India, Ram Nath Kovind, to prepare a draft for 'One Nation, One Election.' The committee has submitted its report to the government. Since Modi become the prime minister, the BJP has been arguing that elections to Parliament and state assemblies should

> be held simultaneously, as that will not only save time, energy and money but also smooth governance. . . . The opposition sees the 'One Nation, One Election' exercise as an excuse to tinker with the constitution for the BJP's long-term goal.[37]

The actions of the Modi government, when read in tandem with those of the Vajpayee-led coalition government that was in power from 1998 to 2004, only compounded the apprehensions of the people about there being a change in the Constitution. During its tenure, the Vajpayee government had instituted a high-power committee under the chairmanship of former Chief Justice of India M.N. Venkatachaliah, to review the functioning of the Constitution and suggest changes. The committee submitted its report, but no action could be taken because the Vajpayee government lost the mandate of the people in the 2004 elections. But the debate continued. Since the formation of the Modi government, several persons closely working with the government have said that, for better functioning, India needed to change the Constitution.

In 2017, RSS chief Mohan Bhagwat had said, 'Our constitution was written based on the understanding of the Bhartiya ethos of our founding fathers, but many of the laws that we are still using are based on foreign sources and were made as per their thinking. Seven decades have passed since our independence . . . this is something we must address.'[38]

Bhagwat was not alone. In 2020, Amitabh Kant, the then CEO of Niti Aayog, had said that India has too much democracy, and tough reforms in the Indian context are difficult.[39]

Bibek Debroy, a member of the prime minister's Economic Advisory Council, too had advocated for a new Constitution for India. In his column for *Mint*, he wrote, 'We no longer possess the one we inherited in 1950. It has been amended, not always for the better, though since 1973 we have been told its "basic structure" cannot be altered, irrespective of what democracy desires through parliament; whether there is a violation will be interpreted by courts.'[40] He concluded by saying, 'Much of what we debate begins and ends with the Constitution. A few amendments won't do. We should go back to the drawing board and start from the first principles, asking what these words in the Preamble mean now: socialist, secular, democratic, justice, liberty and equality. We the People have to give ourselves a new Constitution.'[41]

There is enough archival material to prove that RSS was at the forefront in opposing the Constitution when it was adopted by the Constituent Assembly on 26 November 1949. In fact, RSS and its ideological partners had advocated that, instead of the Constitution, the Manusmriti should be adopted, as it reflected the soul of India. The Manusmriti is based on the hierarchical structure of the society and hence considered a regressive document by its critics. Shamsul Islam, an expert on RSS, said that on 30 November 1949, *The Organiser*, RSS's English mouthpiece, wrote a scathing editorial on the adoption of the Constitution. He quoted the article as saying, 'But in our Constitution, there is no mention of the unique constitutional development in ancient *Bharat*. Manu's Laws were written long before Lycurgus of Sparta or Solon of Persia. To this day his laws as enunciated in the *Manusmriti* excite the admiration of the world and elicit spontaneous obedience and conformity. But to our constitutional pundits that means nothing.'[42]

M.S. Golwalkar was the chief of the RSS then. It is said that he had a spiritual bent of mind and is still considered the moral beacon for RSS. He said, 'Our Constitution too, is just a cumbersome and heterogeneous piecing together of various articles from various Constitutions of Western countries. It has absolutely nothing which can be called our own. Is there a single word of reference in its guiding principles as to what our national mission is and what our keynote in life is?'[43] Golwalkar's statement shows the scant regard he had for the Constitution.

V.D. Savarkar, who was associated with Hindu Mahasabha, was the originator of Hindutva as an ideology and was revered as an iconic figure within the Hindutva fold. Savarkar, too, was unhappy about the Manusmriti not being accorded the place he thought it deserved. He said, '*Manusmriti* is that scripture which is most worship-able after Vedas for our Hindu Nation and which from ancient times has become the basis of our culture-customs, thought and practice. This book for centuries has codified the spiritual and divine march of our nation. Even today the rules which are followed by crores of Hindus in their lives and practice are based on *Manusmriti*. Today *Manusmriti* is Hindu Law.'[44]

If the Manusmriti had been accorded the status of the Constitution of India, the oppressed classes and women would have lived worse lives. If you look at some of the laws given in the Manusmriti to deal with Shudras (Dalits), you'll understand the document's regressive nature:

- Once-born man (a Sudra), who insults a twice-born man with gross invective, shall have his tongue cut out; for he is of low origin.
- If he arrogantly teaches Brahmanas their duty, the king shall cause hot oil to be poured into his mouth and into his ears.
- A low-caste man who tries to place himself on the same seat with a man of a high caste, shall be branded on his hip and be banished, or (the king) shall cause his buttock to be gashed.[45]

Manu's laws were equally regressive for women:

- Day and night women must be kept in dependence by the males (of) their (families), and, if they attach themselves to sensual enjoyments, they must be kept under one's control.
- Through their passion for men, through their mutable temper, through their natural heartlessness, they become disloyal towards their husbands, however carefully they may be guarded in this (world).
- For women no (sacramental) rite (is performed) with sacred texts, thus the law is settled; women (who are) destitute of strength and destitute of (the knowledge of) Vedic texts, (are as impure as) falsehood (itself), that is a fixed rule.[46]

Over the years, the criticism of the Constitution by RSS, its subsidiary organisations and Hindutvavadis has not ebbed. A.G. Noorani wrote that as late as 1992-93, 'The RSS published a white paper denouncing the Constitution . . . In its foreword, Swami Hiranand wrote: "The Constitution is contrary to the country's culture, character, circumstances, situation, etc. It is foreign-oriented."'[47] Swami Hiranand further writes, 'The damage done by 200 years long rule of the British is negligible as compared with the harm done by our Constitution. The conspiracy to convert Bharat into India continues.'[48] Swami Muktanand and Swami Vamdev Maharaj, who were closely associated with RSS, held a press conference in Delhi at Vishwa Samvad Kendra, which was the residence of a BJP MP, on 25 December 1992, and released this white paper.[49]

Professor Rajendra Singh, who was second-in-command in RSS, echoed the same sentiment in an article in *The Indian Express*. Noorani quoted from the article, 'Certain specialties of this country should be reflected in the Constitution. In place of "India that is Bharat," we should have said "Bharat that is Hindustan." Official documents refer to the "composite culture," but ours is certainly not a composite culture. . . . All this shows that changes are needed in the Constitution. A Constitution more suited to the ethos and genius of this country should be scooted in the future.'[50]

After Professor Singh, K.S. Sudarshan became the RSS chief. Without mincing words he said, 'the constitution should be scrapped.'[51] In an article in *The Indian Express*, Karan Thapar recalled how Sudarshan, in an interview for *Hard Talk India*, Thapar's show telecast on BBC, refused to accept the Constitution 'as it stands'.[52]

Much before Professor Singh and Sudarshan, Deen Dayal Upadhyay raised serious questions about the nature of the Constitution. Upadhyay was an RSS pracharak before he founded Jan Sangh along with Syama Prasad Mookerjee in 1951.

Upadhyay was not only a political activist but also a theoretician. He was probably the only one within the Sangh Parivar who tried to systematically demolish the edifice of the Nehruvian model and presented an alternate vision for the nation. He was of the opinion that India had gone through the dark ages, when other civilisations invaded India and ruled over us for over a thousand years, because we had disconnected from our roots, from our thought process. He was of the opinion that, like human beings, every nation has its own 'soul' which defines its basic nature. He called it 'chitti', something that couldn't be acquired. While talking about the Constitution, he said, 'The Constitution has to reflect the basic nature of the nation and if the Constitution goes against the basic nature of the nation and it damages its thought process then it has to be amended.'[53] During a four-day lecture series held in Pune in 1965, Upadhyay propounded the concept of Integral Humanism. In this lecture, he challenged the basic premise of the Constitution, saying, 'The written Constitution cannot go on while opposing the tradition of the country. If it continues while opposing its traditions then it means that the Constitution has not been made according to the Dharma. Only that Constitution can be said to be made according to the Dharma which reflects the thought process of the nation because the thought process is the product of Dharma.'[54]

Upadhyay attacked the Constitution on two counts: secularism and federalism. In his opinion, neither concept reflects the basic nature of our nation. He said that the word 'secular' was borrowed from the West, and in the Indian context it was not needed. He said that the state could not be without dharma, so to call the Indian state *dharma-nirpeksh* (secular) was not right. He was of the opinion that the job of the state was to create a system which was run according to dharma. Then he prophetically announced that the state could only be 'Dharma Rajya'. Though he clarified that this 'Dharma Rajya' was not a theocratic state as is understood in the West, in his lecture, he insisted that unlike in a democracy where sovereignty lies with the people, Dharma would be sovereign. This is a problematic idea.[55] He said, 'Dharma is bigger than people, parliament, majority, judiciary and all other institutions and these have to follow the dictates of the Dharma because Dharma of the nation is bigger than the rest.'[56]

The Indian Constitution is a top-down model. The framers of our Constitution first created the Union and then talked about states. Federalism defines the Centre–state relationship. It assigns the Centre the power to change the geographical boundaries of states with their consent. Indian federalism tries to keep a fine balance between the Centre and the state. But

Upadhyay thought that the basic concept of India as a Union of states was a flawed concept and posed a threat to 'the unity and integrity' of the country. He said, 'In this concept there is no imagination of a live consciousness of Bharat Mata. According to the first article of the Constitution, India that is Bharat is a "Union of States". That means all Matas like Biharmata, Bangmata, Punjabmata, Kannadmata, Tamilmata, etc. will form Bharat Mata. This is a ridiculous imagination . . . that our Constitution should not be federal but unitary.'[57]

Upadhyay's critique of the Constitution of India was not taken seriously, as Jan Sangh then was only a fringe player in Indian politics. However, today, in its new avatar, BJP has acquired the pole position. The party has never disowned Integral Humanism—rather, it swears by it. Hence, the debate on changing the Constitution should not be brushed aside lightly. What has been a murmur since the adoption of the Indian Constitution has now become a loud noise. Looking at the record of the Modi government since 2014, the threat of the Constitution being changed looks real. And it was this very real possibility that played on the minds of the people. The seriousness they accorded to it reflected in the voting behaviour of Dalits and the marginalised people, leading to BJP performing poorly, especially in UP, Maharashtra and a few other states.

In the 2024 election, Indian voters seemed to be telling BJP that the Constitution matters, and the party shouldn't meddle with it.

3

The Divinity Factor

यदा यदा हि धर्मस्य ग्लानिर्भवति भारत ।
अभ्युत्थानमधर्मस्य तदात्मानं सृजाम्यहम् ॥ 4.7 ॥

I manifest myself whenever Dharma starts fading into oblivion and Adharma increases.

परित्राणाय साधूनां विनाशाय च दुष्कृताम् ।
धर्मसंस्थापनार्थाय सम्भवामि युगे युगे ॥ 4.8 ॥

I take birth in every age to protect the virtuous, annihilate the evil-doers, and establish Dharma.

—Bhagavad Gita

On a cruise by the banks of River Ganga in Varanasi, while talking to a reporter, Prime Minister Narendra Modi made a prophetic statement: 'I am convinced that God has sent me.' This statement defines him as a leader and separates him from other leaders, and it will be remembered and quoted in history. The interview, originally in Hindi, was conducted on 14 May 2024, by a *News18* reporter. Here is a translation of some extracts from the interview:

Reporter: Five years back, when I interviewed you, and although many people made fun, I had asked a question because a woman working in a sugarcane field asked me to ask you, that I will ask again. Five years back, I asked you, why don't you tire? After five years, you look even more energetic, you are working more, why don't you get tired?[1]

Prime Minister Modi: Earlier, when my mother was alive, I used to think that I was biologically born. After my mother's death, when I recollected all my experiences, I was convinced I could be wrong. The leftists will make fun of me and pull out my hair, but I am convinced that God has sent me. My energy has not emanated from the biological body. This energy has been ordained to me by God because he wants some work to be done by me, and that is why he has given me skill, potential, a kind heart and inspiration. He has given me the potential to do some work. I am nothing. I am only an instrument. God has decided to get things done through me, and that is why when I do something, I believe that God wants me to do that thing, saying do not worry; it will earn a name for you. But I cannot see God. I am a priest, and I am his devotee. So I treat 140 crore countrymen as my God; they are my God.[2]

Reporter: You are amongst God, and God is with you. Mother is in you. All good wishes.[3]

Prime Minister Modi: Thank You.[4]

This interview received global attention and went viral on social media. Had the prime minister not used the word 'biological', the interview would most likely have gone unnoticed by the news cycles, but it grabbed attention and invited ridicule and scorn. It left even his admirers aghast. Had he said that he wasn't biological to present himself as bigger and grander than the rest, or had he become delusional about his own existence? Was he using the instrument of divinity as a clever ploy for political purposes, or was he a victim of his own narcissistic traits? Sidharth Bhatia wrote in *The Wire*, 'But cynics would be wrong to dismiss Modi's delusions of divine grandeur as mere election talk. Indeed, there have been many clues in the past ten years that Modi has begun to think of himself as someone different, someone much above every other human, who has been blessed with power far beyond the ken of an ordinary human.'[5]

A deeper psychoanalysis of Modi's personality is required to understand the bigger canvas of his statement. Bhatia raises a very important point when he says: 'In his electoral life, ever since he became chief minister of Gujarat in 2001, Modi has never personally lost an election. He has always led his party to victory in the state and, from 2014, at the Centre. He is the BJP's mascot and it would not be wrong to say that the public comes to its rallies to see him. If he were to disappear from the stage, the BJP would likely crumble. No one in his party has the appeal to pull the crowds nor the heft to get his own colleagues together. Besides, no one in his own party can stand up to him and ask him questions—senior leaders are reduced to jelly in his presence. That kind of power can go to someone's head.'[6]

While Bhatia was right when he said Modi had never lost an election, there was no denying that Modi was vulnerable in the 2024 general election. Voter apathy was one of the biggest talking points in this election. It was widely debated that ten years of anti-incumbency against the Modi government was catching up, and the absence of a robust alternative had blunted voters' enthusiasm to vote. It was also reported that even BJP workers and cadre were not enthused enough.

On 2 May, before the third phase of polling, *Reuters* reported: 'More than half a dozen BJP leaders and political analysts that *Reuters* spoke to said a lack of momentum in the two initial phases of the seven-phase-election have dampened hopes of a huge majority for the party, although they said it was still likely to retain power in the world's most populous nation.'[7]

The *Reuters* report clearly said that 'the lower turnout so far in India's long general election has rattled Prime Minister Narendra Modi's campaign managers'. It further stated, 'The lack of momentum has been partly blamed on apathy among party workers believing victory is assured and seems to have prompted Modi to change tack in his campaign speeches to try to fire up the Hindu majority, the party's support base, and get them out to voting stations, political analysts said . . . Modi himself has shifted in his campaign speeches from a focus on the administration's successes in his 10-year tenure to targeting minority Muslims and the opposition Congress party.'[8]

Reporters of independent media like *Reuters* started writing about voter indifference only after witnessing it on the ground in the first two phases of polling. It wouldn't be wrong to assume that the prime minister, with the entire paraphernalia of a very robust state at his disposal, must have got a whiff of it much before the media and accordingly fine-tuned his electoral strategy. Though he is known for his communal speeches during elections, two speeches made by Modi within the span of a fortnight stood out for their virulence. On 6 April 2024, he called the Congress manifesto Jinnah's Muslim League's manifesto. He said, 'The [Congress] manifesto reflects actions similar to those of Muslim League during the struggle for independence. Congress is imposing Muslim League's ideology on the nation, and its manifesto is nothing short of an agenda to push back the country by a century.'[9]

A prime minister who had never missed an opportunity to present himself as the man behind our country's great transformation into a 'New India' and making the country a global player had suddenly changed tack to focus on the opponent's manifesto instead. Traditionally, the manifesto has never been an issue during elections. It is a document that is released and, very quickly, forgotten. However, Modi tried to use the Congress manifesto to polarise voters on religious lines. He tried to paint Congress as a pro-minority party—and by extension, anti-Hindu.

Modi gave another contentious speech on 21 April 2024. Speaking at a rally in Banswara, Rajasthan, he once again attacked the Congress manifesto. 'They have said that if Congress gets to form govt, they would conduct a survey of everyone's assets: how much gold our mothers and sisters have and their value would be computed, including the silver ornaments of our tribal sisters, the assets of govt employees, everything. They don't stop at that. They go on to say that the assets will be equitably redistributed. Is it acceptable to you?'[10] He drew parallels between the Congress manifesto and Dr Manmohan Singh's statement about minorities having the first claim on national resources. 'Does this tell you whom the assets are going to be distributed among? It is going to be distributed among those who have more children, among the infiltrators?'[11] He went on to add, 'I must caution you that even the mangal sutras of our mothers and sisters are not safe from this urban Naxal thinking.[12]

Modi had played on the sentiments of the Hindu voter, especially of women voters, by mentioning their mangalsutras which hold an emotional connect in Hindu marriages. He also othered the Muslims by calling them 'infiltrators'. Moreover, he had given a communal twist to the Congress manifesto.

Congress immediately realised that this could badly damage the party. It reacted aggressively and challenged the prime minister to show that the words 'Hindu' and 'Muslim' were written in its manifesto. Congress spokesperson Pawan Khera reacted angrily: 'Your name will be relegated to the dustbin of history. You are speaking lies after lies just to win an election. You are serving the country such lies about Hindu-Muslim.'[13]

Congress also complained to the Election Commission of India, demanding that 'the PM be disqualified for egregious violations of electoral laws in his speech in Rajasthan.'[14] Bharatiya Janata Party was unapologetic and said that the prime minister 'has echoed people's sentiments'[15]

On 29 May 2024, Hilal Ahmed wrote in *The Times of India*, 'After the first phase of polling, the BJP establishment decided to launch an aggressive political campaign to reach out to its traditional support base. Party brass systematically followed clear anti-Muslim rhetoric to justify the old BJP argument on Muslim appeasement.'[16]

The word 'infiltrators' is not new in the dictionary of RSS/BJP. Since the days of the Rath Yatra from Somnath to Ayodhya, L.K. Advani and his party have been trying to magnify the issue of Bangladeshi immigrants—calling them infiltrators—and through them, targeting the Muslim community. Since 1971, after having freed themselves from the atrocities perpetrated by the Pakistani army in East Pakistan (now Bangladesh) with the military intervention of India, Bangladeshis have illegally migrated in lakhs to India. The migration of Bangladeshis became a huge issue in Assam and in other north-eastern states. However, it would be wrong to say that only Muslims came to India. Hindus, who had decided to stay back in East Pakistan at the time of the partition, also migrated in hordes to India to save their lives. But BJP, in its distorted world view, tried to paint these Bangladeshi immigrants as only Muslims and called them a threat to national security, instead of calling it a demographic crisis.

Even before forming the government at the Centre, BJP had consistently raised the issue and demanded the identification and deportation of Bangladeshi immigrants. During his regime, Modi launched the National Register for Citizens (NRC) to identify such 'foreigners' and Indian citizens. Later, the Modi government promulgated Citizenship (Amendment) Act (CAA) to grant citizenship to those religious minorities who were allegedly persecuted and had migrated from Afghanistan, Pakistan and Bangladesh. But the law did not include religiously persecuted Muslims in these countries. This created a big controversy. Muslims in India viewed this as discriminatory and against the basic tenets of the Constitution. They resorted to agitation. Muslim women from Delhi took the lead and sat on an indefinite dharna at Shaheen Bagh. The Shaheen Bagh movement attracted global attention due to its unique Gandhian way of protest. These women carried a copy of the Constitution and raised the issue that the Modi government, out of its religious bias, was resorting to religious discrimination. This movement had to be aborted due to the COVID-19 pandemic.

Bharatiya Janata Party had always claimed that Congress had compromised on national security by refusing to take action against illegal immigrants when Congress had been in power at the Centre. On 2 April 2024, the prime minister once again accused Congress of supporting 'infiltrators'. He said, 'Our government introduced CAA to grant citizenship to those loyal to Bharat Mata, which is causing the most concern for Congress . . . Congress, which facilitates infiltrators, is now opposing CAA.'[17] With one stroke, the prime minister of India had called the entire Muslim community's existence in the country illegal. He had made them stateless. Which inadvertently meant that Muslims had no right to live in India and should be deported. It is another matter that later he corrected himself and denied that he ever made such a statement.

Modi is a great communicator. He carefully chooses his words to target a particular audience. The motive was political. The purpose was to create an anti-Muslim narrative and influence Hindu voters. Since becoming the prime minister, Modi has avoided attacking Muslims directly in his speeches, unlike in the past when he was the chief minister of Gujarat. But in the 2024 election, his communication strategy changed, and he began attacking Muslims directly once again, though he did this through indirect references and innuendos, and using anti-Muslim slurs.

Before Banswara, this pattern was visible with the prime minister using communal language to paint Congress and Rahul Gandhi as anti-Hindu, but not directly targeting Muslims. In Karauli, Rajasthan, Modi called Rahul Gandhi a 'shehzada' and blamed the Congress for his anti-Ram attitude. *The Times of India* reported, 'He added that Congress had made "objectionable comments" about Ram temple and blamed the party for boycotting the "pran pratishtha of Ram Lalla" in Ayodhya.'[18]

On 13 April 2024, *The Times of India* reported Modi as saying, '*Jo zamanat par hain, aise ek mujrim ke ghar jaake, Sawan ke mahine mein mutton banane ka mauj le rahe hain* (They go to the house of a convict out on bail and have fun cooking mutton in the month of Sawan[19]).' Though he did not take names, the reference was clearly to last year's video of RJD patriarch Lalu Prasad and his son Tejashwi cooking mutton with Rahul Gandhi in the audience. Tejashwi recently courted controversy over another video which showed him enjoying fried fish.[20] *The Times of India* reported, 'PM Modi on Friday accused Congress-led opposition of offending the sentiments of the majority by making a show of cooking meat during auspicious Hindu periods, and said that such acts aimed at appeasing "vote banks" were reflective of "Mughal" invaders "who found perverted joy in demolition of temples and defiling places of worship".'[21]

On 20 April 2024, the prime minister addressed a rally in Chhatrapati Sambhajinagar, Maharashtra, where he called Rahul Gandhi a 'shehzada' again. He said, 'Congress shehzada is facing trouble in Wayanad. Shehzada and his gang are awaiting voting in Wayanad and after that they will announce a safe seat for him.'[22] The use of the Urdu word 'shehzada' is intriguing. He could have called Rahul Gandhi a 'rajkumar', the Hindi equivalent of the word, but he deliberately used 'shehzada' to project Rahul as pro-Muslim and anti-Hindu.

On 23 April, in Rajasthan, he accused Congress of conspiring to snatch SC/ST reservations and giving the quota to Muslims. This speech was given at the Tonk–Sawai Madhopur Lok Sabha constituency, where polling was to happen on 26 April 2024. The prime minister said, 'The right to reservation provided by Babasaheb Ambedkar to Dalits, backwards and Adivasis—Congress and INDI Alliance wanted to give it to Muslims on the basis of religion.'[23] This was not just a passing reference. He dwelt on the subject in detail, and it was apparent that he had done elaborate homework and research. He wanted to create a strong Hindu–Muslim binary and turn it into a major election issue to polarise voters on religious lines and consolidate Hindu voters for his party. It is the Prime Minister who coined the term INDI Alliance so as not to refer to the alliance by its acronym INDIA.

He said, 'Congress party has toyed with Babasaheb Ambedkar's Constitution. When the Constitution was drafted, reservations based on religion was vehemently opposed so that

SCs, STs, and OBCs could get protection. But Manmohan Singh in his speech said—and I was present there as a CM—that Muslims have the first right on the country's resources. This was not a coincidence or an isolated statement. Congress party's thinking has always been of appeasement and vote bank politics. As soon as the Congress came to power at the Centre in 2004, the first thing it did was to try to provide reservation to Muslims by reducing SC/ST reservations in Andhra Pradesh. This was a pilot project, which Congress wanted to try in the entire country. Between 2004 and 2010, Congress tried four times to implement Muslim reservations in Andhra Pradesh. However, due to legal hurdles and awareness of the Supreme Court, they could not succeed in their plans.'[24]

He further said, 'In 2011, Congress tried to implement it across the country . . . Congress made all these efforts despite knowing it was against the basic spirit of the Constitution. But Congress did not care about the Constitution or about Babasaheb Ambedkar. When we got a chance in Karnataka, the first thing we did was end the Muslim quota they had created out of the SC/ST quota.'[25]

Modi's choice of words is interesting. He repeatedly used words like 'Babasaheb Ambedkar', 'Constitution', 'SC/ST reservation' along with 'Muslim'. The strategy was simple—create a bogey of Muslims and paint Congress as anti-Dalit/Adivasi, anti-Constitution and anti–Babasaheb Ambedkar along with being anti-Hindu. This was important because, by then, it was apparent that a section of Dalits, OBCs and Adivasis had started moving away from BJP due to the 'Save Constitution' campaign introduced by Rahul Gandhi and the opposition. It was seen as a fragmentation of Hindu votes, and this could only be stopped by projecting Muslims as the common enemies of Hindus, irrespective of caste fault lines. Therefore, BJP and Modi needed to underline that Modi was the defender of Hindus; the protector of Dalits, Adivasis and OBCs; that the Constitution was safe as long as he was the prime minister, and unlike the Congress, he was the real follower of Babasaheb Ambedkar.

In this endeavour, Modi follows no rules. His speech was a classic example of innuendos, half-truths and lies. While it is true that Congress tried to give reservations to Muslims in Andhra Pradesh, it was not on the basis of religion. This needs to be seen from a historical perspective. Muslims in India are not a monolith community. Like Hindus, Muslims are also divided into many castes and sub-castes. A large number of Hindus who belonged to the Depressed Classes converted to Islam, as they were not treated equally and were subjected to inhuman treatment. Their conversion to Islam was a search for liberation from the oppressive social structures in Hindu society, and to attain social equality and dignity in life. Ironically, the curse of the caste system continued. Dalit thinker Kancha Ilaiah Shepherd writes, '. . . The curse of caste continued to penetrate deeper and deeper into the Muslim community as several caste communities, along with their occupational backgrounds, converted into Islam, particularly during Mughal period. Even after conversion, education and equal opportunities eluded most of them.'[26]

Ali Anwar, a former member of parliament from Bihar and a backward community Muslim, has been leading the movement that demands reservation for Dalit Muslims as recommended by the Mandal Commission. In his book *Masawat ki Jung*, Anwar writes: 'Caste discrimination in Muslim society and the deprived status of a particular section is so evident that it can no longer be overlooked. When the constitution was being drafted, Muslim leaders did not press for any reservation for the Dalits among

Muslims. While one does not suspect the integrity of the Muslim leaders, it is the tendency to glide over the discrimination and inequality within the community, painfully experienced over the past 50 years, that leaves a deep wound.'[27] He further writes, '. . . In independent India, while the constitution provided the Hindu Dalits with the status of Scheduled Castes and even Hindus among Adivasis with the status of Scheduled Tribes and gave them means of upward social mobility, the Muslim untouchables were left to the mercy of Allah.'[28]

This is not to say that the commissions appointed by various governments to study backwardness among different communities ignored social backwardness in the Muslim community. The Kaka Kalelkar Commission, formed in 1953, talked about social backwardness in the Muslim community. However, it restrained itself from recommending reservations for these Muslims. The Mandal Commission, formed in 1977, did not commit the same mistake. It not only identified backwardness among Muslims but also clubbed them along with socially backward groups in Hindus. The Mandal Commission report was revolutionary, not only because it recommended 27 per cent reservation for Hindu OBCs but also because it recommended that Muslims should also avail of reservation facilities. But due to its ideological blindness, BJP has failed to recognise the stark social reality among Indian Muslims. It has failed to understand that Mandal Commission's recommendation for a reservation to a section of Muslims was not based on religion but a recognition of the oppressive nature of the caste system among Muslims. If socially backward Hindus can be given reservations, then why should socially backward Muslims be deprived of the same?

Even the Sachar Committee, formed by the Manmohan Singh government in 2005 to study the socio-economic conditions of

Muslims, underlined in its 2006 report that a section of Muslims is living in worse conditions than Hindu Dalits.

The Congress government in undivided Andhra Pradesh attempted to give reservations to backward Muslims within the framework of the Mandal Commission. Y.S. Rajasekhara Reddy, a powerful leader of Congress, formed his government on 14 May 2004, after defeating N. Chandrababu Naidu. He had promised to give reservations to the backward Muslims. After forming the government, on the basis of Justice Puttaswamy Commission report, he included Muslims in the OBC list and ordered to give 5 per cent reservation to OBCs among Muslims. This government order was nullified by the Andhra Pradesh High Court in September 2004, taking the plea that the government order had exceeded the overall reservation limit of 50 per cent as decided by the nine-judge bench of the Supreme Court in 1992. After the High Court order, the Rajasekhara Reddy government reconstituted the OBC commission under Justice Dalva Subrahmanyam. Based on the Subrahmanyam Commission report, the government issued an ordinance on 20 June 2005, which was replaced by an Act passed by the assembly on 25 October 2005, to give 5 per cent reservation in educational institutions and government jobs to Muslim groups. This was also struck down by the High Court on the plea that no scientific study was done to determine the backwardness of the Muslim groups.[29]

After the High Court's order, the Rajasekhara Reddy government formed an expert committee led by IAS officer P.S. Krishnan, to determine backwardness among Muslims. Based on the report of this expert committee, the Reddy government ordered a 4 per cent reservation to fourteen groups of Muslims in educational institutions and government jobs in 2007. This order was also challenged in the High Court, where it was quashed on 8 February 2010. The state government appealed to the Supreme Court, which allowed the 4 per cent Muslim quota to be reinstated on 20 January 2013 but referred the matter to the Constitution bench to decide the larger question of constitutionality. The matter is still pending before the Supreme Court, and reservation for Muslims continues in Andhra Pradesh and Telangana.

Despite being against reservations for Muslims, Modi has no problem with the Telugu Desam Party (TDP) with which his party entered into an alliance and contested elections together in Andhra Pradesh. Telugu Desam Party, led by Chandrababu Naidu, is in favour of reservation for Muslims, and it had formally announced this in its manifesto. Naidu reiterated his party's promise on 5 May 2024: 'From the beginning, we are supporting a four per cent reservation for Muslims and that will continue.'[30] After Modi formed the government at the Centre, TDP repeated its commitment to Muslim reservations. Naidu's son and TDP's general secretary Nara Lokesh rubbished BJP's argument that it was Muslim appeasement. He said, 'It [reservation for Muslims] has been going around for the last 2 decades and we stand by it. We intend to continue it. . . . It's a fact that minorities continue to suffer and that they have the lowest per capita income. As a government, it is my responsibility to bring them out of poverty. So whatever decisions I take are not for appeasement, but to bring them out of poverty.'[31]

It is so paradoxical that Modi and his party viscerally targeted the Congress manifesto, which has not mentioned the word 'Muslim' even once, or promised to give reservation to Muslims. In contrast, Modi and BJP maintained a mysterious silence on TDP continuing reservation for Muslims. If Muslim reservation was really dangerous for the social fabric of the country, as Modi had claimed it was, then BJP would have criticised TDP for promising to continue reservation for Muslims, and would have refused contesting elections with Naidu. This was electoral opportunism of the highest order. One can conclude that Modi's anti-Muslim reservation campaign had no ideological content; it was the product of fear.

The reality is, even before the first phase of polling, Modi and his party had realised that BJP was in trouble, even in the Hindi-speaking states. This was corroborated by low voter turnout in the first phase of polling. Reports started pouring in that voters were not excited enough to vote for BJP.

In Rajasthan, polling was held in two phases—on 19 April and 26 April 2024. On 18 April 2024, a day before the first phase of polling began, in its debate show conducted by senior journalist Sheetal P. Singh, *SatyaHindi.com* reported: 'There was a definite change in the air and voters were not enthusiastic about BJP and Modi magic was waning.'[32] In the 2014 and 2019 general elections, BJP had won all 25 seats in Rajasthan. As recently as December 2023, the party had won the assembly elections. But according to *SatyaHindi.com*, BJP was on track to lose more than half a dozen seats.

In the neighbouring state of UP, BJP had won 71 out of 80 seats in 2014 and 62 in 2019. However, news from UP was not encouraging either. On 18 April 2024, *SatyaHindi.com* reported that BJP was not performing as per expectations; voters were unhappy with the party and were showing an inclination towards the Samajwadi–Congress partnership.[33] A major loss in UP could hinder BJP's chances of getting a majority in the Parliament.

These reports ultimately proved to be true. In Rajasthan, BJP lost on 11 of the 25 seats, and in UP, it could win only 33 seats.

These reports from UP and Rajasthan must have unnerved the prime minister. He may have realised that the performance-centric narrative would no longer work. Which is why the campaign took a communal tinge. Modi the Prime Minister of India decided to go back to his original avatar of Modi the chief minister of Gujarat.

Modi's diatribe continued. On 29 April 2024, in a long interview with *The Times of India*, he said, 'Our Constitution clearly prohibits reservations based on religion but the Congress govt in Karnataka reversed the law passed by BJP to provide reservation to OBCs and gave it to Muslims, classifying all Muslims as OBC. . . . The Congress govt in Telangana has recently said that it will replicate this move. This proves that Congress wants to reduce the reservation provided to SCs, STs and OBCs across the country and give it to minorities.'[34] Modi was once again speaking half-truths. Like in Andhra Pradesh, in Karnataka, reservation was given to only 36 Muslim communities. These were Muslims who had been categorised as OBCs, subsequent to reports of several commissions—Havanur Commission, Venkataswamy Commission and Justice Chinnappa Reddy Commission. The process of providing reservation to OBC Muslims was initiated by Congress chief minister Veerappa Moily in 1995, but it was implemented by H.D. Deve Gowda. Under his order, 4 per cent seats in educational institutions and government jobs were to be reserved for Muslims. This reservation continued even under two BJP governments in Karnataka.

However, on the eve of assembly elections in 2023, the BJP government led by Basavaraj Bommai removed this 4 per cent reservation. Reservation for Muslims was to be now included within the 10 per cent quota reserved for the economically weaker sections (EWS). This was the party's last-ditch effort to salvage the elections through a brazen communal route, but it did not change their electoral fortune—they ultimately lost. That BJP fought the 2024 general election in Karnataka along with the same H.D. Deve Gowda who implemented the reservation for Muslims when he was the chief minister of the state is another example of the party's political opportunism.

It should be noted that Congress never said that it wanted to reduce reservation for SCs, STs and OBCs to give it to other minorities, as accused by Modi. Chief minister of Telangana Revanth Reddy had only said, 'Neither Shah nor Prime Minister Narendra Modi can scrap the 4% Muslim quota started by the then Congress CM, the late Y.S. Rajasekhara Reddy, in the undivided state.'[35] Rather, it was BJP leader Amit Shah who said in Telangana's Bhongir that BJP would end the Muslim quota. He said, 'In 2019, the public of Telangana gave us four seats. This time, we will win more than 10 Lok Sabha seats in Telangana. This double-digit score in Telangana will make PM Modi cross 400 seats ... Make BJP victorious on more than 10 seats. We will end the Muslim reservation and increase the reservation of SC, ST and OBC.'[36] His statement is another indication of BJP not being confident of the SC, ST and OBC votes in the 2024 elections. The party was using the 'End Muslim Quota' argument as a bargaining chip to lure these Hindu groups into their fold.

During the elections, there was a reason for panic in the BJP camp. Under the leadership of Rahul Gandhi, Congress had decided to reinvent itself by redesigning its ideological position and discovering a new social base. The appointment of Dalit leader Mallikarjun Kharge as the party president was done with the same aim. In its heyday, Congress did not bother to lure OBCs to its fold. The party's social base comprised of Dalits, Muslims and upper castes. But in the 1990s, due to the subaltern politics—the Mandal movement and Dalit politics led by BSP in north India and the Ayodhya Movement—a large section of Dalits, Muslims and upper castes moved away from Congress. Once the bastions of Congress, UP and Bihar, crumbled to the extent that Congress's vote share dipped to less than 10 per cent. In the 2022 UP assembly election, despite Priyanka Gandhi's hard work, Congress's vote share shrunk to an all-time low of 2.33 per cent. The party knew that it could not regain its past glory and emerge as a strong contender for power at the Centre unless it dramatically improved its electoral fortunes in UP and Bihar. Since the upper castes had unequivocally aligned with BJP, Congress had no other option but to explore a new social base. Rahul Gandhi realised that OBCs, which made up almost 50 per cent of the population in the two states, could be a good catch.

Playing a long game, Gandhi decided to work on forging an alliance of OBCs, Dalits, Adivasis and Muslims, which together comprise roughly 80 per cent of the population in these states. Through his two Bharat Jodo Yatras and his frontal attack on Modi, he convinced Muslims, which make up around 14 per cent of the total population of India, that nationally, Congress is the best bet for them. This contributed to the INDIA's massive success in UP in the 2024 elections.

Rahul Gandhi took up the cause of social justice to counter BJP's Hindutva and increase Congress's social base. In this endeavour, Caste Census was a good issue to help gravitate OBCs towards Congress. The demand for a Caste Census was first raised by Nitish Kumar, the OBC leader and chief minister of Bihar. He did this when he was heading the government along with Rashtriya Janta Dal (RJD), which was led by Lalu Prasad Yadav's son Tejashwi Yadav. The Nitish Kumar government got the Caste Census done and published its report in October 2023. With Nitish Kumar joining forces with Modi, Rahul Gandhi took on the cause of the Caste Census. Due to ideological reasons, BJP failed to support the Caste Census, as the party believes that it will further divide Hindu society along caste lines, which will hamper Hindutva's larger project of Hindu unity. But the party also knows that it can't afford to be seen as opposing it either. Therefore, it maintains ambivalence on the issue. Despite tremendous pressure, the Modi government decided not to honour the demand for the Caste Census in its second tenure. Aware of BJP's weakness on this issue, Rahul Gandhi tried to make the Caste Census a major issue during this election, including it in the Congress manifesto too.

After Modi's brazen anti-Muslim attack and his attempt to paint Congress as anti-Dalit, anti-OBC and anti-Adivasi, Gandhi finally reacted on 24 April 2024. *The Times of India* reported, 'Stating that PM Narendra Modi is "shaken, panicked and worried" by Congress's "revolutionary" manifesto, Rahul Gandhi [on] Wednesday said the first decision of the future party govt will be caste census, which is a must to establish the meagre participation of 90% population of SC/ST/OBCs in the country's public and private structure. He said an X-ray of society—a national headcount to determine the socio-economic status of marginalised sections—is "now my life's mission".'[37] Gandhi's attack on Modi was vicious. The article further stated: 'The Gandhi scion accused Modi of duplicity, saying the PM told the country in 2014 that he was an OBC but when the issue of "caste census" came up, the PM started claiming there were no castes in India, except "rich" and "poor". Warning that "the entire BJP movement's mission is to erase the history" of 90% population, he said the SC/ST/OBCs are being invisibilised from the country's past including the freedom struggle, and their real history has to be planted afresh.'[38]

The second phase of polling, held on 26 April 2024, caused further concern in the BJP camp. The voter turnout dipped again in comparison to the second phase of polling in 2019. To counter dithering voters and enthuse party workers in Hindi-speaking states, BJP now had to do something urgently. And once again, the party was left with no option but to sharpen its communal agenda.

Modi was not leaving any stone unturned. In his brutal attack on the Congress in Goa, as reported by *The Times of India*, he said, '. . . Congress wants to extend the "Karnataka model" of offering reservation to all Muslims in the country by "planning a dacoity on 27% OBC quota", and that it "plans to change the Constitution for this appeasement".'[39]

In an interview with *The Times of India*, Modi, targeting Muslims once again, said, 'Our Constitution protects the property of all minorities. This means that when Congress talks of redistribution, it cannot touch the properties of minorities, it cannot consider waqf properties for redistribution but it will eye the properties of other communities. This will sow complete and irreversible communal disharmony.'[40] On 1 May 2024, he challenged the opposition to give in writing that they would neither take away reservation for SC/ST and OBCs nor would they give reservation based on religion. Between the second and fourth phases of polling, Modi's attempt to polarise voters along religious lines was getting more urgent, as seen in these reports/headlines in *The Times of India*:

3 May 2024, Anand/Rajkot

'Call for "vote Jihad" insult to democracy, Constitution: Modi'[41]

'Congress party is a "mureed" of Pakistan: PM Modi'[42]

5 May 2024, Darbhanga

'Lalu tried to save those behind Godhra train arson: PM at rally'[43]

6 May 2024, Etawah

'PM Modi warns OBCs of SP-Congress's Karnataka quota plan for UP.'[44]

8 May 2024, Dhar/Khargone/Ahmednagar/Beed

'Give BJP 400, ensure Congress can't put Babri lock on temple: PM Narendra Modi'[45]

'Modi said, "One of their leaders who has quit Congress has exposed a big conspiracy. He has revealed the intention of Congress's Shehzada to reverse Supreme Court's decision on Ram Mandir as his father did in the Shah Bano case."'[46]

11 May 2024, Hyderabad

'Ram is the idea of India, Congress can't see it as it uses a foreign lens: PM Modi'[47]

Modi was not alone in peddling an anti-Muslim agenda. On 26 April 2024, during the second phase of polling, Amit Shah and Yogi Adityanath too attacked the Congress manifesto. Shah said, 'After the Congress manifesto was released, people's inclination towards the BJP further increased because, in its manifesto, Congress has repeated its old habit of appeasement. The Congress manifesto speaks of taking personal law forward. I would like to ask Rahul Gandhi, Will this country now work as per Sharia?'[48] Yogi Adityanath was more strident. He said, 'Congress has written in its manifesto about bringing personal laws for a particular community. Through this move, Congress aims to impose Sharia law, bringing a Taliban-style rule to India.'[49]

But the big question is, why was it done so unabashedly and openly, and did it help BJP consolidate its Hindu voters? The answer is a resounding no.

Political researcher Asim Ali was emphatic about BJP being in trouble and struggling to get close to 272. He wrote in *The Times of India*: 'The election appears, so far, to constitute a wave-less election. We don't see any pronounced polarisation and consolidation of the electorate along a national axis. Or any manifest hum of voter consensus cutting across horizontal (region/state) and vertical (caste/community) lines around a towering personality. On balance, that is a concerning assessment for BJP-led NDA's prospect of comfortably crossing the majority mark. . . . NDA's campaign (particularly around 400 Paar) has encountered choppier waters among Dalits in the Hindu belt while generating enthusiasm among upper caste and certain backward caste.'[50] Bharat Hun and Uday Chandra's observation was akin to Asim's reading of the elections. They wrote after the fifth phase of polling: 'These elections promise to usher in an era of caste's New Democratic reincarnations. On the one hand, within a broad tent of contemporary Hindutva, Brahmins and Rajputs may make common cause with Dalits or Adivasis. On the other hand, cleavages among OBC and SC groups may foment a fresh wave of anti-BJP politics. Both trends may run simultaneously in different states, throwing up a range of unpredictable electoral possibilities.'[51]

The unpredictability of electoral possibilities weighed heavily on Modi's mind and was the main reason for BJP's extreme communal politics. Use of communal anti-Muslim strategy to polarise voters is not new to BJP, but what was new in this election was the brazenness and the degree of intensity. Having observed and written enough about the 2019 and 2024 elections, I can say with authority that the kind of language that was used to whip up Islamophobia in 2024 was definitely missing in the previous elections.

In 2014, Modi was much ahead of the curve. Compared with the monumental corruption charges against the Manmohan Singh government, Modi projected himself as Vikas Purush. His packaging of the Gujarat Model of Development did wonders for BJP and helped the party win 282 seats. The 2019 elections dramatically changed after the Pulwama episode, in which thirty-nine paramilitary jawans were killed in a terrorist attack. Modi and BJP sensed a great opportunity and unleashed the storm of macho-nationalism after the surgical strike in Balakot, in Pakistan, to demolish terrorist hideouts, and its smart packaging left the opposition stunned.

During the 2014 and 2019 elections, Modi and BJP were riding the national narratives. The failure to weave a similar narrative in 2024 unsettled BJP, and forced Modi and his team of strategists to resort to their time-tested formula of communal agenda. They tried to unleash communal fury, and when that did not work, Modi resorted to the divine route and presented himself as a messenger of God, who is divinely ordained to uplift India from the curse of the past and old establishment, and make India great again. It was an attempt to create a false consciousness, to make voters believe that to vote for Modi meant voting for a larger divine goal, a participation in a cosmic project. Modi calling himself 'not biological' is akin to religious and spiritual leaders who fancy themselves 'destiny's child' or the 'chosen one'.

In 2014, when he was an unknown commodity in national politics despite being the chief minister of Gujarat for three consecutive terms, he used the instrument of divinity for the first time to connect with the masses. He said, 'God chooses certain people to do the difficult work. I believe God has chosen me for this work. Now I only need your blessings.'[52] *The Times of India* reported: 'BJP's PM candidate Narendra Modi on Wednesday sought support for his prime ministerial bid, saying he has been chosen by god to rescue the country from the mess created by UPA and he needed people's blessings for accomplishing the difficult task.' He further said that only a stable government would ensure robust development and so people should ensure BJP gets 300 seats. 'Give such a mandate that we can lay the foundation for the next century of development.'

On 22 October 2018, at the inauguration of the National Police Memorial, he once again used the same language. It has been Modi's endeavour to create the image that under his leadership, the country is safe and has emerged stronger to fight internal and external enemies, whereas previous governments compromised national security and, in the process, weakened the nation. In his opinion, to make the country strong, the first priority of the government and people should be [to] take pride in the sacrifices made by the police force and army. In an attempt to harness the spirit of strong nationalism, he said that the previous governments let the 'files gather dust and when we came to power in 2014 we allocated funds for this task and today we are witnessing the reality. I think probably God has chosen me to do this noble task.'[53]

Another such special occasion was the introduction of the Women's Reservation Bill, 2023, to reserve one-third seats for women in the Parliament and state assemblies. The prime minister said, 'Perhaps God has chosen me for this sacred work, to empower women and harness their power.'[54]

It is no surprise then that the same narrative recurred on an event as auspicious as the inauguration of Ram Mandir in Ayodhya, on 22 January 2024. Before embarking on an eleven-day religious experience, Prime Minister Modi said that God had chosen him as an instrument to represent all Indians during the Pran Pratishtha ceremony and he was undertaking the special religious exercise keeping that in mind.[55]

Two weeks before the 'I am not biological' statement, the prime minister insisted that God had blessed him to do big things. In response to a question about how he takes tough decisions, in an interview with *News18*, he said, 'Just as you are surprised, I too wonder how Modi does this. Then I think, no, maybe God has sent me for this work. Whatever I am doing is inspired by a divine power. This could be God's gift, God wants me to do this work and has sent me with a purpose here. . . . God has shown me this path, that you should not get entangled in other things and you have to do some big work and must remain engaged with that. So, it is God's direction, God's wish, God's plan, and, perhaps, their influence. I am only an instrument.'[56] Even after the 'I am not biological' statement created global controversy and invited scorn and ridicule from his critics, he was not deterred. He kept insisting on his self-divinity. In an interview published in *Navbharat Times*, reproduced in English by *The Times of India*, Modi said, 'I believe that I have been greatly blessed by some divine power, which has made me a medium for public welfare. Over the years, my belief has strengthened that God has chosen me to fulfil a special responsibility.'[57]

Meanwhile, the prime minister continued his anti-Muslim tirade. As seen in *The Times of India* reports:

16 May 2024, Kalyan, Maharashtra

'If Congress is elected, it will make two budgets on the basis of religion. I will not allow the budget to be divided as a "Hindu Budget" and "Muslim Budget".'[58]

18 May 2024, Barabanki, UP

'INDIA bloc allies Congress and SP would "bulldoze the Ram temple" in Ayodhya if they came to office.'[59]

26 May 2024, Mandi, Himachal Pradesh

'Accusing a "communal, casteist and nepotist" Congress of pushing Sharia under the guise of seeking to retain Muslim personal law, PM Narendra Modi pledged Friday that BJP would implement the proposed Uniform Civil Code (UCC) across the country.'[60]

If one digs into the reasons why communal polarisation did not get the desired result for BJP, it is possible that BJP leaders were wrong in assuming that the Hindu–Muslim binary would work universally across the country with the same ferocity. It probably had its own geographical boundaries, and it is fast losing its intensity. In areas where local issues became more important, or the opposition showed a better sense of purpose and unity, and could stitch together a better caste coalition, like in UP, the communal agenda lost its killer edge. While it worked in Madhya Pradesh, Gujarat, Himachal Pradesh, Chhattisgarh, Delhi, Uttarakhand and Karnataka to a certain extent, in Rajasthan, UP, Haryana, Maharashtra, Bihar, West Bengal, Jharkhand, Punjab, Kerala, Tamil Nadu, Telangana and Andhra Pradesh, it either had no impact or worked marginally. States like UP and Maharashtra should be a great learning curve for BJP. In these states, people were fed up with the anti-Muslim venom. The pre-poll survey conducted by CSDS showed that 79 per cent of respondents were of the opinion that India belongs to citizens of all religions equally, not just Hindus. Only 11 per cent said India belongs to only the Hindus.[61]

If BJP were working under the premise that their anti-Muslim rhetoric would be met with reactions from the Muslim community, then they were in for a massive disappointment. A pattern has emerged over the last few years, where the Muslim community has stopped reacting to provocation from BJP leaders and their supporters. In this election, the Muslim community maintained extreme silence. A statement from a group of Muslims in Meerut sums it up. They said, 'It takes nothing for things to flare up. We have never profited from polarised elections. We are silent, we are afraid, and we are careful. But I feel there will be greater voting by us this time. We have chosen candidates and parties with some care. Votes won't be split unnecessarily. Not just in UP, I think that is the guiding thought elsewhere too. Let's see . . .'[62]

Ten years is a long time for any government to not face anti-incumbency. The Modi government was no exception. Giving Modi the benefit of doubt, voters gave him another opportunity in 2019 so he could deliver on his promises. But 2024 was different. The vast gap between the promises made and delivered was stark. The party could have offered a logical explanation to the voters—after all, in a democracy the leaders are answerable to the citizens. However, BJP chose instead to play the divinity card. The voters did not take it.

Modi did not realise that his effort to elevate himself to a divine status exposed his own weakness. People expect a certain level of honesty, integrity, morality, truthfulness and straightforwardness from the 'messenger of God'. Gods are there to offer salvation and liberate souls from angst, miseries and restlessness. In the last ten years, despite the high-decibel promises and pomposity, the Modi government failed at fighting price rise and unemployment. Neither did monthly income increase nor did inflation go down. The Mood of the Nation survey conducted by CVoter for *India Today*, which appeared in August 2023, captured the people's disappointment. As much as 55.5 per cent of the respondents believed that the country's unemployment situation is either very serious. 33.8 per cent believed that the Indian economy would worsen, while 36 per cent thought their household income would not improve. More than 60 per cent said that their current daily expenses became difficult to manage in comparison to the year before.[63] The survey, however, had also predicted that Modi would be back for a third term.

After the results, I wrote, 'And so, we have the voters' verdict. They have disapproved of the way the country was run in the last 10 years. But tragically, the voter is also not greatly impressed with the opposition. The BJP has lost but the opposition has not won. The Indian voter has given a message to both. To Modi, the voters have clearly said that they are no longer willing to be emotionally blackmailed, and the country needs a living leader, not a messenger of God. They want their nation to be reclaimed, a nation in which every religion has its place of pride, where the prime minister belongs not to one religion but to all, and where every human is treated like a citizen. The Indian voter wants their country to be governed by lesser mortals and not God-like figures.'[64]

4

When the Referee Turns Rogue

'Elections belong to the people. It's their decision. If they decide to turn their back on the fire and burn their behinds, then they will just have to sit on their blisters.'

—Abraham Lincoln

SUHAS PALSHIKAR IS A VERY RESPECTED AND SEASONED political analyst. Based in Pune, he has spent more than three decades teaching political science at Savitribai Phule Pune University and is Chief Editor of the journal *Studies in Indian Politics*. No words can describe the election results better than his. In his column for *The Indian Express*, he wrote, 'When dramatic expectations are set through media management, a setback looks like defeat. When parties and leaders are believed to be invincible, retaining power with constraints looks devastating. This is the BJP's predicament.'[1]

On 4 June, when results were declared, BJP was in shock despite emerging as the largest party with 240 seats. And Congress, that could win only 99 seats—which was 141 seats less than BJP's tally—rejoiced. Narendra Modi, who became the prime minister for the third consecutive term, the only prime minister to accomplish this after Jawaharlal Nehru, was seen as defeated.

Before this election, a myth was manufactured—that BJP under the leadership of Modi had evolved a science of elections, that Modi had fundamentally changed the grammar of politics in the country, and that the opposition was in no position to counter that. This was true to a point. But the aura of invincibility that was consciously built around Modi was of another level. According to the narrative, Modi was no ordinary man. He was the myth who had lost no election since becoming the chief minister of Gujarat. Consequently, his victory in this election was taken for granted. Pollsters and analysts, critics and commentators were convinced Modi would win with improved numbers. Opinion polls before the first phase of polling and exit polls after the last phase magnified the myth.

Three exit polls—*India Today*–Axis My India, News 24–Today's Chanakya, and India TV–CNX—all predicted that BJP, along with its alliance partners, could win more than 400 seats. This has happened only once in India's history. No party has ever won just an astounding majority except in 1985, in the aftermath of Indira Gandhi's assassination, when Congress led by Rajiv Gandhi won 404 out of 514 seats.

Axis My India has built a reputation for predicting election results correctly. Its success rate has been stunning. The chairman and managing director of Axis My India, Pradeep Gupta, claimed that since 2013, the company has correctly predicted 65 out of 69 elections (general and state elections), including the 2019 general election results. Gupta claims that, fascinated by Axis My India exit poll predictions, Harvard Business School is doing research on its prediction methodology and processes. It is noteworthy that, unlike other survey agencies, Axis My India restricts itself to exit polls and does not carry out opinion polls.

Like other elections, Axis My India had an enormous sample size, covering all 543 Lok Sabha constituencies. According to Pradeep Gupta, 'Out of 64 crore voters, we spoke to 5.82 lakh voters, which is the representational sample size. We covered 3,607 assembly constituencies, over 22,000 villages. Our on-ground interviews are monitored by a team, there is no possibility of any manipulation or bias.'[2] Axis My India predicted that NDA would get 361 to 400 seats, and the INDIA would end up with 131 to 166 seats. In UP, it assessed that BJP would improve its 2019 tally of 62 and win 67 seats. According to the survey, BJP was heading for its best-ever performance with 322 to 340 seats. But the final result proved disastrous for Axis My India. Bharatiya Janata Party failed to get even the majority number—272—needed to form its own government in Lok Sabha. In 2019, Pradeep Gupta was captured dancing in the TV studio after their exit poll numbers proved to be accurate. Five years later, he cried, again on national television, and admitted that they were wrong this time.

Midway through the election, something strange happened. Allegedly, the Axis My India exit poll had been leaked on social media, and according to the leaked document, BJP would have zero chance to better its tally in thirteen states. Rather, there was a bigger possibility that BJP might lose a few seats in these states. Given the reputation of Axis My India, the information went viral. Nobody was in a position to authenticate the leaked document and its claim. Pradeep Gupta stated that the viral document was fake. He said, 'There is no way any data can get leaked from my office. . . . Everything is recorded, there is nothing on cloud server, only on internal servers. No mobile phones are allowed in office, no computer has internet connection. . . . we are confident about data, there is no question of leakage.'[3] But it so happened that the final result turned out to be closer to the leaked document.

The exit polls stunned everybody, even those who were supporting BJP. Except for a few who bragged that the Modi tsunami was so big and the opposition was in such dire straits that it would not be surprising if BJP were to inch closer to 380 or more seats, more sober analysts were highly sceptical. A friend of mine, who is sympathetic to the RSS ideology of Hindutva, told me a day before counting that BJP would easily cross 272, but he would be surprised if it crossed the 300 mark. According to him, BJP was likely to win 288 seats. He was not very positive when I asked him about the exit polls. Exit and opinion polls have gone wrong in the past too, but it was different this time. In a polarised echo system, those opposed to Modi and BJP believed that survey agencies had been pressurised to inflate numbers to match BJP's claim that NDA would cross 400 seats. The most conservative estimate was done by *Dainik Bhaskar*, which predicted that NDA would get between 281 and 350 seats.

The net result of nine exit polls was that NDA would get 365 seats, the INDIA would get 146 and others only 32. I have been watching exit polls for more than two decades. One can say with authority that exit polls do differ in their predictions; either the direction of the survey is not right or the numbers vary, but this time, each survey was confident that NDA led by Modi would go beyond 350 seats. Not a single exit poll had the courage to say that BJP might not reach the majority number.

Obviously, the opposition had every right to smell a rat. They were enraged and rubbished the exit polls as 'Modi polls'. From the last date of polling, 1 June, to the day of counting, 4 June, the atmosphere was tense. At least I had not witnessed such uncertainty, scepticism and apprehension earlier.

What was most dangerous was the apprehension that if the result turned in favour of the INDIA and BJP was defeated, then would Modi leave power easily? Would the transfer of power lead to chaos and violence, as had happened in the USA after Donald Trump's defeat in 2021? Trump refused to believe that he had been defeated, and his supporters invaded Capitol Hill and vandalised the Congress building. This incident shocked the whole world. It was difficult to believe that such an act could happen in an evolved and old democracy like the USA. If this could happen in the USA, then why not in India?

Shravan Garg, a seasoned journalist and one-time group editor of *Dainik Bhaskar*, one of the most widely circulated Hindi newspapers, hinted at this in his video blog 'Shravan Garg Ki Khari Khari' on 23 May 2024 on *SatyaHindi.com*. He said, 'The verdict which the people are going to give, which will be decisive and will be against the government; and the government knows that it is not getting a majority, their claims [of winning more than 400 seats] are very inflated. Will the government accept [the verdict] democratically or not? The government has to decide; the BJP has to decide, and the prime minister has to decide. After sensing the mood of the nation, the language of the nation, what decision they will take next week—to reverse the verdict or accept the verdict?'[4]

Leaders in the opposition camp, belonging to the INDIA, met on 1 June in a surprise move and rejected the exit polls. On behalf of the alliance, Congress president Mallikarjun Kharge said that they had taken stock of the situation and had reached a conclusion that BJP might emerge as the single largest party, but its number would be much below the majority mark. Kharge claimed that their alliance would get 295 seats. In a brave move, the INDIA leaders claimed that their alliance would form the government. In the meeting, it was also decided that the INDIA partners should be vigilant of any mischief that could occur on the counting day. *The Indian Express* reported, 'The Opposition bloc also decided to approach the Election Commission before counting day [on] Tuesday with a list of demands. These include: asking it to ensure that the time of opening and closing of every balloting unit on voting day is matched with records before counting begins and officers tally their Form 17 C data without fail.'[5] Jairam Ramesh, senior leader of Congress, also accused the home minister, Amit Shah, of calling more than 150 district magistrates. Ramesh said, 'This is blatant and brazen intimidation, showing how desperate the BJP is. Let it be very clear: the will of the people shall prevail, and on June 4th, Mr Modi, Mr Shah, and the BJP will exit, and the INDIA Janbandhan will be victorious. Officers should not get under any pressure and must uphold the Constitution. They are under watch.'[6]

This episode is unfortunate but true. The reason is simple. The nature of Indian politics has changed dramatically since 2014. In this new political system, opponents are not rivals but enemies; they are not to be defeated but vanquished. Civility and niceties of the old school have been replaced by hatred and venom. Moral boundaries have lost the battle to winning. The three pillars of this new system are: arrogance, aggression and abuse. To debate, discuss and disagree are considered signs of weakness.

As a young reporter, I covered the Election Commission of India (ECI) when T.N. Seshan was at the helm of affairs. He was arrogant and rude at times, full of rage and volcanic eruptions, but he never disrespected the opposition members. He listened to their pleas and never had any ideological compulsions. The government of the day could not dictate terms to him. When it came to elections, Seshan was the boss. It was this bipartisan attitude that rid the Indian electoral system of mass-rigging, ballot-looting and violence.

The government did try to control Seshan by appointing two election commissioners alongside him, making the ECI a multi-member body, but by then, Seshan had played his role in history and given so much stature to the commission.

That tradition has surrendered to the might of the state today, and the ECI has had serious allegations levelled against it. In the 2024 election, the opposition believed that it was seriously handicapped by the ECI's attitude. The post-election remarks made by chief election commissioner Rajiv Kumar tells it all. Kumar cast serious aspersion on the opposition, saying, 'We (ECI) factored in fake news, fake narratives between parties to create arguments ... and we contained them. We had even braced our systems against likely false narratives from foreign soil, only to face these from within. We concede that EC failed to stop the mischievous narratives. While I had warned in March that there will be conspiracy balloons in these polls, we never imagined these would burst on EC's head.'[7]

Now juxtapose Rajiv Kumar's statement with the commission's reply to Congress president Mallikarjun Kharge's letter to the leaders of the INDIA bloc, on the issue of the delayed publication of increased voter turnout from the first and second phases of polling. For the first phase, the delay was eleven days, and the increase in turnout was 5.5 per cent. The turnout data of the second phase was released after four days, citing an increase of 5.7 per cent. Normally, the voter turnout data is released the same day with a caveat that the final data will be released the next day. Inevitably, the next day, turnout data increases slightly. The release of the first phase turnout data after eleven days with an increase of more than 5 per cent was abnormal, and opposition parties had every right to raise questions. It was widely debated in mainstream media and on social media. Conspiracy theorists had a field day. Motives were questioned and aspersions cast. In an atmosphere of distrust and toxicity, it was inevitable. But the bigger and more logical question is: should a constitutional institution also react in the same manner as political parties do?

In his letter, Kharge asked opposition leaders to raise their voice against the discrepancies in the data. He raised two important questions. First, why was there a delay in the release of turnout data? Second, why did the ECI not issue clarification for the cause of the delay? Kharge also asked leaders to be vigilant. *The Times of India* reported, 'Kharge urged the bloc leaders to collectively, unitedly, and unequivocally raise their voices against discrepancies, emphasizing the importance of safeguarding democracy and protecting the independent functioning of the Election Commission of India.'[8]

Kharge's letter indicates the lack of trust between the Modi government and the opposition, with the opposition believing that the Modi government could go to any extent to win elections. The manipulation of constitutional bodies is new to Indian politics. In the past, booths were looted, elections were rigged, and local administrations were accused of influencing results at the altar of the government of the day. However, constitutional bodies being used to win the national election was unheard of. Kharge wrote, 'We all know how PM Modi and the BJP are visibly flustered and frustrated by the voting trends and their receding electoral fortunes in the first two phases. The entire nation knows that an autocratic regime, drunk with power, can go to any extent to stay in the chair."[9]

Of course, it was a strongly worded letter. And it had to be responded to. The question is: who should have responded—the Modi government, BJP or the ECI? Kharge's letter was a political letter, and the Modi government should have rebutted in equal measure, but the response came from the ECI. *The Times of India* reported, 'Coming down heavily on Congress president Mallikarjun Kharge, Election Commission on Friday dismissed his allegations around voter turnout data as "baseless" and said it could create an "anarchic situation, besides doubts and disharmony". "Through innuendos and insinuations, the contents of the post tend to create disharmony in respect of the delicate space of election management, can plant doubts in the minds of voters and political parties ..." EC said.'[10]

It is the ECI's responsibility to conduct free and fair elections. But it is not a political organisation and isn't expected to make a political statement. It was well within ECI's right to respond to Kharge's letter, but the language it used was offensive and political. As a non-political organisation, the ECI ought to have ensured it remained objective and non-partisan. It hadn't managed to do this, which is why its response was exposed to interpretations and accusations about its political and ideological leaning. 'The Commission accused Kharge of pushing a "biased narrative" under the guise of seeking clarifications,'[11] *The Times of India* reported the ECI also having said, 'As a senior parliamentarian, a very seasoned politician, with experience of 52 years in electoral politics and electoral process, and as the head of a prominent national political party, you must be aware that EC follows the most transparent process of preparation of electoral roll and well designed and well tested participation of political parties/candidates at every stage of the process.'[12] To use such language—'create an anarchic situation', 'pushing biased narrative', 'plant doubts in the mind of voters'—and to sermonise one of the most senior politicians in the country, holding the constitutional post of leader of the opposition in the Rajya Sabha, was not appropriate.

Congress's reaction was equally bitter. The party said that the ECI's response was a 'permanent blot' on the face of the institution that was there to ensure a level playing field for all political parties.[13] Opposition leaders also met the ECI to raise their concern about delayed and increased voter turnout data. A petition was filed in the Supreme Court by the Association of Democratic Reforms (ADR) seeking the direction of the court to publish turnout data within forty-eight hours of the polls closing. The Supreme Court sought the ECI's response to explain the increase in voting but received the baffling reply that it was not legally mandated to publish turnout data booth-wise after every phase of polling. The Supreme Court concurred with the ECI and refused to give any direction at a time when the election process was ongoing. In this matter, legalistic interpretation is not valid. If the ECI was not bound by law to publish booth-wise voter turnout data, why had it been doing so for decades, and why did the present commission also do it? It is because a well-established convention was being followed by the ECI, and it is because voters and all the stakeholders in a democracy have the right to know the number of votes polled in the area, and nationally, too. The ECI's response defies the basic logic of democracy and reflects their non-understanding and respect for voters' rights. While it might be legally right, it was against the spirit of democracy.

The whole controversy was unnecessary and is symptomatic of the malaise that has crept into our political system, which is corroding Indian democracy from the inside.

Democracy is the name of contesting ideas, searching for new concepts, and questioning the present one. To imagine that questioning discredits and destabilises the system and institutions is an unsettling idea.

Since Modi-led BJP surprisingly won 282 seats in 2014, serious questions have been asked about the efficacy of the electronic voting machines (EVMs). The opposition found it hard to come to terms with the fact that BJP, which had been struggling to make its presence felt in UP till the assembly elections held two years earlier, suddenly won 73 of 80 seats in the Lok Sabha elections along with its alliance partner Apna Dal. In the 2017 UP assembly elections, BJP won 313 seats out of 403. What surprised BJP's critics and opposition was that this victory came at a time when the nation was still reeling from the aftereffects of demonetisation.

Seeing that the Punjab election results seemed to be anomaly given the context of what individuals and the economy had suffered due to demonitisation (and how it was implemented overnight), Aam Aadmi Party (AAP) seriously pushed the issue of EVM manipulation. I was then a part of AAP, and the party was very hopeful of forming the government in Punjab. Opinion and exit polls had hinted towards AAP's win in the state. That the party could manage only 20 of 117 seats with 23.7 per cent votes was shocking, to say the least. I was in the party office, about to go live on a TV channel as the spokesperson of AAP to share the party's perspective, when I got a call from Arvind Kejriwal's office. I was told to say that the EVMs were manipulated to defeat AAP in Punjab. I was not convinced, and tried to argue that it was not right to blame the EVMs because by that logic, it would be futile to contest any election in the future. I also thought this argument would demoralise the party cadre and candidates; if they were told that the EVMs are rigged, then why would they campaign and fight elections? But I was told that it was the party's decision and I had to toe the line, and so I did. Since then, AAP used every platform to discredit EVMs. Even the floor of the Delhi assembly was used to prove that an EVM can be hacked, rigged and manipulated. Other opposition parties also picked up the issue. In the age of social media, the issue of EVMs was sold like a hot cake and it found its takers too, especially among those who found it hard to digest that Modi and BJP could get a majority in two consecutive national elections, and that BJP could turn around the tables in assembly elections in states like Haryana and Tripura, where it had negligible presence earlier.

But the present opposition is not the only one to cast aspersions on the efficacy of the EVMs. When BJP lost the Lok Sabha election to the Congress in 2009, L.K. Advani too had raised doubts about EVMs at a press conference. *The Indian Express* reported, 'BJP leader L.K. Advani has demanded the reintroduction of ballot papers in elections, beginning with the Maharashtra Assembly elections in October, and three other states later this year. . . . We should revert to ballot paper unless the Election Commission is able to ensure that Electronic Voting Machines (EVMs) are foolproof . . . '[14] G.V.L. Narasimha Rao, who later became BJP spokesperson and MP, wrote a book on the manipulation of EVMs, and Advani wrote the foreword of the book. Another BJP leader, Subramanian Swamy took the EVM issue to the Supreme Court. He requested the court that EVMs should have a paper trail to ensure free and fair elections. *Business Standard* reported, 'The Supreme Court today directed the Election Commission to introduce in a phased manner a paper trail in EVMs for the next general elections in 2014, saying it will ensure free and fair polls.'[15]

But the controversy did not end. Since 2004, when EVMs were introduced in all 543 Lok Sabha constituencies for the first time, they have been subjected to transparency debates and insinuations. The Supreme Court has presided over nine cases related to Voter Verifiable Paper Audit Trail (VVPAT) since 2013. As late as 26 April 2024, the day of the second phase of polling, the Supreme Court dismissed a petition filed by ADR, demanding either a return to ballot papers or 100 per cent verification of VVPAT. The petition also requested that the voter be allowed to place the VVPAT in a separate sealed box, to add more transparency. The court categorically said that the possibility of hacking or tampering of EVMs was unfounded.[16] But to bring more transparency in the system, the Supreme Court directed symbol loading units to be sealed and stored in strong rooms for forty-five days after results, to facilitate checks of discrepancies alleged later. The court allowed candidates who finish second and third in a poll to seek C&V of burnt memory and microcontroller of up to 5 per cent of EVMs used in an assembly segment.[17] Simply put, candidates who stood second and third could ask engineers of EVM manufacturers to check microcontroller chips (in 5 per cent of EVMs per assembly segment of each Lok Sabha constituency). The requests were to be made within seven days of the result. Candidates were to pay for it and would get their money back only if EVMs were found faulty. The Supreme Court also asked the ECI to explore if VVPAT slips could be counted electronically and if each party could be assigned a unique bar code alongside the symbol in the VVPAT machine.

Justice Dipankar Datta observed, 'It is of immediate relevance to note that in recent years, a trend has been fast developing of certain vested interest groups endeavouring to undermine the achievements and accomplishments of the nation earned through the hard work and dedication of its sincere workforce. . . . No constitutional court, far less this court, would allow such attempt to succeed as long as it (the court) has a say in the matter.'[18] With all due respect to Justice Datta, the observation was unwarranted. To doubt the ADR's credentials was uncalled for. Due to the ADR's efforts, many electoral reforms have been carried out. And even in this case, it was because of ADR's petition that the Supreme Court ordered three new steps to make the system more transparent and nip any doubts about the EVMs in the bud. In the Supreme Court's verdict, the prime minister and BJP found a ready argument to discredit the opposition. The prime minister said it was a 'tight slap' to the opposition's face.

The fact remains, the matter was serious enough for the involvement and directives of the Supreme Court mid-elections. This entire exercise is indicative of the fact that a large section of society, including political parties, are convinced that EVMs are being manipulated, possibly with the help of the ECI. The survey conducted by CSDS Lokniti indicates this dangerous trend. In response to the question 'How likely is it that EVMs can be manipulated by the ruling party?' 17 per cent said 'a lot' and 28 per cent said 'somewhat'. In total, 45 per cent of respondents believed that EVMs can be manipulated by the ruling party. Only 16 per cent said that EVMs cannot be manipulated. Compared with 2019, fewer people are willing to trust the ECI as well. According to the CSDS Lokniti pre-poll survey in 2019, 51 per cent of respondents said that they trusted the ECI to a great extent, but that number drastically slipped to 28 per cent in 2024. Those who don't trust the ECI increased from 7 per cent to 14 per cent, and those who don't trust it at all increased from 5 per cent to 9 per cent in 2024.[19]

If the perception about the credibility of the ECI declined, then nobody but the Modi government and the ECI are responsible. The Supreme Court, in its wisdom, had decided on 2 March 2023 that the appointment of the chief election commissioner and election commissioners should be made on the advice of a selection panel composed of the prime minister, the leader of opposition in the Lok Sabha—and if the leader of the opposition is not available, then leader of the largest party in the Lok Sabha—and the Chief Justice of India. Until this verdict, election commissioners were appointed by the government of the day. The Supreme Court's historic judgment was an exercise to annul any perception that the ECI works under the authority of the government, making it a truly independent constitutional body. It was an exercise to make elections free and fair, but the Modi government did not like this decision. The government used the very same Supreme Court verdict to nullify the purpose of the whole exercise. In its order, the Supreme Court said, 'All the Members were of the clear view that elections must be conducted by an independent Commission. It was a radical departure from the regime prevailing under the Government of India Act, 1935.'[20]

It was left to the Parliament to make a law. The law was never made, for unknown reasons and, after Independence, the governments kept appointing election commissioners and chief election commissioners. It was the Supreme Court's endeavour to correct this anomaly in the system, which is why it passed the judgment. However, it also said, 'We make it clear that this will be subject to any law to be made by Parliament.'[21]

In December 2023, the Modi government passed a law according to which the selection panel would not have the Chief Justice of India as one of the members; instead, a cabinet minister nominated by the prime minister would take the Chief Justice's place. This meant the government would always have a majority and an upper hand in appointing the election commissioners.

In my opinion, the Supreme Court's verdict should not have been tinkered with. It was a progressive order and the government should have passed the same through the Parliament. The change introduced by the government has diluted the independent nature of the ECI and marred its reputation.

The actions of the ECI too have been of no help. During the 2024 elections, a perception was created that the ECI was not willing to take action against the ruling party, while the opposition would not be spared. One shining example was when the prime minister made that infamous statement in Banswara, Rajasthan, where he referred to Muslims as 'infiltrators'. The Election Commission did not take any cognisance of the statement suo moto. Even though it was a brazen attempt by the prime minister to polarise voters on religious lines—peddling Islamophobia and leading to disharmony between communities—the ECI maintained royal silence. When Congress reported this to the ECI and asked for the prime minister to be disqualified, the ECI's response of serving a notice to the party president deepened suspicions. It has always been the norm for the ECI to serve a notice to the offender in the case of a violation. But Modi was spared.

The Times of India wrote, 'Setting a new trend to make party presidents accountable for alleged violation of the model code of conduct by their candidates and star campaigners, Election Commission on Thursday issued notices to the chiefs of BJP and Congress seeking their response to alleged violations made by Prime Minister Narendra Modi and Congress leader Rahul Gandhi.'[22] Bizarrely, neither the prime minister nor Rahul Gandhi were mentioned by name in these notices, with the ECI only referring to 'some of the star campaigners'.

Anurag Kundu wrote in *The Indian Express*, '. . . It is expected that the Election Commission should be independent. Setting aside the Supreme Court's constitutional bench judgement, the unilateral appointment by the Executive of the two Election Commissioners two days before the announcement of election dates cast a shadow on its independence. The continued silence on several complaints by the Opposition against the BJP and its alacrity in acting on the latter's complaints raise serious questions of bias. So far, the EC has a different approach in responding to the BJP and Opposition's complaints of violation of the Model Code of Conduct.'[23]

The 2024 election will always be remembered for the anti-Muslim campaign unleashed by the BJP leaders, including Prime Minister Modi and Home Minister Amit Shah. But it will also be memorable for the ECI's silence. No action was initiated to stop the vilification. No leader of the BJP was ever punished. The atmosphere of hatred, venom, threat, intimidation and social disharmony continued unhindered and unchecked. As Suhas Palshikar put it, 'An ECI busy responding to Congress President has no time attending to the full-blown anti-Muslim campaign. Not even a meek murmur.' Political scientist Zoya Hasan, Professor Emerita, JNU, in the same article, remarked, 'The current ECI has lost credibility because its behaviour is perceived as being partisan. Without executive self-restraint or harder institutional firewalls to safeguard the independence of the ECI, India's democracy remains under threat.' Another eminent scholar Giles Verniers said, 'Honest question: has there been a lower moment for the ECI? The scepticism they face is self-inflicted.'[24]

I know Seshan is not around to course-correct at a time when his great legacy has been mortgaged to the political class. What is sad is that I don't see a Seshan rising again in the future to reignite the great institution's independence. The decline is deep, and the shoulders responsible for sharing the burden of democracy are too weak. This election was another reflection of how institutions have crumbled in the last ten years and surrendered to the whims of one man, who claims not to be human.

5

A Rigged Playing Field?

DAVID SELBOURNE'S *AN EYE TO INDIA: THE UNMASKING OF A Tyranny* is a scathing book about the Emergency in India. The book is a study of how a political party develops hubris over a period of time, eventually believing that it is the destiny of the country, and that the party's history is the history of the country. One leader, in their illusionary world, starts believing that they are 'superhuman' and that only they can take the country into the future; without them, the country will disintegrate. By its nature, this hubris discards and destroys space for opposition, dissent and disagreement; the party and the leader have the monopoly over wisdom, and others are obstructions and hindrances. This self-belief treats citizens as their captive audience and uses violence to counter any form of protest. The party and the leader pretend to function in a democratic set-up; their motto is to run a 'one-party state' in a multi-party system. If one juxtaposes this exposition about Emergency days to the present set-up in India, one will be horrified to see the similarities.

Selbourne writes, '. . . If "only the Congress can be in charge of India" then the opposition could be ideologically perceived as having nothing to say. It was "wholly negative" or "recalcitrant." It used "obstructionist tactics [which were] an impediment to smooth functioning, and [did] not fit into democratic system governed by the Constitution"; "reform was never possible before because we were busy, always busy, fighting the opposition." Thus, the opposition was not merely "without a better policy or programme"—the normal language of inter-party contention—but with "no support from people" and "unconcerned with any of the major problems of India". It was not merely "divisive and disruptive", but "trying to break the morale of the people", and engineering strikes generating violence. And then, one reaches a theoretical nadir in which opposition was perceived to be undermining not a unitary system (in which the argument would be at least theoretically plausible) but "the democratic system which our people have chosen", and "which we intend to make a success of by dealing with those forces seeking to undermine".'[1]

Selbourne has summarised how the ruling dispensation perceived the opposition during the incumbency of Indira Gandhi in the 1970s. More than fifty years after the Emergency, the debate on how democracy has backslid remains alive. Not only that, the ruling dispensation has moved a few steps further. The Emergency was a reprehensible act that shook the foundations of Indian democracy. It taught the country how an autocratic leader and party can use the Constitution and tools of democracy to undermine the same democratic process that helped them to occupy the position of ultimate power.

Since the days of the Emergency, one of the lessons that political leaders and parties have learnt is that the formal constitutional imposition of an emergency will not be tolerated by the citizens. Therefore, attempts have been made in the last few years to compromise the democratic set-up without taking the constitutional route. This new approach involves using the instruments of the state to weaken the state itself, and circumvent the whole state system to its advantage. It is a myth that the State means only the government at the Centre. In reality, the State has legitimate rights for coercive powers. The cabinet is part of the State, not the whole of the State, chosen by the people; however, a large part of the State is unelected. Other than the Parliament and the assemblies, constitutional institutions have equal stakes in the democratic system; they have well-defined structures and operate within the limits of well-defined boundaries. If these constitutional institutions are not led by men and women of conviction, then there is always a danger that these institutions will crumble under the pressures of a cabinet led by a powerful leader. What India has witnessed in the last few years is that the cabinet led by a totalitarian leader has become enormously powerful, while other institutions have surrendered or greatly weakened in equal measure. This has happened not only at the Centre but in states too.

On 26 June 1975, at 7 a.m., the Emergency was officially imposed after the signature of President Fakhruddin Ali Ahmed. Thousands of political leaders and workers including Jayprakash Narayan (JP), Morarji Desai, Raj Narain, Piloo Mody, L.K. Advani, Jyotirmoy Basu and others were arrested under draconian laws, leading to a rebellion against Indira Gandhi. Her own continuity as the prime minister was in danger due to the Allahabad High Court's order to invalidate her membership of the Lok Sabha and debar her for six years from holding the prime minister's office. Though the Supreme Court passed a stay order on the matter, she still could not vote in Parliament. There was a great murmur that more than a hundred MPs of her own party were preparing to demand her resignation and replacement in the wake of the high court's order. JP had given a call to the army and police not to follow illegal orders, and a disintegrated group of political parties opposed to Gandhi were gravitating towards unity under his moral leadership. A mass movement spurred by price rise, inflation and corruption had already paralysed the functioning of the governments in many states. Gandhi's supporters had already concocted the conspiracy theory that US's Central Intelligence Agency (CIA) was in cahoots with the opposition to unseat her from power. The possibility that the opposition, for the first time, might defeat Gandhi in coming parliamentary elections was looming large.

If we jump to 2024, the situation is vastly different. None of the situations described on the eve of Emergency existed on the eve of the parliamentary elections. Prime Minister Narendra Modi was extremely popular, as surveys suggested. He was riding the saffron wave due to the Ram Mandir consecration in Ayodhya, and the opposition was in total disarray. Nitish Kumar, who had been the pivot of unity among the opposition parties, had deserted the INDIA in January. The prime minister had total control over his party, and there was no threat to his leadership from any corner, neither from BJP nor from RSS. Though economic distress was making the lives of citizens difficult, there was no mass movement to unseat Modi. And most of all, there was no JP. The only moral force that made its presence felt was Rahul Gandhi, who travelled from one corner of the country to the other, not once but twice. But even he was in no position to challenge Modi's political hegemony. Rahul Gandhi's leadership was not universally acceptable, even in his own party.

It was beyond comprehension why Enforcement Directorate (ED) arrested two sitting chief ministers, Arvind Kejriwal and Hemant Soren, who also happened to be the most popular leaders of their own parties, and why Congress's accounts were frozen. And all this was done in an open democratic society!

Kejriwal, the enigmatic leader of Aam Aadmi Party (AAP) and chief minister of Delhi, was arrested on 21 March 2024, and Soren, the chief minister of Jharkhand and supreme leader of Jharkhand Mukti Morcha (JMM), was taken into custody on 31 January 2024. Both leaders were charged with corrupt practices. They were arrested by ED under the draconian Prevention of Money Laundering Act (PMLA), under which it is difficult to get bail unless the court is prima facie convinced that the arrested is innocent. In between these two arrests, Congress accused the Modi government of having a hand in their accounts being frozen on flimsy grounds. Was it due to the alacrity of the overenthusiastic officers who wanted to prove themselves loyal to the king, or was it designed from the top to influence the election that was to follow in April and May? The answer is simple.

Modi has such a vice-like grip over his government and the party that no individual or officer worth their salt dare take a decision that has serious political consequences without direct clearance from the prime minister's office. These were political decisions taken after weighing all the permutations and combinations. I believe these steps were mala fide in intent and were meant to influence the elections directly.

And here lies the riddle of this election. Even though it was widely speculated that BJP was confident of retaining power after the elections, they couldn't wait until after the elections to execute these steps. If the party was truly confident about its victory, why would it do something that was bound to invite criticism? The question then is, was the prime minister privy to certain information about the public's mood, which required dramatic action to divert public attention from the negatives of the government? Was it an attempt to counter the anti-incumbency against the BJP government, which would have vitiated the party's election campaign?

Hemant Soren, a popular Adivasi leader, had formed the government along with Congress and other partners after defeating BJP in Jharkhand. Hemant Soren had invited the ire of the Modi government since he decided to align with the INDIA. On 31 January, ED arrested him in a case of sale and purchase of 8.5 acres of army land. According to *The Indian Express* report,[2]

> The ED had been investigating various cases in Jharkhand, including illegal mining, an MGNREGA 'scam' of 2009, and the alleged illegal sale and purchase of an Army plot in Ranchi. It was during the Army land investigation the name of then revenue sub-inspector of Bargain Circle Office, Bhanu Pratap Prasad, popped up. Prasad was eventually linked to Soren.
>
> The ED claimed that Prasad was part of a syndicate involved in acquiring properties illegally, through force as well as by falsifying government records. According to the agency, Prasad was the custodian of several original registers—also known as Panji 2—in which land records (particularly ownership details) were falsified.
>
> During searches on April 13, 2023, ED said that 11 trucks of property documents along with 17 Panji 2 were seized from him. This information was shared by the ED with the then Chief Secretary of State, and accordingly an FIR was registered on June 1 last year. This FIR became the genesis of the registration of the ECIR—ED's equivalent of an FIR—in which Soren was arrested.
>
> According to the ED, Soren is among the people Bhanu Pratap 'hatched conspiracies with' to take over

> properties. . . . The land parcels, totalling an area of 8.5 acres in Bargaain area of Ranchi, were physically verified by Prasad on instructions from the CMO, the ED alleged. It said its survey of the area under the PMLA confirmed that Soren had illegal possession of the land.

Hemant Soren challenged the ED to produce proof that he held the land, but he was interrogated for seven hours. Before being arrested, he resigned and passed the baton to party loyalist Champai Soren to become the chief minister in his place.

During the entirety of the election campaign, Hemant Soren remained in jail, and he got bail after the election on 28 June 2024. The court observation is an eye-opener for all those who believe in democracy.

The Jharkhand High Court's order reads: 'The overall conspectus of the case based on the broad probabilities does not specifically or indirectly assign the petitioner to be involved in the acquisition and possession as well as concealment of 8.86 acre of land connected to the "proceeds of crime." None of the register/revenue records bear imprint of the direct involvement of the petitioner in the acquisition and possession of the said land. . . . The consequences of the findings recorded by this Court satisfies the condition as at Section 45 PMLA, 2002 to the effect that there is "reason to believe" that petitioner is not guilty of the offence as alleged.'[3]

The court, in a way, indicted the ED, and that proved the argument that Hemant Soren was arrested for other reasons, not for corrupt practices.

Similarly, Delhi chief minister Arvind Kejriwal was arrested on 21 March. He was arrested once the election process had formally begun. On 16 March, ECI announced the election schedule. Before he was arrested, Kejriwal had been sent nine summons to appear before the ED, in none of which he had been named an accused or a witness. Kejriwal's deputy Manish Sisodia and MP Sanjay Singh had already been arrested in this case. Sanjay Singh later got bail. Like the Hemant Soren case, the court did not declare that Sanjay Singh was innocent, but it hinted at the fact that the case against Sanjay Singh would not stand under the scrutiny of the court. But Sisodia remained in jail. For reasons unknown, Kejriwal did not appear before the ED even once. Finally, when the Delhi High Court refused to give him any legal protection from arrest, the ED went to the chief minister's residence the same evening, interrogated him for two and a half hours, and arrested him. Kejriwal had been interrogated earlier by the CBI in the same case. He is the only chief minister to be arrested by an enforcement agency while he was still in office and had not resigned.

If Modi is cold-blooded and calculative, Kejriwal is volatile and impulsive, and revels in theatrics. Unlike Hemant Soren who had passed on the baton to Champai Soren, Kejriwal refused to resign. In fact, before Kejriwal was arrested, AAP had declared that he would not step down and would run the government from jail.[4]

Constitutionally, there is no provision that requires a sitting chief minister to resign if they have to go to jail.[5]

After Kejriwal's arrest, people assumed that once he was sent to judicial custody, he might decide to resign, but that too did not happen. On 1 April 2024, Kejriwal was sent to Tihar Jail. Aam Aadmi Party argued that sending Kejriwal to jail was part of a bigger conspiracy by Prime Minister Modi to destabilise the AAP government in Delhi, and Kejriwal's resignation would mean falling into the trap laid by BJP. It is true that Kejriwal could continue as chief minister constitutionally, but it was against the basic ethos of the Constitution. Yes, there is a written Constitution which has to be followed verbatim, but in a well-established democracy like ours, conventions also become constitutional norms that have to be followed rigorously to preserve the sanctity of the Constitution.

Since the adoption of the Constitution, it has been the norm that if a chief minister is sent to jail during the process of investigation for any offence, then they resign, and someone else is sworn in as chief minister. Former chief minister of Tamil Nadu, J. Jayalalithaa, and former chief minister of Bihar, Lalu Prasad Yadav, did the same; they resigned as chief minister before going to jail, and the party chose another leader to run the government. But Kejriwal was writing a new chapter in India's constitutional history.

Ideally, the Modi government should have invoked Article 356 to sack his government, as his continuance in jail amounted to a total breakdown of constitutional machinery in the state. No chief minister can run a government from jail. They can't hold cabinet meetings or freely meet their ministers or senior officers of the government, unless permission is granted by the court. They cannot sign any documents or hold any meetings through video conferencing either.

But the Modi government did nothing. A senior BJP leader and former cabinet minister told me that the government would not oblige Kejriwal with such an act because they wanted to expose him thoroughly. Kejirwal had been accused of being an anarchist in the past and his response to the situation was only solidifying the belief. Bharatiya Janata Party wanted to show the people of Delhi how little Kejriwal believed in and respected the Constitution.

Kejriwal challenged his arrest in the Supreme Court. Meanwhile, electioneering was in full swing. Polling was to be held for seven seats in Delhi on 25 May and in Punjab on 1 June 2024. On 10 May, the Supreme Court granted Kejriwal interim bail to participate and campaign for his party. The court said, 'General elections supply vis viva (living force) to a democracy. Given the prodigious importance, we reject the argument . . . that grant of interim bail/release on this account would . . . (mean) placing the politicians in a benefic position compared with ordinary citizens.'[6]

This was an unprecedented verdict by the Supreme Court, which must have gladdened the hearts of AAP supporters, but it was a shock to the Modi government and BJP. Was the court writing a script that was against BJP's plan? It is to be noted that Kejriwal did not ask for bail; his petition was to challenge his arrest, which he called illegal. The court neither passed a judgment about his arrest nor granted him 'permanent bail'; he was freed for only twenty-one days so he could campaign for the party as the leader. In their usual theatrical style, Kejriwal and his party immediately projected his release as a great victory. Kejriwal addressed his supporters outside Tihar jail, thundering in messianic style, 'I am back. Crores of people prayed for me. I'm fighting against dictatorship with all I have, now 140 crores of us have to do that.'[7]

Kejriwal's arrest has exposed his commitment to 'new politics'. In 2012, when the party was formed, Kejriwal had declared that he had entered the arena not to do politics but rather to change it. He was dead set against dynastic politics and high-command culture. The party was so committed to the cause that it wrote in its constitution that 'no two members of a family would contest elections'. However, the party removed this clause from its constitution in January 2021.[8]

The party changed as it swam into the ocean of politics. Instead of them changing politics, politics changed them.

Once Kejriwal went to jail, another trait of his political persona was revealed to the people. His wife Sunita Kejriwal appeared on the political landscape. She was seen sitting on the CM's chair with pictures of Bhagat Singh and Babasaheb Ambedkar in the backdrop, reading Kejriwal's message. She became his spokesperson. She was seen mingling with the top leaders of the country when the INDIA bloc organised a protest rally against the arrests of Kejriwal and Hemant Soren at Ramlila Maidan, Delhi.[9] She was seen doing road shows and addressing rallies for AAP during elections. There is nothing wrong with a wife defending her husband and fighting for him. But here she was being projected as the successor to Arvind Kejriwal. If he were to resign, it would be Sunita Kejriwal taking his place, much like Rabri Devi had done when Lalu went to jail in the fodder scam.[10]

But did these theatrics work for Kejriwal? Sadly no. Despite being in an alliance with Congress in the national capital, AAP could not win even a single seat out of seven. This was the third consecutive parliamentary election in which AAP failed to win a single Lok Sabha seat in Delhi. If the party was expecting waves of sympathy due to Kejriwal's arrest, it was left disappointed. It is quite clear that Kejriwal is no longer perceived as a national alternative, and that his charisma is diminishing. With fatigue setting in, AAP might have to confront serious problems in the assembly elections. In politics, theatrics have a shelf life; they do not work beyond a point in the absence of substance.

Irrespective of his politics and theatrics, Kejriwal is no ordinary leader. There was a time when he and his party were perceived as a national alternative to Congress, and as a main challenger to the might of BJP and Modi. Unlike Hemant Soren, Kejriwal's arrest created global headlines. United Nations Secretary General Antonio Guterres's spokesperson reacted sharply, saying, 'We very much hope that in India, as in any country that is having elections, everyone's rights are protected, including political and civil rights, and everyone is able to vote in an atmosphere that is free and fair.'[11] The United States' Department of State spokesperson said they were monitoring reports of Kejriwal's arrest and has encouraged its Indian counterpart to ensure 'a fair, transparent, and timely legal process' for the jailed Delhi Chief Minister.[12] Taking note of Kejriwal's arrest, Germany's Foreign Office spokesperson said, 'We assume and expect that the standards relating to the independence of the judiciary and basic democratic principles will also be applied in this case.'[13]

The Indian Ministry of Foreign Affairs strongly reacted to these statements and termed them as an interference in India's internal matters.

Kejriwal's arrest sparked protests across the country too. Aam Aadmi Party staged protests. The INDIA bloc condemned Kejriwal's arrest, calling it an assault on India's democracy. Rahul Gandhi said, 'A scared dictator wants to create a dead democracy.'[14]

The next day, the INDIA bloc delegation met the ECI and gave a memorandum. It alleged that the arrests of Kejriwal and Soren would erode the level playing field during elections. 'There emerges a clear, deliberate and sinister pattern, where the ruling regime is abusing its power, and completely destroying any semblance of a level playing field for other political parties contesting the Lok Sabha elections. Never before has such high-handedness ever been witnessed.'[15]

Whether one calls it the politics of vendetta, a devious game of winning elections at any cost, or just the actions of an overzealous government department, the income tax department freezing the accounts of the Congress party on a frivolous charge, on the eve of the elections, was a serious jolt to Indian democracy which had the potential to derail the whole electoral process. It was an attempt to immobilise Congress's election campaign, which was the fulcrum of the opposition. When Ajay Maken, the national treasurer of Congress, held a press conference in Delhi, I was shocked. Maken said, 'The government hasn't just frozen our accounts, but democracy has been frozen if the principal Opposition party's account is frozen just weeks before the general elections. Will our country have a single party rule?'[16]

He told reporters, 'We received information yesterday that banks are not honouring the cheque we are issuing. On further investigation, we got to know that the Youth Congress's bank accounts have been frozen. The accounts of the Congress party have also been seized. Income Tax asked for ₹210 crore recovery from the Youth Congress and the Congress. The money in our accounts, sourced through crowd-funding, has been frozen. Freezing the accounts of an Opposition party just a couple of weeks before the Lok Sabha elections are notified is akin to freezing democracy.'[17]

Maken lamented, 'We don't have money to pay salaries to our office-bearers and dedicated cadres. Not just the Nyay Yatra but all our scheduled political activities will be impacted as a result of this.'[18]

The matter was related to only ₹14 lakhs. *The Economic Times* reported,

> The case dates back to financial year 2017-2018, when the party did not file its return by the extended deadline of Dec 2018, a precondition to claim tax deduction available to registered political parties. It also failed to meet another requirement related to acceptance of cash donations

above Rs 20,000. The department said the party accepted cash donations of over Rs 14 lakh, resulting in a loss of its 'exempt' status. It is now treated as an 'association of persons' and faces normal tax liability.

In July 2021, a demand of Rs 105 crore was raised following assessment of the party's returns and it paid only Rs 2.5 crore. It had to pay Rs 21 crore, that is 20% of the original demand of Rs 105 crore before the commissioner (appeals) to keep the case in abeyance. The demand, including interest, has now swelled to Rs 135 crore and the interest component will keep rising till the final payment is made or the case is dismissed. . . . After a recovery notice was issued by the tax department on February 13, multiple bank accounts of Congress were attached and frozen as part of routine procedure followed by the tax department to recover dues, if an assessee fails to pay due tax.[19]

The Economic Times report stated that the income tax department had attached and frozen multiple bank accounts of Congress due to the non-payment of outstanding dues.[20] Bharatiya Janata Party spokesperson Sambit Patra clarified, 'These bank accounts have not been frozen, they are operational. You [Congress] can deposit money in these accounts and withdraw too, except ₹125 crores, which has been attached by the Income Tax Department due to the non-payment of dues as per Income Tax rules.'[21]

Congress appealed before the Income Tax Appellate Tribunal against this action, requesting a stay, but on 8 March, the appeal was turned down. Congress did not get any relief from the Delhi High Court in this matter either. Their problem was further compounded when the party received fresh notices to the tune of ₹1,700 crore. The income tax department claimed that it had found fresh discrepancies in the Congress party's income tax returns filed for the financial years 2017 and 2021. Before this, the party was slapped with another notice concerning an amount of ₹523.87 crore, for some 'unaccounted transactions' between 2014 and 2021. Congress called it 'tax terrorism'. Congress leader Jairam Ramesh said, 'The BJP is engaged in tax terrorism and efforts are being made to financially cripple the Congress.'[22]

The Congress treasurer made the accusation that such actions were not pursued against BJP, despite flagrant breaches of tax regulations, and in his opinion, if the income tax department pursued the matter, then they could demand over ₹4600 crores from the BJP.[23]

There is absolutely no doubt that Congress was at fault to begin with, but with elections around the corner, the income tax department could have waited on taking action. The department did not realise—or perhaps chose to ignore—the fact that it could lead to serious repercussions in the coming elections. How could a party contest election when its accounts were frozen? This had a direct bearing on the principle of a level playing field, which is the basic requirement for elections.

It is common knowledge in India that no officer dares to freeze the accounts of a political party that has national status without informing the minister concerned with the current dispensation. Moreover, such has become the system of governance since 2014 that no minister can give a go-ahead to the department without getting clearance from the prime minister's office. It feels good to say that there is no interference and departments are doing their job without fear and favour, but there isn't any truth to that statement. Irrespective of which party is in power and who the prime minister is, given the politicisation of the system of bureaucracy, no officer will take such a call without permission from the top; if they do, it would jeopardise their career.

The suspicion is stronger as the entire opposition has been subjected to much harassment since Modi became prime minister. Investigating agencies have been unleashed on them. Particularly the ED, armed with draconian PMLA, has been weaponised to terrorise the opposition, break parties, ensure defection to BJP and topple state governments where BJP isn't in power. This tax incident is not a stand-alone case. In 2019, on the eve of the Maharashtra and Haryana assembly elections, the houses of five employees in the accounts department of Congress's headquarters were raided. Anand Sharma, a senior Congress leader, accused the BJP government: 'It is election time, we have to give funds to our candidates, we have to spend on publicity, but the accounts section is closed. All our accountants have been summoned. Income Tax people are sitting at their homes. . . . This government . . . works with vendetta in mind, selectively identifying and targeting its political opponents. It is not only the Indian National Congress and its leaders; in recent years, it goes across political parties but only those parties which are opposed to them—whether it is the Trinamool Congress, TDP, BSP, or SP, the list is long.'[24]

Enforcement Directorate had not even spared Sonia Gandhi and Rahul Gandhi in the *National Herald* case in 2022. For over fifty hours over five consecutive days, Rahul Gandhi was interrogated by ED in its office. Congress president Mallikarjun Kharge was not spared either. Both leaders are promoters of the Young India company that owns *National Herald*.

Before 2014, except during the Emergency, opposition leaders were not terrorised at such a massive scale by investigative agencies. Arresting two sitting CMs of the opposition camp and freezing accounts of Congress on the eve of elections are unparalleled events in Indian electoral history. Those who compare this with the Emergency forget that once the Emergency was lifted by Indira Gandhi and elections were announced in 1977, all the opposition leaders who had been arrested were freed, and they freely contested elections. In contrast, in 2024, opposition leaders were arrested just before the elections. This difference between 1977 and 2024 has to be underlined because it tells a story about the nature of the two regimes.

6

The Roadblock to Hindutva's Juggernaut

'If Hindu Raj does become a fact, it will, no doubt, be the greatest calamity for this country . . . Hindu Raj must be prevented at any cost.'

—Dr B.R. Ambedkar

'THIS IS JUST A MIRACLE.' ON 4 JUNE, AFTER PARTICIPATING in an election debate, I spoke to a Samajwadi Party (SP) leader outside the TV studio. He said, 'Till the first two phases of polling in UP, we were neither very hopeful nor speaking much. But when we saw the response to Rahul's speeches, we realised that the weather has changed, and we have a fair chance. Then we got into aggressive mode.' This was the day when the miracle happened, and UP was the talk of the town. Most unexpectedly, voters had given a verdict against BJP in a state where—the party was convinced—it couldn't be defeated. By noon, BJP found itself struggling to get even 35 seats. The news of the day was that the almighty, omnipotent, divinely ordained prime minister could barely win in Varanasi, the very city in which he had pompously announced that 'Mother Ganga has called me and adopted me.' Modi finally won by 1.52 lakh votes.

I can't name the SP leader, as we were engaged in an informal chat, but I was immediately reminded of a conversation I had with another SP leader over phone. This was in January 2024. The Ram Mandir consecration had not yet taken place, and from streets to TV studios, the saffron wave was turning into a tsunami. Bharatiya Janata Party's massive victory had been declared inevitable, and the opposition was disheartened.

On the phone, the SP leader did not sound too optimistic either. When I asked him how many seats they expected, he could not count more than seven. I said, 'If that is the case, then no power on earth could stop Modi from winning a third term with more than 300 seats.' When I asked him which seats he thought the party could win, he was unsure. By March, I was told by another SP leader that the party would have an alliance with Congress as Muslims are more inclined towards Rahul Gandhi, and the party was planning to identify 25 to 30 seats strategically, pool all resources and try to win as many seats as possible, instead of contesting all 80 seats. This clearly indicated that SP had given up on giving a good fight to BJP in UP, and their battle was one of survival. But 4 June told a different story. Together, SP and Congress wrote a chapter that would haunt BJP for years.

Why and how did this happen?

Uttar Pradesh was undoubtedly BJP's most powerful bastion after Gujarat. It was considered another Hindutva laboratory. On the eve of the elections, BJP was complacent. It seemed to believe that electoral history was on its side. The party had the genius of two Hindutva leaders—Modi and Yogi—along with Lord Ram's blessing in the form of the consecration.

When Modi began his campaign for the Lok Sabha in 2014, he strategically decided to contest from Varanasi, along with Baroda in his home state of Gujarat. Modi knew that he could not become the prime minister unless he conquered UP. After the initial breakthrough in the early 1990s due to the Ram Mandir movement, BJP had not been a major force in the state for almost a decade and a half. As late as the 2009 parliamentary elections, they could only win 10 seats in UP with 17.5 per cent votes, while Congress had won 21 seats and SP, under Mulayam Singh Yadav's leadership, 23 seats. Even Bahujan Samajwadi Party (BSP), led by Mayawati, won 20 seats. In the 2012 assembly elections, BJP's vote share shrank to 15 per cent, and the party could win only 47 seats. With 224 seats and 29.15 per cent votes, SP had formed the government.

Bharatiya Janata Party had no hope of emerging with a majority in 2014. Afterall, just two years prior, in 2012, its vote share had been only 15 per cent. But thanks to the highly personalised and presidential style of campaigning, Modi turned the tide, and BJP's vote share almost trebled to 42.63 per cent. The party won 71 seats, which was nothing less than a miracle. In 2017, Modi's magic worked again, and BJP ended up winning on 312 out of 403 seats in the UP assembly. In 2019, BJP's juggernaut continued, despite SP and BSP getting into a formidable alliance. Bharatiya Janata Party won 62 seats, and its vote share jumped to 49.98 per cent. Belying all speculations, BJP again formed government in the 2022 assembly elections with 255 seats. This time, BJP's seat share might have reduced, but its vote share increased to 41.29 per cent compared to 39.67 per cent in the 2017 assembly elections.

Since 2014, BJP has been in a pole position in UP, with the opposition struggling to give it a tough fight. Compared with the 2017 assembly elections, SP improved its vote share by 10 per cent in 2022. It did this by forming smart alliances with small caste-based political parties, gaining a 32.1 per cent vote share. But it had to be satisfied with 111 seats. Meanwhile, Congress suffered its most humiliating defeat in UP. Despite Priyanka Gandhi leading the campaign, the party could win only 2 seats with 2.33 per cent votes. On the eve of the 2024 Lok Sabha elections, data clearly suggested that BJP had the upper hand.

Combining the statistics with the fact that BJP had at its disposal two Hindutva icons—Narendra Modi and Yogi Adityanath—there was no stopping them.

Yogi is no ordinary leader within the Hindutva fold. Today, he is seen as the future prime minister and, arguably, a worthy successor to Modi. Rashtriya Swayamsevak Sangh pressurised Modi and Shah to appoint Yogi as the chief minister in 2017. For them, he is the party's next-generation leader. If Modi has adopted UP, then Yogi, by virtue of being the Peethadhiswar of Gorakhnath Math in Gorakhpur, is the son of the soil.

By being the Peethadhiswar, Yogi has inherited a revolutionary tradition in the Hindu fold which 'revolted against the distortions in Brahminism and Buddhism' and 'opposed caste discrimination'.[1] Sant Gorakhnath, who associated himself with the Nath sect, is considered to be one of Hinduism's greatest spiritual leaders. Yogi was anointed as the Peethadhiswar after the demise of Mahant Avaidyanath on 12 September 2014. It is ironical that Yogi is known for his anti-Muslim rhetoric even as Gorakhnath had 'laid the foundation of Hindu-Muslim unity'.[2] Even today, the tradition continues and 'no Muslim is denied audience or response at the temple janata darbar', and 'there is no discrimination in dealing with the complaints'.[3] Yogi comes from the Hindu Mahasabha stream, but today he is an integral part of BJP and RSS.

A question that is worth asking is: why couldn't the two leaders—Modi and Yogi—win UP for the party? Especially, in the land of the Ram Mandir movement—the very movement that catapulted BJP to the pinnacle of power. Before the Ram Mandir movement, BJP had been reduced to 2 seats in the Lok Sabha, with only 7.74 per cent votes, in 1984. Advani wrote, 'Reconstructing the temple for Sri Rama became the symbol of this rising consciousness—ridding the country of the perversities to which it was being subjected in the name of Secularism, forging a strong and united country. The object of the movement thus became not just to construct yet another temple, the object became to put our country back on its feet, to purify our public life, our public discourse. This is how in 1989 the Bharatiya Janata Party formally decided to lend its shoulder to the cause the Party was responding to the deepest urges of our people.'[4]

Nilanjan Mukhopadhyay, who has keenly observed the Ram Janmabhoomi Movement and also written a book on the subject, believes that the 'Ram Mandir movement was India's biggest post-independence mass agitation.'[5] He is of the opinion that, after Independence, BJP/RSS used the Ram Mandir movement to change the dominant public discourse on secularism and Hindu–Muslim unity. He writes, 'The Ayodhya movement [Ram Mandir movement] is unprecedented in the annals of Indian history. The success of the Sangh Parivar lies in having ensured that the passion and paranoia aroused in the course of the agitation for the Ram temple, was not limited to merely demolishing the Babri Masjid and constructing a new temple in its place. In addition to it, sentiments stirred in the minds of a large section of Hindus have become integral in their psyche. From a time when the dominant section of Hindus was in principle, of the view that it was obligatory for the majority to safeguard the interest of the minorities, the same people have now begun to think that the obligation is on minorities, to ensure that sentiments of the majority are not hurt.'[6]

Before one dives deep to find out the reason for BJP's unexpected performance in UP in the 2024 elections, one must remember that the party was also best prepared arithmetically. At one pole was SP, which was unsure of having a stable alliance with Congress despite being a member of the INDIA bloc. During the assembly election, SP had a serious face-off with Congress in Madhya Pradesh, where the local unit of Congress led by Kamal Nath was unwilling to accommodate SP. In fact, when he was asked if he was willing to give seats to Akhilesh Yadav's party, he said, '*Are bhai chhodo Akhilesh Vakhilesh* [forget about Akhilesh].'[7]

This was blockbuster masala for mainstream TV channels to unleash a narrative of how fragile the opposition's alliance was, and a godsent opportunity for BJP to discredit SP and the INDIA. Akhilesh had every reason to be upset. He said, 'If Congress continues to behave like this, then who will trust them? If we fight with confusion in mind against the BJP, then we won't succeed.'[8]

On the other hand, BJP was indulging in smart politics. It created a meta-narrative around Ram Mandir and stitched brilliant caste alliances to counter the social justice narrative weaved around the Caste Census by the INDIA bloc. Originally brought into focus by Nitish Kumar, the Caste Census was highjacked by Rahul Gandhi and Akhilesh Yadav once Nitish joined forces with BJP. Bharatiya Janata Party was aware that SP had increased its vote share by more than 10 per cent in the 2022 assembly elections by weaving together a bigger rainbow coalition with smaller caste-based parties like Suheldev Bharatiya Samaj Party (SBSP), Rashtriya Lok Dal (RLD),

Mahan Dal, Apna Dal (Kamerawadi), Janvadi Socialist Party, Jan Adhikar Party of Babu Singh Kushwaha, along with other caste leaders like Swami Prasad Maurya, Dara Singh Chauhan and Dharam Singh Saini. As the alliance of more than two dozen parties took shape, BJP started weaning away a few caste-based parties from the SP camp.

In July 2023, BJP lured SBSP of Om Prakash Rajbhar, and Dara Singh Chauhan. It already had among its allies Anupriya Patel's Apna Dal and the NISHAD Party. Its biggest catch was RLD, a party that seeks to represent the interests of the Jat community in western UP. While Jats constitute only 2 per cent of UP's population, they are a dominant caste and exert influence on other castes too. Their presence is decisive in 10 Lok Sabha constituencies in western UP.

Rashtriya Lok Dal leader Jayant Chaudhary had been on very good terms with Akhilesh Yadav. The two parties contested the 2019 and 2022 elections as allies, and SP even nominated Chaudhary to the Rajya Sabha. In the 2022 election, RLD commanded 2.85 per cent votes and won 8 assembly seats.

Since 2014, BJP had been getting Jat votes. However, it expected some disillusionment in this group of voters owing to the farmers' protest. 'Our empirical study shows 91% of the community supported BJP in 2019. This dropped to 71% in 2022 assembly polls,' said Professor A.K. Verma of the Centre for Study of Society and Politics. He blamed the erosion on farmers' protest and demand for reservation for Jats.[9] 'BJP is also likely to benefit from its alliance with Jayant Chaudhary's RLD.'[10] Bharatiya Janata Party smartly played its card. To provoke Jayant Chaudhary and Nitish Kumar to desert the INDIA bandwagon, the Modi government announced Bharat Ratna for Bihar's backward caste leader Karpoori Thakur and former prime minister Charan Singh. Karpoori Thakur was awarded the Bharat Ratna on 23 January 2024, the day after the Ram Mandir's consecration. The announcement for the Bharat Ratna being awarded to Charan Singh was made on 9 February 2024. By then, Nitish Kumar had already moved to NDA.

Prime Minister Modi wrote on X, 'This honour is dedicated to his incomparable contribution to the country . . . His dedication to our farmer brothers and sisters and his commitment to democracy during the Emergency is inspiring to the entire nation.'[11] Prime Minister Modi had attempted to kill three birds with one stone. Firstly, he created an exit route from the alliance for Jayant Chaudhary, who happens to be Charan Singh's grandson. Secondly, through this, BJP was offering an olive branch to angry farmers of western UP who had participated in the farmers' protest on the issue of three farm laws, which had lasted over a year, until the laws had been withdrawn by the government. Lastly, it was an attempt to blunt Congress's attack that Modi and BJP were anti-democracy and anti-Constitution by reminding citizens about the Emergency imposed by the Congress government, which had been opposed by Charan Singh. Charan Singh, who had assiduously built his image as a farmers' leader, was originally with the Congress and had moved to the opposition benches later. In 1967, he went on to become the first non-Congress chief minister of UP. In a country where caste identity influences voting behaviour, the Bharat Ratna was conferred to Charan Singh to win over the Jat community, which has the 'potential of influencing results in nearly 40 Lok Sabha seats and around 160 Assembly seats, spread across UP, Haryana, Rajasthan and Delhi.'[12]

With Apna Dal, RLD and SBSP on its side, BJP managed to have an electorally powerful caste alliance of Kurmi, Jat and Rajbhar against the Yadav caste, which has been loyal to SP. And yet, the party did not get the desired result.

One of the reasons was a more sophisticated social engineering by SP. Akhilesh Yadav, who had realised the potential of caste alliances in the 2022 assembly election, decided not to put money on caste leaders of small parties; if they were with him, it was well and good, and if not, he was not much bothered. He worked on a dual strategy. His first aim was to neutralise BJP's strategy of polarising non-Yadav castes within the OBC community.

Ever since Modi became the supreme leader, BJP has successfully worked on a divide-and-rule policy. The party's stance of Hindu unity against Muslims and Christians is well known. What remains lesser known is that the party has no qualms about dividing Hindus too. The party is willing to self-destruct its own ideological position of a Hindu civilisation for electoral gains. When it comes to applying the divide-and-rule policy within the Hindu fold, it is done with great finesse. The strategy is simple: identify the most dominant caste in a state that has not been voting for BJP, isolate that dominant caste, and build an umbrella front against that caste by labelling the dominant caste as a 'usurper'.

Bharatiya Janata Party has used this strategy in Haryana, Jharkhand, UP and Bihar. In Haryana, the party isolated Jats; in Jharkhand, they created a coalition against Adivasis, who had strong ties with Jharkhand Mukti Morcha (JMM). In UP, they tried to build a coalition of non-Yadav within backward castes and non-Jatav caste within Dalits. Similarly, in Bihar they did the same against Yadavs, who are strongly aligned with the Rashtriya Janta Dal (RJD). In UP and Bihar, the MY combination of Muslims and Yadavs has been solidly with SP and RJD. In order to find a winning space for itself, BJP created negativity against the MY combination, stigmatised them with goondaism and hooliganism, and called them a menace to society and dangerous for the security of the common man. As part of BJP's propaganda, if the Lalu regime was called 'Jungle Raj', then in UP, SP's rule was popularised as 'Goonda Raj'. This strategy worked in UP in the 2014, 2017, 2019 and 2022 elections.

In the 2024 elections, Akhilesh Yadav tried to get out of this trap. He introduced social engineering of a new kind within the politics of social justice. One could call it Mandal 3.0.

While Mandal 1.0, which had Mulayam Singh Yadav, Lalu Prasad Yadav and Mayawati as its icons, ignited the latent energy of backward castes and Dalits, democratised their consciousness and made them realise the power of their demographic strength, it was handicapped by the supremacy of what was the dominant caste among the backward castes. As a counter to that, Modi and BJP tried Mandal 2.0, which was to appropriate backward politics by challenging the hegemony of the dominant caste, creating a chimaera of empowering other castes among backwards and Dalits. This was done within the Hindutva framework. In UP, it succeeded to a large extent. In contrast to these two versions, Mandal 3.0 is more egalitarian in its intent. Here, dominant backward castes like Yadavs are willing to take a backseat and give more space to other castes.

Akhilesh Yadav's PDA—Pichhda + Dalit + Alpsankhyak—is a radical concept. It tries to integrate three distinct identities of backward castes, Dalits and Muslims into one 'discriminated' meta identity. It doesn't seek to assimilate three different identities into one, but to preserve these identities in their distinctive forms. It recognises all three as victims of the hegemonic meta identity, which is represented by the upper castes and the upper class on a larger canvas. All three social groups together comprise 80 per cent of the population but their share in the power structure is abysmally low. If Mandal

1.0 is defined purely by social discrimination, then Mandal 3.0 adds the dimension of economic elements to social identity and broadens its social foundation by having a coalition with Muslims as an active component. Muslims have an electoral association with the politics of social justice, especially in UP and Bihar. In these two states, Muslims have consistently voted for SP and RJD. Since Modi became the prime minister, Muslims have felt institutional discrimination; they are constantly socially ostracised. Historically, Muslims have been economically backward but not publicly discriminated against. That position has changed in the last ten years. Akhilesh Yadav and Rahul Gandhi have tried to accommodate Muslims in their larger fight for social justice.

Yadav's PDA meets Gandhi's Jitni Abadi, Utna Haq (the rights of any group are proportionate to its population) midway and creates a beautiful social chemistry which, if it succeeds in the long term, will be detrimental to BJP's Hindutva. 'Rahul Gandhi's call for "jitni abadi, utna haq" (distribution of public resources proportionate to the population) coupled with various opposition parties' (SP, RJD and Congress) collective demand for a caste census has brought back the question of social justice and redistribution of public resources to the forefront of Indian politics . . . Akhilesh Yadav's PDA strategy—standing for the welfare of Pichhade (backward), Dalits, Alpsankhyak (minorities) and Adhi Abadi (women)—may be the key to wooing voters beyond the SP's core support base of Yadavs and Muslims.'[13]

Akhilesh took a risk by ignoring caste-based small parties. Instead of establishing communication through their leaders, he tried to communicate directly with these communities. This was opposed to his 2022 election strategy when he had tried to form a conglomeration of caste-based parties. Akhilesh's experience with such parties had been less than perfect in the past. Mostly led by self-seekers and power-hungry politicians bereft of any ideological conviction, there have been many cases of such parties acting as power brokers, ready to sell their conscience at a throwaway price. In fact, many leaders who had joined the SP camp prior to the 2022 assembly elections moved to BJP once it emerged victorious.

Akhilesh Yadav showed strategic thinking in ticket distribution in the 2024 elections. Realising how BJP polarises voters against the MY combination, Akhilesh majorly focused on giving tickets to non-Yadav OBCs and Dalits. In 2024, SP, being in alliance with Congress, contested only 62 seats. They gave tickets to 27 candidates belonging to non-Yadav castes. Compared with the 2014 and 2019 elections, where SP had given tickets to 12 and 10 Yadav candidates respectively, only 5 Yadav candidates got tickets in 2024. Other than Yadav OBCs, SP gave 10 tickets to the Kurmi community, the second most powerful OBC caste after Yadavs, and the rest were distributed among Kushwaha, Pal, Maurya, Nishad, Shakya, Rajbhar, Bind, Gurjar, Jat and others. In an attempt to reach out to Dalits, the party gave them 17 tickets. Akhilesh Yadav took another bold step. He nominated two Dalit candidates from the general seats of Faizabad and Meerut. 'The distribution of tickets reflects a deliberate effort to accommodate a diverse spectrum of caste groups, with allocation made to Kurmis, Dalits, Yadavs, Muslims, upper castes and Other Backward Classes (OBCs). This strategic manoeuvring is aimed at dispelling the perception of the SP as a 'Yadav-centric' party and fostering a sense of inclusivity among marginalized communities.[14]

No wonder seasoned editor Prabhu Chawla praises Akhilesh Yadav for reinventing his father's party with a new 'modern mind'. He writes, 'For SP [Samajwadi Party], Yadavism is dead, long live new Yadav. Akhilesh now leads a minimised Yadavised outfit.'[15]

In the 2024 election, one of the worries of Akhilesh Yadav was that BJP would succeed in painting SP as a party that favours Muslims over Hindus. Giving the Muslim tag to opposition parties helps BJP polarise Hindu voters. Bishwajit Banerjee writes, 'This time, Akhilesh Yadav has made an attempt to ward off pro-Muslim image and one promoting Muslim politics and gave only four tickets to the Muslims as against 20 percent of the community population in the state.'[16]

In the 2024 elections, SP's challenge was to break BJP's inroads among non-Yadav OBCs. According to the Centre for Studies of Developing Societies (CSDS), in 2014, 61 per cent non-Yadav OBCs voted for BJP in UP. This number increased to 72 per cent in 2019. Kurmis and Koeries, the two OBC castes that are politically most powerful after Yadavs in the state, were solidly aligned with BJP. In 2014, 53 per cent of Kurmis and Koeries voted for BJP; in 2019, the number went up to 80 per cent.

Rajiv Kumar writes,

> It's the non-Yadav OBCs, though, that of late have evolved as a major political force in the state. Constituting around 35% of UP's population, this rainbow of various heterogeneous non-dominant castes, including Kurmis, Mauryas, Kashyaps, Sainis, Sahus, and so forth, could single-handedly decide which party will have an upper hand in the polls.
>
> Following the Mandal movement, most of these groups started backing the socialist parties, including the SP. However, given the massive influence of the Yadavs in the Akhilesh Yadav-led party and the BJP's outreach towards them, they have overwhelmingly entered the saffron camp.[17]

> Prime Minister Narendra Modi himself coming from the OBC community too has impacted their voting preference besides the NDA government aggressively wooing them with posts and policies. In the 2019 Lok Sabha polls, the BJP fielded 27 non-OBCs in Uttar Pradesh, nine more than the opposition Mahagathbandhan that included the SP and BSP, according to an *Indian Express* report.[17]

Amitabh Tewari's analysis in *India Today* is also along the same lines. He writes,

> In Lok Sabha polls, the BJP's vote share in UP increased from 18 per cent in 2009 to 42 per cent in 2014 and 50 per cent in 2019. It received 60 per cent support from non-Yadav OBCs (a gain of 31 per cent) and 45 per cent support from non-Jatav Scheduled Castes (a gain of 37 per cent) in the 2014 general elections.
>
> The saffron party expanded its social base beyond the Brahmin-Baniya samaj to include non-Yadav OBCs and non-Jatav Dalits in its fold, creating an unbeatable combination accounting for roughly 60 per cent of the state population. It weaned these groups away from Samajwadi Party and the Bahujan Samaj Party by highlighting how Yadavs and Jatavs occupied prominent power positions in these parties, driving a wedge between Yadavs and non-Yadav OBCs, and Jatavs and non-Jatav Dalits.[18]

But in the 2024 elections, BJP's performance in UP was greatly disappointing. One of the major reasons was the reverse weaning away of non-Yadav OBCs and non-Jatav Dalits from the party. 'Data from the CSDS post-poll survey shows that the

BJP received 61 per cent support from the Kurmi-Koeris (a loss of 19 per cent), 59 per cent support from non-Yadav OBCs (a loss of 13 per cent) and 29 per cent support from non-Jatav Dalits (a loss of 19 per cent). '... The INDIA bloc's Kurmi-Koeri and non-Yadav OBCs votes went up 6 per cent and 13 per cent compared with 2019. Of 37 Samajwadi Party wins in the Lok Sabha, 21 winners were OBCs (including five Yadavs), seven Dalits, four Muslims and five upper-caste candidates.'[19]

It seems BJP paid the price for taking non-Yadav OBCs and non-Jatav Dalits for granted. This happened at a time when SP, along with Congress, was course correcting. Bharatiya Janata Party became a victim of its own success. In the 2024 elections, it gave 33 per cent of tickets to OBC candidates in contrast to the SP's 50 per cent. The ticket distribution by BJP in UP was heavily tilted towards the upper castes, giving them 45 per cent of the tickets. The same pattern was visible in ticket distribution in the 2022 assembly elections too. Then, 35 per cent of tickets were given to OBCs despite them comprising 45 per cent to 50 per cent of the population in UP, and upper castes, which constitute approximately 20 per cent of the population, were given 44 per cent tickets. The cabinet formation also reflected the same imbalance. Despite being more in number, only 22 ministers were OBCs, and the same number of the upper caste were made ministers. Among the top three posts, two went to the upper caste candidates. Yogi Adityanath, an upper-caste Rajput, was made chief minister; Brajesh Pathak, another upper caste, was appointed deputy chief minister; and Keshav Prasad Maurya, an OBC, was made deputy chief minister.

Dr Laxman Yadav, who is fast emerging as a young political thinker, has written a bestseller called *Professor ki Dairy* wherein he has tried to explain the PDA phenomenon from a historical perspective. In his opinion, PDA has two social forces that have drifted away from each other in the last decade due to the conspiratorial politics of Hindutva. According to Dr Yadav, the two forces realised their mistakes and, in the 2024 election, tried to come together. In a long essay, which he wrote at my request, he argues, 'Mandal movement is the dividing line in independent India. Christophe Jaffrelot calls the Mandal movement a silent revolution. In fact, the Mandal movement has successfully tried to address Phule and Ambedkar's agenda of uniting backward castes and Dalits. The Mandal movement not only laid the foundation of bringing together different backward castes, but it also tried to articulate the demands of the 90% of Bahujans. Dr Ram Manohar Lohia tried to organise the politics of North India around the slogan, "Pichhde paven Sau me Sath" [backwards should get 60% of 100], which was further expanded by the socio-cultural intellectuals and organisations like Arjak Sangh, Triveni Sangh, Jagdev Prasad Kushwaha, Ram Swarup Verma, Lalai Singh Yadav and others, within the socialistic thought that "Sau me nabbe Shoshit hain, shoshiton ne Lalkara hai; Dhan, Dharti aur Rajpath me nabbe bhag hamara hai [90 out of 100 are the exploited, the exploited have challenged; in wealth, land and in the functioning of the government, we should have 90% share]". The Mandal movement talks about these 90%, which is why Vishwanath Pratap Singh said that he had changed the grammar of politics. But right-wing politics propped up the Kamandal movement to counter the Mandal movement. In this era of Mandal and Kamandal, the slogan of "mile Mulayam Kanshi Ram, Jai Sri Ram hawa me ud gaye [when Mulayam and Kanshi Ram met, Jai Sri Ram was blown away in thin air]" defeated BJP just after the demolition of Babri Masjid. It was the beginning of an ideological relationship between Dalit and Backward votes, and the togetherness of Muslim and progressive Hindus kept the BJP and the Congress away from power for long. This was the reflection of a socio-cultural unity that was getting deepened in the society. Due to education, reservations among employment and socio-cultural movements, the political consciousness further strengthened, but over a period of time, BJP tried to put SP and BSP, one against the other, resultantly SP and BSP became enemies for two and half decades. . . . In 2014 BJP polarised Dalits and Backwards on the line of religious identity of Hindu along with Patriotism. BJP was successful in making inroads among Dalits and backwards. The same thing was repeated in 2019.'

Dr Yadav believes that it was a temporary phenomenon. Dalits and backwards were to be disillusioned soon. This is what happened in 2024 when Akhilesh Yadav, along with Rahul Gandhi, tried to cobble up Dalits and backward classes by pushing the agenda of the Caste Census, breaking the 50 per cent reservation ceiling. He argues, 'In reality, the right-wing ideology of BJP/RSS and ideology of socialist and Ambedkar-wadis are fundamentally opposed to each other. . . . This was the time when ideas and struggles of Ambedkar, Phule, Periyar, Lohia, Kanshi Ram and Mulayam were reaching to these social groups thanks to social media and social organisations. The anger in this section of society due to their rights being robbed was increasing. Anger was waiting for a leader. Akhilesh Yadav and Rahul Gandhi filled that gap . . . PDA had brought back the old equation of Mulayam and Kanshi Ram, which had failed in 2019 despite the alliance of SP and BSP.'

Dr Laxman's views are echoed by Dalit thinker Professor Ravikant Chandan, who teaches at Lucknow University. He is one of the very few who, during the elections, said that BJP would not win more than 35 seats in UP. He was of the opinion that the aggressive Hindutva politics of Yogi Adityanath and BJP/RSS had alienated a large section of Dalits from BJP and had ignited a new wave of Dalit consciousness, which was crystallising as a counter-force to Hindutva. Since this whole movement was not a one-face movement and no political party owned it, it was largely ignored by the mainstream media. It should be noted that Dalits constitute almost 20 per cent, or approximately 4.1 crores, of UP's population.

When I requested Professor Ravikant to analyse the reasons for the INDIA's unexpected success in UP, he wrote a long piece for me.

'After winning Lok Sabha elections in 2019, open announcements for the establishment of Hindu Rashtra became a regular thing. Atrocities and exploitation of Dalits increased. It was said that on the occasion of 100 years of RSS, India would be declared a Hindu Rashtra. The Dalit community was aware of the danger of Hindu Rashtra, and the educated and alert section of the society became very active. As a result, regular seminars were conducted to spread the ideas and concerns of Babasaheb Ambedkar. Awareness campaigns were launched to save the Constitution, reservation, education, dignity and self-respect. After a long time, the Dalit community came forward to fulfil the dream of Babasaheb Ambedkar. It was for the first time that attraction towards Buddhism, outside Maharashtra, increased, and regular seminars for Buddhism were being organised. In these seminars and congregations, twenty-two promises of Babasaheb Ambedkar were recited. The government tried to discourage this. The organisers were harassed. To quieten Dalit intellectuals and to break their morale, they were targeted. Cases were foisted on them. They had to go through the torture of police and courts. But with increased atrocities, they became more vocal. Dalits were left with two options, either to choose slavery of Hindutva or embrace independence of the Constitution. They were worried about their future. Between

2019, when the Supreme Court delivered its verdict about Ram Mandir, and 2024, when the consecration of Ram Mandir happened, there arose a new wave which was not discernible to others.'

Like Professor Ravikant, Sheetal P. Singh was one of the very few journalists who had correctly read the mood of UP voters and had reached the conclusion that BJP was heading for big trouble in the state. He had said he would be surprised if BJP got more than 40 seats. Like Professor Ravikant and Dr Yadav, Singh also replied in writing to my questions about BJP's poor performance in UP. 'The most important fact was the explosion of political consciousness among the educated and employed members of the Dalit community. They have an abundance of information about how the reservation was being blunted in jobs, the one-sided capture of university faculties by upper castes and the total domination of Brahmins and Thakurs in police stations and tehsils. They also had saved in their phones statements of BJP leaders in which they were bragging about their intent to change the Constitution.'

Professor Ravikant explained that this new wave was not sponsored by anyone. It was spontaneous and self-generating, and was the result of deep scars of the past. It was taking shape at a very different level, and if the politics of Hindutva did not take cognisance of this subterranean but potentially powerful movement, then BJP would surely remain in trouble in the future too. Professor Ravikant's vivid description and illustration of this wave is eye opening. He writes, 'Bahujan Samaj and, especially, a large section among Dalits, have stopped celebrating big Hindu festivals like Holi-Diwali, on a big scale. They are moving away from Hindu gods and goddesses, and their place is being taken over by revolutionary heroes and spiritual gurus and saints of Bahujan Samaj. The birth anniversaries of Buddha, Kabir, Ravidas to Bahujan heroes of modern India, like Jyotiba Phule, Savitri Bai, Ramaswami Naicker, Chhatrapati Shahu Maharaj, Babasaheb Ambedkar, Sant Gadge, Ram Swarup Verma, Periyar, Lalai Singh, Karpoori Thakur, Maharaj Singh Kushwaha, Jhalkari Bai, Uda Devi Pasi are today celebrated as their new festivals. On their birth anniversaries, seminars are organised where preambles of the Constitution are read out, Buddha Vandana is chanted, and it is pledged that they would not let India be made a Hindu Rashtra. April, the month of Babasaheb's birth anniversary, has become bigger than Eid and Diwali for Dalits. According to *Financial Times*, more than ₹5,000 crores are spent on 14 April to celebrate Babasaheb Ambedkar's birth anniversary. Today, the youth take out processions holding blue flags, along with DJs and music. In the last five years, these birth anniversaries and processions of Bahujan heroes have become an occasion to prove their commitment to their identity, existence and their rights. In the last five years, the number of such seminars, congregations and rallies has grown exponentially. In such congregations, 'protection of the Constitution', 'opposition to Hindus Rashtra' and views of Babasaheb Ambedkar are the main themes that are discussed and debated, a pledge is taken, the politics of BJP and RSS are fiercely criticised and attacked, and commitment to the unity of Bahujan is reminded and repeated. It is apparent that either BJP could not anticipate this movement among Dalit–Bahujans or had no idea about the power of this leaderless movement.'

It is paradoxical that this new wave of Dalit–Bahujan consciousness was crystallising at a time when BSP, led by Mayawati, the original commander of the Dalit movement in UP, was weakening. Kanshi Ram, the originator of this unique Dalit experiment, had succeeded where Babasaheb Ambedkar had failed. During the freedom movement, Ambedkar was fighting for the upliftment of the Dalits. A fierce critic of Mahatma Gandhi, Ambedkar was of the opinion that Dalits have been treated worse than animals in the Hindu religion for thousands of years and that the caste system is so powerful and oppressive that it is impossible for Dalits to seek salvation within the Hindu fold. According to him, leaving the Hindu religion was the only option for Dalits. He said, 'If I am disgusted with Hindus and Hinduism, it is because I am convinced that they cherish wrong ideals and live a wrong social life. My quarrel with Hindus and Hinduism is not over imperfections of their social conduct. It is much more fundamental. It is over their ideals.'[20]

Babasaheb had said that he was born a Hindu, but he would not die a Hindu. A few days before his death, on 14 October 1956, he turned Buddhist with lakhs of his supporters at Deekshabhoomi, Nagpur. Today, Ambedkar is worshipped as God by Dalits and Bahujans, but he could not convert his movement into a political party. He even failed to win elections for himself after leaving Nehru's cabinet in 1951. He contested the Lok Sabha election twice—first from Bombay North in 1952 and second from Bhandara in a by-election in 1954, but he lost both.

Kanshi Ram turned the Dalit movement into a successful political movement. In 1984, he formed BSP, contested the election, and his successor, Mayawati, became chief minister of UP four times. In 2007, she even formed a government on her own. The party winning majority seats in the UP assembly was no small achievement. But since then, BSP has been on the decline, and in the 2024 elections, they seemed on the verge of fading out. They could only get 9.39 per cent votes and failed to win a single Lok Sabha seat. Even Mayawati's own Jatav community, which constitutes 11 per cent of UP's population and has been a committed vote bank of BSP, is now getting disillusioned with her politics and is looking for an alternative. The CSDS post-poll survey for the 2024 elections captured this disenchantment among Jatavs. In the 2019 elections, 65.3 per cent of Jatavs voted for the SP–BSP alliance and only 14.1 per cent polled for BJP. In 2024, 44 per cent of Jatavs opted for BSP. The number of Jatav votes for BJP-led NDA increased to 24 per cent, whereas 25 per cent voted for the INDIA. In 2019, Jatavs voted in bulk for SP–BSP, only because of BSP. This number should have remained intact or increased in 2024 when BSP was contesting alone. Instead, it dropped to 44 per cent, a dip of 21 cent. Arguably, this was caused by the mysterious inactivity of Mayawati. For reasons unknown, she has confined herself within the four walls of her residence, except for issuing press releases. She is not even vocal on Dalit issues. Many conspiracy theories have been floated about her tacit understanding with BJP, but there is no concrete proof of this. Professor Ravikant writes, 'Mayawati was sworn in as a chief minister of UP four times; at one point, she was seen as a future prime minister, too. But after losing the 2012 assembly elections, she is constantly declining. In 2014, Modi became the prime minister, and in 2017, Yogi was anointed as CM of UP, but in these years, Mayawati's silence and her inactivity pushed Dalit politics on the margin. But the Dalit consciousness continues to grow.'

Brajesh Shukla is an astute observer of UP politics. He loves to wander during elections and speak directly with voters. He is not a theoretician. His observations are based on his first-hand contact with voters. Even he is mystified. He wrote, 'BSP has reached its 1989 situation. Then BSP had 9.90 per cent votes, whereas in this election, it has 9.39 per cent. It is difficult to assess BSP's strategy now, but the question is why BSP, which has been fighting for the interests of Dalits, has weakened so much.'[21]

Mayawati's enigmatic silence has also been explained by saying that she has been silenced by the central investigating agencies like the Enforcement Directorate (ED), Income Tax department and Central Bureau of Investigation (CBI) at the behest of the Modi government due to corruption cases. It is also being said that since 2007, BSP has compromised with the Bahujan ideology, and the party has allegedly been hijacked by Brahmins; therefore, Dalits have started drifting away from the party. Professor Vivek Kumar of Jawaharlal Nehru University, who is a Dalit and has written a book on BSP, writes in an unpublished article, 'There is a dearth of theoretical and empirical analysis of reasons why BSP has not been able to gain its lost ground since 2012 although it took many bold decisions during its various governments which really empowered Bahujans in Uttar Pradesh and at the national level. . . . Singling out a leader for the failure of a movement in a caste-ridden hierarchical democracy can be erroneous.'[22]

He argues that once a disempowered movement attains success, it logically leads to disintegration. In favour of his argument, Professor Kumar cites examples of several Bahujan leaders like Swami Prasad Maurya, Babu Singh Kushwaha, Sone Lal Patel, Om Prakash Rajbhar and Sanjay Nishad, who left BSP after earning recognition in the party, to carve out their own identity and gain more autonomy and political power.

Irrespective of Mayawati's silence, the Dalit and Bahujan roar was loud and clear. They were worried about BJP's claims of winning more than 400 seats, and their aim to change the Constitution. In a report on the online platform *Scroll.in*, Devraj, who belongs to the Pasi community from Barabanki district, responded in anger about the prospective change in the

Constitution when asked whom he would vote for. The report analyses:

> He attributed the desire to change the Constitution to chhuaa chhut, or caste discrimination. 'It is because the Constitution has been written by Babasaheb, who belonged to a lower caste,' he said, referring to BR Ambedkar, who served as the chairperson of the committee that drafted the Indian Constitution, 'that these people don't like it'. 'They don't like that the Constitution provides for reservation [in government jobs and educational institutions],' he continued. 'That's why they want to change it.'[23]

The same sentiment was echoed by Gautam Mane. He said, 'They want to change the constitution of India and stop job reservation.'[24]

The question is: why did the Dalits not choose BSP? Rane said that many Dalit voters had ditched the Bahujan Samaj Party, which has for long led the community in UP, because they felt it was too weak now to take on the BJP.[25]

If we compare the voting behaviour of Dalits of UP with that of Maharashtra, a pattern seems to emerge. Dalit voters of Maharashtra were also looking for a party or alliance that could defeat BJP's Hindutva. In Maharashtra, Prakash Ambedkar's party Vanchit Bahujan Aghadi's (VBA) vote percentage also dropped like it did in UP for BSP. In 2019, VBA had tied up with All India Majlis-e-Ittehadul Muslimeen (AIMIM) to contest on 47 seats. In 2024, it contested 42 seats alone. If in 2019 it got 6.99 per cent votes, then in 2024 it shrunk to 3 per cent. Ajinkya Gaikwad, a political science researcher at Mumbai's SIES College, argues, '. . . we cannot forget that Dalit voters have been the Congress's vote bank for years, and so there was a sense among them that they should keep the ideology of aligning with Ambedkar aside and go for a secular party to defeat Hindutva forces. It would also mean that votes are not wasted.'[26]

Mayawati further caused herself damage when she removed her nephew Akash Anand as her political successor midway through the elections. Akash Anand had been vehemently attacking BJP in his public rallies, and his removal by Mayawati further strengthened the perception that she was not seriously fighting BJP.

It is now crystal clear that two issues—the 'Change the Constitution' campaign and the scourge of Hindutva—had the Dalit–Bahujan community seriously thinking, and they concluded that the continuance of the BJP rule would take the community into dark ages, in which they would be accorded no dignity. There is no doubt that initially, they were seduced by the high-sounding words of Hindutva, packaged into a glamorous wrap of 'Sabka Sath, Sabka Vikas', lured by the false attraction of being adopted by the same Hindu ritualistic order that had refused to accord them human status in the past. But ten years of Hindutva rule at the Centre and seven years in UP was enough to make them take note of how they were being used as fodder to achieve Hindu Rashtra, a concept that Ambedkar vehemently opposed. Ambedkar had said, 'If Hindu Raj does become a fact, it will, no doubt, be the greatest calamity for this country. . . . Hindu Raj must be prevented at any cost.'[27]

In the course of time, the community has also realised that BSP could no longer fight for their civilisational cause because its politics had become transactional. It so happened that at the same time, Akhilesh Yadav and Rahul Gandhi were not only seen to be articulating their concerns and worries but also as ready to calibrate their thought process and political strategies to accommodate the interests of Dalits and Bahujans. If Akhilesh was looking beyond Muslims and Yadavs through the prism of PDA and was ready to share power with other marginalised and weaker castes, then Gandhi had also moved beyond the past mistakes of Congress on the Mandal Commission and was willing to fight for the Caste Census and embrace the politics of social justice. In contrast, BJP was mired in the past; it failed to see the new wave of consciousness among Dalits and Bahujans. Because of their ideological hubris, the party was not ready to address the civilisational anxieties of the 'mooknayaks'.

Bharatiya Janata Party's defeat was so heavy that seven central ministers—Smriti Irani (Amethi), Mahendra Nath Pandey (Chandauli), Sanjeev Balyan (Muzaffarnagar), Bhanu Pratap Singh (Jalaun), Sadhvi Niranjan (Fatehpur), Ajay Mishra (Lakhimpur Kheri), Kaushal Kishore (Mohanlalganj)—and two UP state ministers—Jayveer Singh (Mainpuri) and Dinesh Pratap Singh (Raebareli)—lost. Even for those who won, including Prime Minister Narendra Modi and Defence Minister Rajnath Singh, the victory margins had shrunk. Prime Minister Modi, who had won by 4,79,505 votes in 2019 in Varanasi, had to be satisfied with a victory margin of 1,52,513 votes only in 2024. Rajnath Singh's margin was reduced to 1.3 lakh votes from 3.47 lakhs five years earlier.

The election results undoubtedly shocked BJP. The party constituted a committee to find out the reasons for the defeat. The committee prepared a fifteen-page report based on its interaction with 40,000 people. The committee's report can be summed up in ten bullet points, as enumerated by the *Mint*:[28]

1. Opposition's narrative that reservations would be removed and comments by BJP leaders on constitutional amendments.
2. Paper leaks in competitive exams.

3. The issue around the recruitment of contract workers.
4. Large-scale dissatisfaction among BJP workers over the conduct of government officials.
5. Hasty ticket distribution affected the morale of BJP workers.
6. Discontent among party workers towards the BJP government in the state regarding police stations and tehsil offices.
7. Voters in the Thakur community distancing from the party.
8. No support from backward communities such as Kurmis and Kushwahas.
9. Pasis and Valmikis, among SC votes, shifted their support to the Samajwadi Party and the Congress.
10. BSP candidates in Lok Sabha polls did not split the Muslim votes. Instead, they had an impact on seats where BJP had strong candidate support.

The whispers in the BJP circle were that reports like these were mere paperwork and they were later thrown into the dustbin of the party archives. The issues raised in the report were not addressed; rather a search for a scapegoat began. Immediately after the report was released, factional politics raised its head, and the blame game started. This was a new development in BJP. It was a signal that the party, which was known for its discipline under the iron grip of Modi, had given way to the old politics. A section of BJP leaders believed that internal sabotage was the real reason for the party's humiliation. In personal chats, BJP leaders hinted to me that Yogi Adityanath, the powerful chief minister of UP, was the initiator of this move. The committee report hints at this when it blames government officials in bullet points 4 and 6. I was also told that the message from Lucknow was clear—that the state administration should be neutral during elections.

A very senior journalist based in Lucknow told me that in the top echelons of BJP, there was no confusion that Yogi was behind the debacle of the party in Lok Sabha elections, and he was basically paying back for the 2022 assembly elections when attempts were made to defeat him. The journalist was of the opinion that the growing stature of Yogi as a Hindutva icon has threatened many in the party who are positioning themselves for the post-Modi era. This journalist, who is quite entrenched in the power corridors of BJP, wished to stay anonymous.

Vinod Agnihotri, who belongs to UP, has the experience of covering UP politics for over three decades and has written a book on the farmers' protests. He did not mince his words when I asked him how he analysed the factional fight in UP. He said, 'Internal bickering, which has intensified in UP after Lok Sabha results, is a struggle more for Delhi than for Lucknow. This struggle is linked with "who after Modi" politics. Modi is playing his third innings for the BJP at the Centre. Amit Shah is the second most powerful leader after Modi right now. It is like Advani after Atal Bihari Vajpayee. All those leaders who could have been the claimants for that space have been neutralised one after the other, but Yogi is the only one whose popularity goes beyond UP, and he was the most sought-after star campaigner for the BJP after Modi in the elections.'

Another senior journalist who has access to the chief minister and is based in Lucknow told me that the chief minister was aware of the move to remove him. According to this journalist, Yogi, through his emissaries, has sent the message to the top leadership that if he is removed from the chief minister's chair, he will return to his math in Gorakhpur. This was interpreted as a direct threat that he was not like Shivraj Singh Chouhan, the former chief minister of Madhya Pradesh who did not retain the position after the massive victory of BJP in Madhya

Pradesh in 2023, or like Vasundhara Raje Scindia, former chief minister of Rajasthan, who was totally sidelined while a political featherweight leader, Bhajan Lal Sharma, was anointed in her place. He would not quietly surrender to the dictates of Delhi.

Vinod Agnihotri says, 'In the last seven years, the style of governance which Yogi has developed has made him the biggest face of Hindutva in the RSS scheme of things. Like Modi, who, as a chief minister of Gujarat, has evolved Gujarat's model of governance, Yogi has also developed a model that is being copied by other BJP leaders. His popularity and emergence as a Hindutvavadi leader are not liked by those in the race to succeed Modi.'

In fact, after becoming the chief minister of UP, Yogi Adityanath has consciously built an image of himself as a saviour of Hindus vis-à-vis the Muslims. He has used strong-arm tactics to deal with 'bahubalis' from the Muslim community like Atiq Ahmed, Mukhtar Ansari and Mohd. Azam Khan. He did not flinch in using the bulldozer to demolish houses of Muslims accused of wrongdoings. He takes great pride in criminals being killed and injured in police encounters and is also accused of using the police encounters to majorly target outlaws from the Muslim community. To a certain extent, within the Hindutva support base, he is rated better than Modi in dealing with Muslims and their supporters. In fact, during the murmur to remove him after the Lok Sabha results, his supporters vented their anger on social media and even criticised Modi.

When the deputy chief minister Keshav Prasad Maurya said in the party's working committee meeting, which he later tweeted too, that 'organisation is bigger than the government' and 'pain of the workers is my pain', it was interpreted as a result of internal bickering, and seen as an attack on Yogi.[29]

Yogi also did not want to be left behind. He said, 'Overconfidence caused harm in elections.' This was interpreted as a jibe at the party's central leadership.[30]

The saga continued. The impression was that Keshav Maurya was targeting Yogi on behalf of the central leadership. Keshav Maurya was no match for Yogi, and he did not have the wherewithal to face Yogi—unless he was supported by powerful leaders in Delhi. Though Maurya did have an axe to grind. In 2017, when BJP won the assembly election with 312 seats, he was the BJP president and a natural claimant to the seat of chief minister. But that chair, most unexpectedly, was offered to Yogi. He was made the deputy chief minister, but Yogi did not let him function independently. In the 2022 assembly elections, Maurya lost the Sirathu seat, though he remained the deputy chief minister. The massive loss in the Lok Sabha election was a good opportunity for him to convince the central leadership that the party could only be saved in 2027 if Yogi, an upper-caste leader, was replaced by an OBC leader, and he fit the bill.

Politics in UP is delicately poised. Bharatiya Janata Party's aggressive Hindutva has been successfully challenged by the newly revitalised politics of social justice, which has helped unite a large section of Dalits, OBCs and Muslims. It is easy for BJP to deal with the challenge posed by Muslim unity. What poses a problem to BJP/RSS is not Muslims but the large section of Hindus who are not ready to join Hindutva's bandwagon. It is the disillusionment among this section of Hindus, specifically, Dalits, Bahujans and OBCs, which has organically engaged with the trauma of Muslims. This has generated a tricky situation for BJP/RSS, which is faced with the dilemma that if it takes the social justice route, then its Hindu unity project is jeopardised, and if it continues with an aggressive Hindutva path, then its electoral victory will be hampered. It is because of this dilemma that RSS, after its Kerala meet, conceded that a Caste Census could be carried out, but only for welfare measures and not for politics. At the same time, it also raised the slogan of 'batenge to katenge' (divided we fall). It is Yogi at the forefront of the 'batenge' rhetoric that is being endorsed by RSS and Modi. Unless this dilemma is resolved, the road ahead for BJP in UP will be arduous and bumpy. Mandal 3.0 has stopped the juggernaut of Hindutva in UP, at least for some time.

7

Varanasi's (Un)Expected Verdict

'Had my sister [Priyanka] contested the Varanasi seat, the prime minister would have been defeated by 2 to 3 lakh votes.'

—Rahul Gandhi, 11 June 2024[1]

IF CONGRESS HAD SHOWN COURAGE AND GAMBLED BY PITTING Priyanka Gandhi against Narendra Modi to contest from Varanasi, who is to say what turn India would have taken after 4 June 2024. But Congress did not do that, and the Modi era continues. By the time Rahul Gandhi made this statement a week after the results were declared, Modi was ensconced in the saddle, though not so comfortably. Bharatiya Janata Party couldn't manage a clear majority on its own, and while Modi was re-elected for a third term as the prime minister, his sheen was gone. The RSS chief Mohan Bhagwat seemed to be telling Modi to mend his ways when he said that a true sevak does not have 'ahankara' (arrogance) and works without causing any hurt to others.[2]

Yes, the Congress did not show an iron will, but the people of Varanasi were ready to do the impossible. Ajai Rai, who was a lightweight candidate, lost by only 1.52 lakh votes. Instead of soaring to new heights, Modi's victory margin shrunk. Bharatiya Janata Party had wanted Modi to win by more than ten lakh votes. As Manoj Bhadra wrote, 'Having coined a new slogan "Abki baar, 10 lakh paar", the BJP is leaving no stone unturned to meet its target by all means as a challenge. The attendant tension is no deterrent on the party's efforts to increase the victory margin of Modi.'[3]

To create history in Varanasi, BJP put in tremendous efforts from the get go. A grand show was organised on the day of Modi's nomination. 'Around 16 national party presidents, three CMs, and four Union ministers including the Defence Minister were present at the time of the nomination.'[4]

But despite the tall claims and boasting of monstrous proportions, what was most surprising was that, when the prime minister proceeded to his meditation retreat at Vivekananda Rock Memorial in Kanyakumari after campaigning, Amit Shah, who is the second most powerful man in the government, stayed back to hold the fort in Varanasi along with many union ministers and heavyweight party office bearers. As Bhupendra Pandey reported, 'The PM left the responsibility of supervising the election in Varanasi to Union Home Minister Amit Shah, his second-in-command who in the past couple of days held meetings with senior leaders, Union Ministers Piyush Goel [Goyal] and Giriraj Singh, and BJP national general secretary Sunil Bansal. The three, along with a team of key BJP and RSS functionaries, have been managing the party's affairs in the run-up to voting.'[5]

If Varanasi was truly going to be a cakewalk as BJP had proclaimed publicly, then why was Shah deputed to lead the Modi Army in the city? Why was he gathering the party's alliance partners too? As reported by Pandey, 'Among the others who held a meeting with Shah were BJP ally and Suheldev Bhartiya Samaj Party (SBSP) chief Om Prakash Rajbhar and former Samajwadi Party (SP) leader Narad Rai, who joined the BJP on Tuesday. Sources in the BJP said Shah assigned tasks to his senior party colleagues, Rajbhar, and Rai who is from the Bhumihar community.'[6] Clearly, Modi alone was not enough. The party tried to bring in workers from other states to mobilise people of their states. 'In the past few days, the BJP has mobilised workers from different states and districts of Uttar Pradesh to help with the campaign. Party workers from Puducherry, Tamil Nadu, Telangana, Andhra Pradesh and Rajasthan are making rounds of areas where Tamils, Telugu people and people from Rajasthan live.'[7] It is another matter that the local BJP office bearers were boastful. '*Hum log kayde se campaign hi nahin kar rahe hain, koi fight hi nahi hai. Bas jeet ka margin badhana hai* (We are not properly campaigning since there is no fight. The only task is to increase the victory margin).'[8] But wouldn't Amit Shah have visited other constituencies, helping the party win more seats, instead of being stuck in Varanasi, if it was only about the winning margin and not about victory itself?

There is no denying that even the opposition had considered the holy city a lost fight. Congress had chosen Ajay Rai as its candidate from Varanasi not to defeat Modi but for mere tokenism. Rai was the state Congress party president who had contested against Modi in 2014 and 2019 as well. In both elections, he came in third, with 75,614 votes (7.34 per cent) in 2014 and 1,52,548 votes (14.38 per cent) in 2019. In 2024, his votes jumped to 4,60,457, with a vote share of 40.74 per cent. In 2014, there was no alliance between the opposition parties. In 2019, despite the SP–BSP alliance, the joint candidate Shalini Yadav could get only 1,95,159 votes, and lost the elections by 4,79,505 votes. In 2024, when SP entered into an alliance with Congress, which had managed to get only 2.33 per cent votes in the 2022 assembly elections, it was not thought of as a formidable alliance. But as elections marched past, the alliance in UP proved to be the nemesis for BJP, and in Varanasi, the opposition candidate Ajay Rai gave jitters to Modi on counting day. Rai got 4,60,457 votes, and lost only by 1,52,513 votes. Modi received 6,12,970 votes, 61,694 votes less than 2019.

At a time when Modi's victory in Varanasi was taken for granted, and the debate hinged on how much the margin would improve compared with 2019, very few reporters showed the courage to present the true picture of Varanasi. It seems reporters working with mainstream media either lacked the awareness about the ground reality, had fallen to editorial cowardice or surrendered to ideological bias.

A few good men held their fort and reported the truth—and the truth was that there was massive discontent with the prime minister. This feeling of dissatisfaction had its roots in the development initiatives that had ignored the very ethos of the city. According to mythology, Varanasi was established by Lord Shiva. Over the centuries, various people have contributed to the city's unique character. The city belongs to Kabir, one of the greatest spiritual saints. It is also the city where Tulsidas wrote *Ramcharitmanas*, the story of Lord Ram. The city was also home to the mystic poet-saint Ravidas. It's the city about which poet Kedarnath Singh wrote:[9]

[. . .]
yeh aadha jal mein hain
aadha mantra mein
aadhaa phool mein hai
aadha shav mein

aadhaa neend mein
aadha shankh mein
agar dhyaan se dekho
to yah aadhaa hai
aur aadha nahin hai

[. . .]

shatabdiyon se isi tarah
ganga ke jal mein
apni ek taang par khada hai yah shahar
apni doosri taang se
bilkul bekhabar

[. . .]

it is submerged
half in water
half in flowers
half in mantra.

Half in death
half in sleep
half in conch shell.

If you look again
it half remains
and half does not.

[. . .]

And for centuries now
praying to the unseen sun

the city has stood
in the water
on one leg
completely oblivious
to the other.

The modernisation of the city had ignored all these aspects, and through the election results, the spiritual city seemed to have expressed displeasure at the attempts made to change its character. Varanasi is no ordinary city. In hindsight, it seems Varanasi was enraged about being taken for granted. It reacted the way it ought to have. One of the greatest holy cities in the world was out to teach a lesson. It was out to prove that if lesser mortals, out of sheer arrogance and delusion, discover divinity in themselves, then the law of the cosmos will prove how hollow and brittle those who proclaim to be invincible are.

A week before polling day in Varanasi, senior journalist Anand Sahay hinted that Modi was no longer invincible in his own burrow, and that the road ahead for him was not going to be smooth and easy. He wrote, 'If Varanasi weren't the prime minister's constituency in the Modi era, in which no tactics to win can be deemed underhand, an observer may well be led to think that there is a fight on. This owes to the sharply dropping graph of the leader of the government in New Delhi, not particularly to any stalwart nature of the challenge he faces from the Congress party's Ajay Rai, although the Congress is in a firm alliance with UP's influential Samajwadi Party which is holding up very well—a sharp contrast from the time of the UP state poll of 2017.'[10]

Sahay also wrote, 'If you are in a big city, avidly read the papers and closely follow television news, the election campaign playing out in the countryside in Uttar Pradesh can be the bigger surprise. Varanasi in this state of large size and considerable diversity illustrates this perfectly.'

No doubt, in the ten years since Modi became the member of parliament from Varanasi, projects to the cost of ₹48,000 crore have been sanctioned and approximately ₹41,000 crore has been spent. A lot of development work has taken place. Today, other than the Kashi Vishwanath Corridor, widened roads, clean ghats and a highway to the airports has given a new dimension to the city. The number of tourists has also tremendously increased in last few years. But these changes in the city's landscape have made a section of the citizens unhappy. Their complaint is that the city's unique identity has been altered. Banaras, after all, is not a commercial city; it breathes spirituality, and ancientness is its identity. But an attempt to bring modern amenities to the city has ruined its uniqueness. Vishambhar Mishra, a professor at the city's Indian Institute of Technology and head of the Sankat Mochan Trust, said, '. . . these changes have robbed the city of its identity. . . . Varanasi used to be the city of lanes and bylanes. People could start from wherever and negotiate the lanes to reach the ghats to take a dip in the Ganges.'[11]

Modi's approach to Varanasi, as elsewhere, is likely driven by his aspiration to be remembered alongside the likes of Jawaharlal Nehru and Indira Gandhi. This urge to have a place amongst the biggest leaders propels him to create massive buildings. History bears testimony to the fact that great architecture and landmarks remind people of those who built them, the emperors of the past being a shining example of this. For instance, the Mughal emperor Shahjahan, though not a great ruler, is still remembered for the Taj Mahal. Modi knew that the Ram Mandir would go down in history so he ensured that he led the consecration of the temple. Of course, the move was intended to reap benefits during the parliamentary elections too, but the bigger intent was to go down in history as someone who built the Ram Mandir for Hindus. The new Parliament building had the same intent behind it.

Modi knows better than anyone else that the Kashi Vishwanath temple occupies a unique place in Hindu tradition. It is not only situated in one of the holiest cities in the world but is close to the holiest of rivers in Hindu mythology. Kashi Vishwanath is also one of the twelve Jyotirlingas. The Kashi Vishwanath Corridor would always remind pilgrims of the man who built it, and that man is none other than Narendra Damodardas Modi. Like the Ram Temple consecration, the Kashi Vishwanath Corridor too was created with the elections in mind, but the bigger motive for Modi was to place himself among one of the greatest saviours of Hindu civilisation, who fought and restored the glory of Hindus. Lord Ram and Lord Shiva are part of the Hindu holy trinity of Brahma, Vishnu and Mahesh, and Modi has managed to connect himself to two of them through the Kashi and Ayodhya temples. In this context, the prime minister's words while inaugurating the corridor on 14 December 2021 are extremely significant. He said, 'When you come here, you will not see only faith, you will also feel the glory of your past here—how antiquity and novelty come alive together, how the inspirations of the ancient are giving direction to the future. . . . This entire new complex of Vishwanath Dham is . . . also a symbol of sanatan (ancient) culture of India. This is a symbol of our spiritual soul, a symbol of India's antiquity, traditions, India's energy and dynamism.'[12]

In his forty-five-minute speech, Modi also reminded Hindus about the wrongs that had been done in history. He said, 'Tyrants attacked this city, tried to destroy it. History is witness to Aurangzeb's atrocities, his terror. He tried to change civilisation with the sword. But the soil of this country is different from the rest of the world. Here if an Aurangzeb comes, a Shivaji also rises. . . . If any Salar Masud comes, then the brave warriors like King Suheldev make him taste the might of India's unity . . .'[13]

The reference to Aurangzeb is typical of the RSS ideology. And Modi never forgets to package himself as the greatest Hindutvavadi in RSS. This helps him cement his position within the Sangh Parivar too. *Organiser*, RSS's supposed mouthpiece, wrote, 'The day today will be marked in the history as another step towards rejuvenation and renaissance of Bharat as a nation and Hindu society as the longest surviving culture in the world.'[14]

The prime minister laid the foundation stone of the Kashi Vishwanath Corridor on 8 March 2019. The Kashi Vishwanath temple is surrounded by narrow lanes and by-lanes, which used to get very congested when the pilgrims thronged the temple on auspicious occasions for the holy darshan of Lord Shiva. The prime minister ordered rebuilding the entire area for easy access to the temple. For this purpose, the premises of 3,000 square feet was converted into 5,00,000 square feet. 'The project involved purchase and acquisitions of more than 300 properties around Shri Kashi Vishwanath Temple. The rehabilitation of around 1400 shopkeepers, tenants and homeowners was done amicably. . . . During the process of destruction of the old properties, more than 40 ancient temples were rediscovered. These temples have been restored and beautified, while ensuring that there is no change in the original structure.'[15]

Against Modi's claim of igniting 'civilisational resurgence', his critics and opponents tried to project the entire construction as 'anti-Kashi'. Ajay Rai and his team tried to create a narrative on social media, and in an on-ground campaign, that Modi has harmed the city instead of spearheading the perceived revival.

'Before the *lokarpan* of the Kashi Vishwanath corridor, Modi was presented as a destroyer of the "pauranic nagri" by a section of locals. The Kashi Vishwanath corridor was seen as anti-local and anti-Kashi in the social media narratives by these sections. The alliance came together to make use of such emotions.'[16]

The idea of presenting Modi as an outsider disconnected from the roots of Kashi succeeded and helped the INDIA swallow Modi's votes. 'In South Varanasi, the heart of spiritual rejuvenation and the cradle of ghats and temples, and development centered on pilgrimage and tourist inflow, the BJP managed to scrape through "with nearly 16,000 votes". In 2019, this number was close to 60,000.'[17]

During elections, residents of Varanasi were divided about the development work around the temple and the city. A few who supported BJP were gung-ho about the whole thing, others had complaints. Aishwarya Sharma, a twenty-four-year-old who set up a homestay business near the Kashi Vishwanath Temple, was quoted in the *Economic Times* saying, 'The development, particularly of Kashi Vishwanath Corridor, has come as a blessing. The consistent flow of tourists has helped us set up a thriving homestay business. . . . In 10 years, change is clearly visible in Kashi. Sewage infrastructure has strengthened. Underground cabling has been done. We have new roads around the temple. Most importantly, Kashi now has a huge influx of Indian tourists.'[18]

The report presented the other side, too, and made it clear that not everyone was on the same page.

'However, not everyone is entirely convinced. Some, like Arvind Yogi and Jyoti Sharma, expressed concerns about whether the development aligns with Varanasi's spiritual essence and raised issues of crowd management. Anil Kumar Singh, a faculty member of BHU, emphasised the need for better infrastructure management to sustain Varanasi's growth. "No doubt development has taken place, but do they conform to Kashi's spiritual image?" he asked.'[19]

In the midst of this debate, the INDIA leaders added a new twist. Modi was presented as an outsider who had ignored the local population and given contracts for construction and other work to his friends from Gujarat. 'For example, in a video, Rai was seen attacking Modi and "Gujarat ke mitr" for the rejuvenation efforts of the Pushkar Kund in Varanasi. Rai says that Modi's friends from Gujarat swallowed crores in the rejuvenation of the pond—"*karodon rupiya dakaar liya*"—yet the pond has algae floating on it. Small complaint against gargantuan development brought by Modi, may be? But when project "Gujarati" is the aim, the green algae on the pond works like gold on social media.'[20]

A section of residents concurred with Ajay Rai. The city, which had felt proud when the prime minister had contested from Varanasi in 2014 and, after winning, surrendered the Baroda seat for Varanasi, was talking about how Gujaratis were being preferred in new business opportunities and being awarded contracts in Varanasi. Though I have no information if it was done at the prompting of the prime minister's office or the result of an overenthusiastic local administration, it had surely damaged Modi's reputation. *Business Standard* reported, 'Mazhar, a 30-year-old trader . . . said Varanasi witnessed rapid development after Modi became the PM and that it was a matter of pride that he represented the local constituency. "Sadly, there is an overdose of mandir-masjid narrative during polls which does no good to any community. There is much to be done for the local weavers, textile manufacturers, and traders. Most of the big contracts are going to companies from other states, especially Gujarat," he lamented.'[21]

As the elections progressed, Varanasi seemed to be on a different tangent. Modi, being hailed as a unique one in generations of leaders, was uncomfortable in his own turf. If the majority of the Indian media was hesitant to state the obvious, the foreign media wrote bluntly on the last day of polling, 1 June 2024. *ABC News* of Australia wrote, '. . . The mood of the country seems to be different than it has been over the last 10 years of Mr Modi's rule with bread-and-butter issues—such as unemployment and inflation—on people's minds more than religious issues. This is the case even in the prime minister's own constituency of Varanasi. . . . In Varanasi city, it is the city's educated youths who seem most disillusioned. . . . The rising cost of living is also hitting those who live in the city hard.'[22] *ABC News* further noted, '. . . the BJP appears to be nervous in the prime minister's own seat. . . . While most, even many Opposition voters, believe Mr Modi will win the seat as usual, there's a strong sense of disillusionment in the air.'

Anand Sahay interviewed a BJP municipal councillor in Varanasi for *The Wire*, and when he asked the councillor why there seemed to be no enthusiasm for the prime minister, the reply betrayed BJP's helplessness. The councillor said, 'For some reason, the scene this time seems different from 2019; I can't say why. I don't know.'[23] Though the councillor did add, 'We will win here, you will see. It's only a question of margin.'

After driving for more than 1,000 km in UP, Anand Sahay inferred that the Ram Mandir consecration at Ayodhya was 'not an election issue' and Prime Minister Modi was not guaranteed to win elections for the BJP. He wrote, '. . . The prime minister's name brings up indifference or even annoyance, no matter where one travels in the state. Right up until now, Modi's campaign pitch was to urge voters to cast their ballots in his name. The candidate didn't matter. This was an essential part of the panoply of the building of the cult of personality. Not any more. The trick has collapsed completely.'[24]

I found Sahay's choice of words—'indifference' and 'annoyance'—about Modi striking. After reading reports by him and others, I was reminded of my experience as a political worker when I was in Varanasi in 2014. I was with Aam Aadmi Party (AAP) and had gone to Varanasi to campaign for Arvind Kejriwal. What I witnessed was something new, something surreal. Modi had not become the prime minister yet, but he was phenomenally popular. It was next to impossible to criticise him in public without confronting violence and abuse. I captured this mood of Modi's supporters in my book *The Crown Prince, the Gladiator and the Hope*.

'In conversation with a friend at the village market, he [a young boy] had praised Arvind [Kejriwal] and deprecated Modi. All of a sudden, a total stranger who had been standing nearby threatened to slap him if he dared to criticise Modi. The young man told us that such hooligans given to violence were at large around the village markets, terrorising those who dared to condemn Modi openly. Kailash [Patel] and I were dumbfounded; I was reminded of Hitler's storm troopers. These were ominous signs for a democracy. I had covered many elections in the past as a journalist but never was a leader and his supporters attacked in such numbers and never had I heard of people being threatened by unruly elements just because he or she had criticised a prominent leader. I found myself wondering whether the behaviour of Modi's supporters was just an aberration or if there was a strategy to it and whether the gradually emerging pattern was something that would become more visible in a systemic form in the future where no difference of opinion would be tolerated. For the present, we had no certain answer.'[25]

There emerged a pattern after 2014, where those who criticised the prime minister publicly faced the wrath of the state and of his supporters, but in this election, that fervour was missing. The common man was openly critical of him in Varanasi, UP and other places too. The reason was obvious. 'Now, in absentia, Modi is being grilled for his failed policies leading to the most dismal employment data in 45 years and the widespread collapse of the small businesses since demonetisation from which most are yet to fully recover. . . . The regularly rising prices offer no respite. These are the very issues that Modi ducks and resorts instead to low grade communal propaganda, gimmicky slogans, and sings paeans of praise to himself, while launching into diatribes against Rahul Gandhi all the time.'[26]

The result in Varanasi reflected the widespread disillusionment with Modi and his style of politics. Had somebody other than him contested from Varanasi, defeat was certain. People were unhappy and angry. The prime minister had probably been briefed in advance, which is why Amit Shah was sent to do damage control. It was Shah's presence and the aura of Modi that saved the day, even if their win was greatly diminished. But the message was clear. Around Varanasi, BJP miserably failed, and even Modi's magic did not work. There are 12 Lok Sabha seats in the Varanasi region, of which BJP could win only three—Mirzapur, Bhadohi and Varanasi. In Mirzapur, Union Minister Anupriya Patel won by only 37,810 votes. In Bhadohi, the INDIA had given the ticket to Trinamool Congress. Lalitesh Pati Tripathi did not use the better-recognised party symbol of the cycle of SP or the hand of Congress, instead fighting elections with the two-leaf symbol of TMC. He might have won if he had chosen the cycle or palm. He lost by only 44,072 votes.

Modi did win in Varanasi, but it was a moral defeat for the man whose name was a guarantee for other people's victory.

No wonder, *The Times of India* reported, 'At Gulab Bagh, where victory celebrations took place late evening, it was evident the jubilation lacked the vigour of the past two elections.'[27]

The same report also stated, 'BJP Kashi region unit president Dilip Singh Patel said, "We are scheduling an organisation meeting in which all reasons for the 2024 LS poll performance in Varanasi seat will be reviewed."' But nobody knows what happened in that review as the report was not made public. The forty-member task force, which was formed to review BJP's performance in UP, also did not visit Varanasi, as Varanasi and Lucknow, where Defence Minister Rajnath Singh contested, were barred from the review. The big question is—why?

8

Ayodhya and the Politics of Arrogance

'Let me explain what I mean by religion. It is not the Hindu religion which I certainly prize above all other religions, but the religion which transcends Hinduism, which changes one's very nature, which binds one indissolubly to the truth within and which even purifies. It is the permanent element in human nature which counts no cost too great in order to find full expression and which leaves the soul utterly restless until it has found itself, known its Maker and appreciated the true correspondence between the Maker and itself.'

—Mahatma Gandhi

'AFTER TAKING A BATH IN THE SARYU RIVER, GO STRAIGHT TO see Ram Lalla, there is no need to buy anything in Ayodhya, take the Prasad from your home, after offering there, come straight back home, Ram traitors should also realise what a big crime they have committed. Buying anything from the shopkeepers in Ayodhya is like strengthening these Ram traitors.'[1]

On 6 June 2024, two days after the results of the general elections were announced, a gentleman named Chandan Sharma wrote this on the social media platform X. His name is not important. What is significant is the outpouring of hate and the call for an economic boycott. The latter has become common since Modi became the prime minister in 2014. But the target of the boycott so far had been mostly Muslims. These calls were made by hate-mongers, self-proclaimed Hindutvavadis who had the tacit support of the state. But this was a curious case. For it was not Muslims who were being targeted but an entire city. The city of Ayodhya, no less.

Here is another social media post: 'You have shitted on the same people who fed you. Caste is bigger than the religion and country for you. . . . . Today, you made the party which had opened fire at the Karsevaks win while you defeated the party which brought Lord Ram back home.'[2]

This 'gentle' man is called Daksh Chaudhry, and his words are a part of a viral video. His outrage was against the Samajwadi Party candidate who had won the Ayodhya seat. He demanded to know why the BJP candidate had been defeated. In his tweet, there is a reference to an incident that happened on 30 October 1990, when Karsevaks led by Vishva Hindu Parishad (VHP) tried to storm Babri Masjid, and the UP government, led by the then minister Mulayam Singh Yadav, ordered the police to open fire on the Karsevaks. In the firing, six Karsevaks were killed. V.P. Singh was the prime minister then, and BJP, led by L.K. Advani, had extended support to his government to keep Congress out of power. After the incident, BJP withdrew support from the government. Mulayam Singh Yadav subsequently left the Janata Dal and formed his own party, which came to be called the Samajwadi Party.

In another tweet, Hindutvavadis went after the residents of Ayodhya, citing a reference from Ramcharitmanas, to claim they had always been traitors. A user tweeted that if residents of Ayodhya can accuse Mother Sita, then one shouldn't expect them to help Hindus. And that the residents of UP were to be condemned.[3]

On social media, there was no dearth of such self-proclaimed Hindutvavadis who were openly abusive of the residents of Ayodhya. One tweet called them 'eunuchs'. Another said that the residents of Ayodhya should drown in shame, and that they are not worthy of being called Hindus.[4]

These tweets are testimony to the fact that the loss of BJP candidate Lallu Singh, to SP candidate Awadhesh Prasad Pasi, in Ayodhya was a bolt from the blue and had struck Hindutvavadis where it hurt them the most. Surprisingly, residents of Ayodhya were not upset by such posts and videos. *Outlook* magazine's reporter captured the mood of the people in Ayodhya:

'An entrance to the Ram *Mandir* opens on the same road. Most devotees have arrived from different parts of the country. And, over the last few days, they saw a message on social media platforms: that if they visit Ayodhya, they shouldn't give business to the locals. "Before I came here," says Vivek Kumar, a salesman from Chandigarh, "my friend told me, 'Don't buy any *prasad* from local shopkeeper.'" He did not. "They defeated the BJP; we won't let them thrive." It makes no sense to a shopkeeper on the main road: "Because the winning candidate [Awadhesh Prasad] is also a Hindu."'[5]

The report further stated, 'A man on the Delhi-Ayodhya flight kept watching and "liking" videos on the topic . . . Another man in a hotel lobby assured someone on the phone: "Ayodhya-*vaasi* are not at fault. They still belong to Shri Ram." The boycott call amuses Shri Pal Das, a priest at the Prajapati Temple: "Sure, don't buy anything from us. But will you leave everything connected to our town—how about the roads that pass through it? Will you come by helicopter, do darshan and return?"'[6]

The consecration of the Ram Mandir was supposed to unleash such energy that would drown the entire opposition in UP. Instead, BJP performed badly in UP, the centre of the Ram Janmabhoomi movement, and it lost in Ayodhya, the birthplace of Lord Ram. Nothing could be more humiliating and disillusioning for Hindutvavadis. In their opinion, the centre of the ideological gravity of Hindutva had betrayed them. This demolishes the edifice of the whole argument that India has changed, Nehruvian secularism is dead, and India is now the abode of resurgent Hindus. The whole project of constructing a 'proud Hindu' who works like a monolith and behaves like one unit failed at the very place that was supposed to inspire the entire Hindu civilisation.

Writing for *The Wire*, Omar Rashid says, 'Ram featured in the BJP's election campaign in many aspects. Not only did the party solicit Hindu votes as a reward for getting the temple constructed, which, lest we forget, was built following a Supreme Court judgement in 2019, but also demonised Opposition leaders for not attending the politically loaded pran pratishtha ceremony. The election was a contest between Ram Bhakts (devotees) and Ram drohis (traitors), claimed chief minister Adityanath, in rally after rally.'[7]

Awadhesh Prasad resents the idea that BJP took credit for the construction of the Ram Mandir. He said, 'As far as the *mandir* (temple) goes, they claim that they have built it. The *mandir* was not built by them but after the judgement and directions of the Supreme Court. No matter which government was ruling the country, the temple would have still been constructed.'[8]

Awadhesh Prasad Pasi is a very seasoned leader of Ayodhya. He belongs to a Dalit family and has been a member of the legislative assembly (MLA) for nine terms and a minister six times. It is also remarkable that this time, despite being a Dalit, he contested elections from a general seat, Faizabad, where Ayodhya is situated, not from a constituency reserved for Dalits, and yet he won by 54,000 votes. On the question of Hindutvavadis abusing residents of Ayodhya, he gracefully reacted, 'I pray to Prabhu Shri Ram, Hanuman Ji and Saryu Mai (mother river Saryu) that they correct the mentality of such people and develop in them a feeling of harmony.'[9]

The chief priest of the Ram Mandir, Acharya Satyendra Das, said that those who were abusing people of Ayodhya and blaming them for the election result were displaying their 'foolishness'.[10]

He further said, 'They obviously do not understand the bhakti of Bhagwan Ram. Such people who view Ram only as an election issue are petty and despicable.'

Many posts by such people used casteist slurs as well. Awadhesh Pasi was also the target of such posts. Fortunately, these posts did not lead to any social tension and no untoward incident was reported. Bharatiya Janata Party also did not show any support to such individuals. Though a newly elected member of Parliament from Unnao, Sakshi Maharaj was an exception. He said, 'BJP's defeat in Ayodhya is a matter of concern. In Ayodhya, a Ram Bhakt lost, and those who shed blood in Saryu won.'[11]

The police took note of such posts and videos and arrested two persons.

Unlike BJP's campaign, Awadhesh Prasad Pasi's whole campaign hinged on secular issues. He coined a slogan that was the anti-thesis of BJP's Hindutva narrative. He said, 'Na Mathura, Na Kashi, abki bar Awadhesh Pasi [Neither Mathura, nor Kashi, this time Awadhesh Pasi]'. Along with the Ram Mandir, BJP and RSS have been talking about 'liberating' Kashi Vishwanath temple in Varanasi and Krishna Janmasthan temple in Mathura. According to them, like Ram Mandir in Ayodhya, these two temples were also demolished, and mosques were built by Mughal rulers in their place. The Supreme Court has given its verdict about the Ram Mandir, but the matter is still pending in court for the other two. In both cases, the courts have given orders to give a report after verifying the nature of the religious structures in the two places.

Awadhesh Pasi was challenging the basic premise of the BJP/RSS campaign in the heart of the Hindutva cradle. Initially, this slogan did not catch my attention. I was pleasantly surprised when a very senior bureaucrat, who retired as a secretary in the Government of India, called me to talk about the election results. During our conversation, he said, 'The slogan in Ayodhya, "Na Mathura, na Kashi, abki bar Awadhesh Pasi", is revolutionary. People have not noticed this enough. At a time when Hindutva ideology is the dominant feature of the politics in India, to coin and raise such a slogan which negates the fundamentals of Hindutva, is very creative and daring.' I could not agree more. Then he added, 'Don't forget this was happening in Ayodhya, the land of Ram Mandir, which was the reason for the ascendance of the BJP. Believe me, something is changing, and BJP should be worried.' The chat continued for long and after I put the phone down, I did a Google search to confirm what he said about the slogan. And when I found it correct, I called a few friends in UP and Ayodhya. They all confirmed that the slogan was discussed and used extensively during the campaign. I was told that the slogan was cleverly used by SP to connect with the Dalit samaj, Muslims and OBCs. In Ayodhya, the Pasi samaj has a population of approximately 2.5

lakh. Traditionally associated with toddy tapping, pig-rearing and petty agriculture, Pasis are the second largest Scheduled Caste community in UP, constituting around 16 per cent of the Dalits as per the 2001 Census.

Former principal of Ayodhya's Saket College V.N. Arora said, 'Samajwadi Party's chief Akhilesh Yadav played a master stroke by nominating a Pasi candidate from the general seat. Afterwards, the "Na Mathura, na Kashi, abki bar Awadhesh Pasi" slogan touched the chord of Dalit voters. The message that Awadhesh Pasi belonged to Pasi samaj really worked. When Dalits and other backward caste voters met with Samajwadi Party's original voters, the Yadavs and Muslims, then it became a winning combination for Awadhesh Pasi.'[12]

Lallu Singh has won two consecutive elections for the Lok Sabha, in 2014 and 2019. In 2014, he got 48.08 per cent votes, and in 2019, he managed to get 48.66 per cent votes, but in 2024, his vote share shrunk to 43.81 per cent. Awadhesh Prasad Pasi, in contrast, received 48.59 per cent votes. He has been elected to Parliament for the first time. In 2017, when BJP came back to power in UP after a long time, with 312 seats, and Yogi Adityanath became the chief minister, the party had won all five assembly seats in Faizabad. But in the 2022 assembly elections, when BJP once again won and formed a government, they lost two seats in Faizabad. Gosaiganj and Milkipur assembly seats were won by SP. In 2023, BJP, surprisingly, lost in the Ram Abhiram Das ward in the Ayodhya Municipal Corporation elections to an independent Muslim candidate called Sultan Ansari. What is more shocking is that the party lost in the ward despite Yogi Adityanath having campaigned himself. It is important to remember that these defeats occurred after the Supreme Court had unanimously pronounced a verdict in favour of Hindus for the construction of Ram Mandir on 9 November

2019, and after the Bhumi Pujan[13] for the Ram Mandir was performed on 5 August 2020. Bharatiya Janata Party's slogan in this election for the voters of Ayodhya was '*Jo Ram ko laaye hain, hum unko laayenge* [We will elect those who got Ram here]'. But that did not happen.

The Ram Mandir consecration was the summit of the Ram Mandir movement. Though BJP was formed in 1980 after a split in Janta Party, the party has been in existence since 1951 in its earlier avatar as Jan Sangh. Syama Prasad Mookerjee was its founder-president. But in six parliamentary elections, from 1951-52, BJP/Jan Sangh could never get more than 35 seats. In fact, in 1984, the party was reduced to only 2 seats. Its biggest leader, Atal Bihari Vajpayee, lost elections in Gwalior to Madhavrao Scindia. But as the Ram Mandir movement gained momentum, slowly but steadily, the course of Indian politics started changing. In 1989, the party won 85 seats, but its vote percentage was still only 11.36 per cent.

The Babri Masjid/Ram Mandir conflict was more than five hundred years old, as claimed by BJP/RSS. But it caught the attention of RSS only in 1984. The story goes that RSS had organised a winter meet in Parade Ground, Allahabad, in January 1984. In this meeting, RSS chief Balasaheb Deoras asked the senior office bearers a question: 'I heard there is a lock on Ram Janmabhoomi Mandir in Ayodhya.' When the answer was affirmative, he commented, 'How long would the lock continue to be there?'[14] RSS chiefs are not known to make causal remarks. Though I have no way to confirm, I assume that Deoras must have thought the whole issue through, and he might have internally discussed it with the organisation's senior leadership before talking about it with RSS office bearers. This was the time when terrorism in Punjab posed a serious threat to the unity and integrity of the country. Deoras's comment was also preceded by the conversion of four hundred Hindu families to Islam in Meenakshipuram, Tamil Naidu, in 1981, which had shaken RSS.

Deoras was no M.S. Golwalkar. He is perhaps the most political RSS chief. The lock on the Ram Janmabhoomi temple might have given him an idea to counter what he considered was the menace of Islamisation, and to unite Hindus within their own ideological thinking and help BJP grow after the hugely successful Ekatmata Yatra in 1983. By then, RSS had learnt that piggybacking on secular parties, as it did in 1977 when Jan Sangh merged itself into Janta Party, would not take the party far. Finally, in 1980, with a split in Janta Party, Jan Sangh was reborn with a new name—Bharatiya Janta Party (BJP). After Deoras's comment, things moved fast. In April 1984, two significant events took place, which laid the foundation for the future Ram Janmabhoomi movement. In April, Virat Hindu Samaj was formed in Delhi, of which Congress leader Karna Singh was made the president, and in Vigyan Bhawan, Delhi, approximately five hundred sadhu/sant assembled, and a resolution was passed that three religious places of the Hindus—Ram Janmabhoomi in Ayodhya, Krishna Janmabhoomi in Mathura, and Kashi Vishwanath temple in Varanasi—should be handed over to Hindus. This congregation was called Dharma Sansad. Ashok Singhal, who later emerged as one of the top leaders of the Ram Mandir movement, was instrumental in both events. Singhal, who was part of RSS, was asked by Deoras to lead Vishva Hindu Parishad (VHP). Though formed in 1964, VHP had been a defunct organisation for a long time. Singhal should be credited for the success of the movement. But it is interesting to know that Ram Janmabhoomi Mandir was not on RSS's agenda till 1984. In fact, it was V.D. Savarkar's Hindu Mahasabha that was instrumental in first raising the issue just after Independence, and later pushing for the installation of the Ram Lalla idol in Babri Masjid.

Nilanjan Mukhopadhyay claims in his book *The Demolition and the Verdict* that Savarkar was of the opinion that Hindu religious places, like the Ram Janmabhoomi, should be liberated, and a resolution in this regard was passed by the United Province Hindu Mahasabha on the eve of the second anniversary of India's independence in 1949. 'This endorsed a prior demand of the All India body of Mahasabha for "restoration of the temples of Shri Vishwanath at Kashi, Shri Ram Janmabhoomi at Ayodhya and Shri Krishna Mandir at Mathura which were converted into a mosque in the Mughal times and remains of which are still there."'[15] Mahant Digvijaynath, an influential member of the Hindu Mahasabha in North India, was part of the group that installed the Ram Lalla idol on 23 December 1949 in Babri Masjid.

In his book *Ayodhya: 6 December 1992*, former prime minister P.V. Narasimha Rao vividly describes that night: 'On that cold night, a bag containing water from Saryu river, the idol of Ram Lalla and a copper urn moved towards the Babri Masjid from the Ram Chabutra. Two dozen odd policemen posted at the shrine paid no attention to the stealthy movements of that shadowy group, who entered the poorly guarded precincts of the shrine by scaling the boundary wall between the inner and outer courtyard. With the light of the lantern, a few of them washed the floor of the sanctum sanctorum and placed the idol on a sacred piece of cloth. They reverentially covered it with another piece of cloth and lit incense sticks in front of it. Only when the group broke into chants of "Prakat Kripala, Deen Dayala", there was a flurry of activity among policemen outside. It was past 3.30 a.m.'[16]

Installation of the idol was part of the bigger conspiracy in which the local administration of Faizabad was deeply involved.

It is speculated that the whole episode was planned at the top level, and involvement of the top Congress leaders in the state, who were part of the ministry, could not be ruled out, along with the leaders of Hindu Mahasabha. Govind Ballabh Pant was then the chief minister, Bhagwan Sahay was the chief secretary, and K.K. Nayar was the district magistrate of Faizabad. The idol could not be removed despite Prime Minister Jawaharlal Nehru's order. Out of frustration, Nehru told Lal Bahadur Shastri, the then home minister in UP, 'I fear that we are heading again for some kind of disaster.'[17]

It is widely speculated that Nayar was transferred in advance to Faizabad from Gonda for this purpose only. Pant was ideologically close to P.D. Tandon, who later became the Congress president in 1950 against Nehru's wishes, and was considered sympathetic to the Hindu cause. He belonged to Sardar Patel's camp in the Congress. Chief secretary Sahay asked Nayar twice to remove the idol, but he did not comply. On 27 December 1949, he offered to resign in his communication to Sahay. 'I would, if the government decided to remove the idol at any cost, request that I be relieved and replaced by any officer who may be able to see the solution a merit which I can't discern.'[18] Nayar took voluntary retirement from service and went on to become a member of the fourth Parliament on a Jan Sangh ticket.

Narasimha Rao writes, 'The shrine was attached under Section 145 of the Code of Criminal Procedure on 28 December 1949.'[19] Priya Datta Ram, the then chairman of the municipal board of Faizabad, was appointed receiver of the property. And later, as per the magistrate's order, the gate of the mosque was locked. The receiver and the priest were allowed to enter the property and offer prayers to the idol at a designated time. Hindus could offer puja from outside the iron gate.

This picture of the idol placed behind the iron grille of the gate was projected by VHP, saying that Ram was imprisoned at his birthplace in Ayodhya and had to be freed. On 11 July 1984, they decided to launch a mass campaign to inform and enlighten the public at large about Ram Janmabhoomi and build support for the movement. On 25 September 1984, Shri Ram Janki Yatra started from Sitamarhi, the birthplace of Sita in Bihar, to reach Ayodhya. Ram–Janki were mounted on a matador in such a way that both were seen as imprisoned behind bars. On 7 October 1984, sadhus and sants converged at Ayodhya on the banks of Saryu as planned and took a pledge to free Ram Janmabhoomi. This yatra was a roaring success. Rashtriya Swayamsevak Sangh realised the potential of the movement, and from here on, there was no stopping. Meanwhile, Indira Gandhi was assassinated on 31 October 1984, and general elections were held. Congress returned to power with more than 400 seats, this time led by Rajiv Gandhi.

During Rajiv Gandhi's tenure, two major developments helped the movement gain momentum. One was the Parliament's decision to reverse the Supreme Court verdict on the Shah Bano case, which was interpreted as an act to appease Muslims for votes. Two, the Lucknow district court ordered the unlocking of the Babri Masjid to let Hindus offer prayers to the deity on 1 February 1986. Within forty minutes of the order, the lock was opened in front of (Doordarshan) cameras, which was reason enough for critics to believe that the whole exercise was a sham and done at the behest of someone very powerful in Delhi. Obviously, the unlocking was done to appease Hindus, to neutralise the negativity generated against Congress after the Shah Bano case.

Once doors were unlocked, the demand for the construction of Ram Mandir was raised vociferously. The Rajiv Gandhi government was caught in a whirlpool of the Bofors scam and desertion of its own top leaders like V.P. Singh and others. Due to these factors, the government was in no position to not acquiesce to the demand of shilanyas, that is, laying of the foundation stone, for the Ram Mandir on 9 November 1989, just before the general elections. And yet, Congress lost the elections. V.P. Singh became the prime minister with the support of BJP, which had won 85 seats, its best ever electoral performance till then. It was clear that the Ram Mandir movement was what BJP needed to fulfil its ambition to capture power at the Centre. When Singh implemented the recommendations of the Mandal Commission to give 27 per cent reservations to OBCs, L.K. Advani started his famous Rath Yatra from Somnath to Ayodhya. And, as they say, the rest is history. On 6 December 1992, Babri Masjid was demolished by Karsevaks. And in 1996, Atal Bihari Vajpayee took oath as the prime minister, leading a BJP government for the first time at the Centre. While the Vajpayee government survived only thirteen days, it was clear that, sooner or later, BJP was set to become the dominant party. In 1998, they formed a coalition government. After waiting for decades, BJP had finally arrived as a national party, and Congress was in a terminal decline.

Bharatiya Janata Party forming the government on its own, led by Modi in 2014, was no accident. Other than the follies of Congress and other parties, the Ram Mandir movement was the major reason for BJP's ascendance. That Ayodhya did not oblige BJP with a victory in 2024 even as the Ram Mandir movement had attained its ultimate goal is indeed puzzling. Can Ayodhya's rejection of BJP be construed as the rejection of Hindutva? Does it indicate that Hindutva has failed in its core function of uniting Hindus? Or is Hindutva a work in progress, and is it too early to predict its demise?

Ram Mandir is not Hindutva's ultimate destination, after all. It is only part of the process. Its ultimate goal is to correct the weakness of the Hindu society, which is thought to be the reason for its surrender before other religions for hundreds of years. The whole journey is inspired by two human impulses—nostalgia and vengeance. The concept of Vishwa Guru is part of the nostalgia that India was a superpower before a foreign religion—Islam—came to India with invaders; that India was a land of prosperity, where rivers of honey and ghee used to flow. That India was the capital of world knowledge. This conception does not necessarily have to be true, but when it becomes part of the emotional world of an individual, organisation or society, it works as an engine that keeps pushing its creator. But when nostalgia is faced with the present reality, it gives birth to vengeance. The incompatibility of the nostalgia and the present reality creates a disconnect between the emotional and cognitive world, which leads to irritation, frustration, restlessness, disintegration, destruction and, ultimately, violence. This disconnect creates a void in the emotional world, and revenge is the only refuge to fill that void. Vengeance becomes a creative option for the construction of a better future.

In the RSS's conception, the last thousand years have been a paradise lost. Islam has been the reason for thousands of years of trauma that triggers the impulse of revenge; Muslims have to be taught a lesson for what they did, and the lesson should be taught in such a way that they dare not repeat the past. To mitigate its weakness, Hindus have to be awakened; they need to be told that they are the inheritors of a great civilisation, and they have to unite if they wish to emerge as a great nation. The Ram Janmabhoomi movement, up to a great extent, has spurred that consciousness, and RSS has succeeded in making Hindus take great pride in being Hindu.

According to Neeladri Bhattacharya, 'The battle for the Ramjanmabhumi is part of a wider political struggle for a constitution of "Hindu" consciousness and identity, for the construction of a unified Hindu tradition, and for the assertion of "Hindu" power over all other communities in India.'[20] When the movement was in its nascent stage in 1986, RSS's top leader H.V. Sheshadri forcefully wrote, 'The present agitation to liberate the Sri Rama Janmabhoomi . . . is no less than a battle for national self assertion. . . . nothing short of a phase of struggle for the liberation of the National Soul.'[21]

For RSS and Hindutvavadis, independence meant only freedom from the British. But if India had to get rid of the scourge of history, then Hindus, which comprised 85 per cent of the population, had to think alike as a nation. However, in RSS's understanding, Hindus were caught in a web of the sin called secularism which '. . . has led to a civilisational crisis in India; secularism "is draining away the nation's 'elan vital' of Hindu spirit".'[22]

If Advani's Rath Yatra was an instrument to enrage Hindus, to make them rise up and realise their Hinduness, then it was also a weapon to discredit Nehruvian secularism. Advani popularised the word 'pseudo-secularism'. He wrote, 'Reconstructing the temple for Sri Rama became the symbol of this rising consciousness—ridding the country of the perversities to which it was being subjected in the name of Secularism, forging a strong and united country.'[23]

Advani knew that secularism was not the answer to the civilisational malaise that Hindus have been inflicted with for centuries. However, unlike Modi, he was living in an era where discarding secularism outrightly was not an option. Bharatiya Janata Party was caught in a situation where, despite the Ram Mandir movement, it had to earn credibility and respectability in the eyes of the public, which had been fed with strong doses of secularism. The leaders told the public at large that secularism was the only way forward if India was to survive as a nation. It was not easy to erase that consciousness in an impulse. It needed time and constant hammering. Advani was sharp. He did not attack secularism as a concept, per se, but called it pseudo-secularism. He was trying to convey to the people that India had been pursuing the wrong secularism, which was based on the appeasement of Muslims and the hate of Hinduism.

It is this secularism that was to be discarded. On the ground, foot soldiers of Hindutva were spreading canards against secularism, calling secularists traitors and agents of the West. 'Secularists are identified as "Hindu baiters", traitors, Muslim communalists. They are "trojan horses" who "weaken Hindu strength from within". These "traitors" have to be attacked to defend the Hindu nation.'[24]

Common people in the street were told that India would survive not by secularism but by igniting nationalism, which meant the resurgence of Hindutva and the exclusion of Muslims and Christians. Advani confessed that the purpose of the Ram Janmabhoomi movement was not limited to building a temple. He wrote, 'The object of the movement thus became not just to construct yet another temple, the object became to put our country back on its feet, to purify our public life, our public discourse. This is how in 1989 the Bharatiya Janata Party formally decided to lend its shoulder to the cause[;] the Party was responding to the deepest urges of our people.'[25]

Neeladri Bhattacharya's diagnosis was bang on when he wrote, 'The politics of Ramjanmabhumi . . . seeks to reconstitute Hindu identity as an aggressive, masculine identity. It speaks the language of vengeance and retributive justice.'[26] The process that RSS started and Advani carried forward through his Rath

Yatra has reaped fruits during Modi's regime, when secularism has turned into an abuse and secularists are openly called traitors, anti-national and supporters of Pakistan. Since 2014, baiters of secularism have the hegemonic force and the backing of a robust state; therefore, it is not wondrous that Ayodhya is abused after BJP's defeat there. Because, within Hindutva, choosing a secularist 'Hindu baiter' who says 'Na Mathura, na Kashi, abki baar Awadhesh Pasi' is not an option.

However, the forces of Hindutva have to realise that India is still a secular country; that Hindutva still has the support of only 36.57 per cent while 63.43 per cent have not voted for them. It is not Ram bhakts who are violent or vengeful. It is BJP's andh bhakts who indulge in hate. 'People are abusing us sitting in Delhi and Gujarat. If they think that only the BJP folks are Ram *bhakts*, then they're wrong. They're not Ram bhakts; they're *andh bhakts* [blind devotees].'[27]

Ayodhya resident Suman Gupta is the editor of the newspaper *Janmorcha Daily*. In an interview with me before the results were announced, she had predicted BJP's downfall. She firmly told me that BJP would lose despite the Pran Pratishtha ceremony in Faizabad. After the result, on my request to cite reasons for the defeat, she wrote, 'People far away from Ayodhya are surprised by BJP's defeat because they are not aware of the true nature of Ayodhya. Therefore, they could not imagine that the BJP could lose in Ayodhya. Ayodhya has been the citadel of composite Ganga-Jamuni Sanskriti. Though the entire Ram Janmabhoomi movement in Ayodhya and outside was fought in the name of Ayodhya, that composite culture remained alive in Ayodhya.'

It is also a rejection of the arrogance of Lallu Singh, who had said that BJP needed 400 seats to change the Constitution. His statement alienated Dalits in Ayodhya, who make up approximately 21 per cent of the total population. A shopkeeper in Ayodhya was angry with the way Lallu Singh led his election campaign and conducted himself as an MP. *Outlook* magazine reported him saying: '"The BJP's arrogance led to its downfall." Referring to a famous Hindutva song, *Jo Ram Ko Laaye Hain/ Hum Unko Layenge* [We'll elect those who brought Ram], he asks, "Can someone bring Ram? He is the one who has brought us all." And finally: "I don't want the BJP's certificate that I'm a Hindu."'[28]

People in Ayodhya were deeply upset about the way they had been taken for granted. They resented the thought process that BJP, by constructing the Ram Mandir, had done some 'ahsan' (obligation), and all Hindus should be indebted to them and vote for them. Since they called their bluff, now they are being called 'ungrateful'. During the consecration, the only people who were absent from the ceremony were the local residents of Ayodhya. The whole city had been converted into a military camp. Residents were not free to move; they were confined to their homes. This is what the people had to say: 'The BJP put our entire town under curfew . . . not for one or two days but forever,' and 'The police beat them with *lathis* [sticks] . . . they made us dogs in our own home.'[29]

The same arrogance was on full display while displacing people in the name of beautification of the city for the Pran Pratishtha and for the movement of the VIPs. 'Without doubt, the anger of shop owners and businessmen who were displaced owing to the demolition of their shops and establishments for the construction and widening of Ram Path, Janmabhoomi Path and Bhakti Path leading to Ram Mandir, and who were facing a livelihood crisis due to lack of proper rehabilitation and adequate compensation, is being cited as a major reason for the party's defeat in the Lok Sabha elections.'[30]

Suman Gupta also says, 'During the election, people of Ayodhya were living in fear because they had seen how houses and shops were demolished, and few had to do it by themselves. People were feeling helpless. The compensation was not given properly, and even that was also given to their own. Nobody was in a position to oppose. Therefore, people were waiting for the right moment, waiting for the iron to get hot so that they could use their hammer, and this is what they did.'

Swarajya summarised the irony of the affair: 'Although the temple's construction fulfilled a long-standing desire and brought a sense of pride, for many locals, it has become a symbol of their displacement and marginalisation.'[31]

Ayodhya is not a city of traitors. Traitors are those who do not understand the meaning of true religion. True Ram bhakts are those who do not harbour arrogance about bringing Ram to Ayodhya. Ram is omnipresent. Ram is omnipotent. Ram is omniscient. And Ram resides in the hearts of those who are pure and simple. Tulsidas says,

काम कोह मद मान न मोहा। लोभ न छोभ न राग न द्रोहा ॥
जिन्ह कें कपट दंभ नहिं माया। तिन्ह कें हृदय बसहु रघराया॥[32]

If BJP wants to move beyond Ram Janmabhoomi and Ayodhya, then it has to listen to the voices of Ayodhya who have rejected the politics of arrogance. It is the true message of Ayodhya and of Lord Ram.

9

The Tacit Retaliation of Muslims

'This will always remain one of the best jokes of democracy, that it gave its deadly enemies the means by which it was destroyed.'

—Joseph Goebbels

'*Iss time pe Muslim ki zuban band ki hai* (Our lips are sealed),' said a businessman in Siyana, Bulandshahar. Salman Gauri of Aligarh Muslim University said, 'In a way, Muslims have been forced to keep their mouths shut.' A director of a charitable hospital in Meerut said, 'Have Muslims gone quiet in UP? Certainly.'[1]

In several areas in western Uttar Pradesh—where the community constitutes about 30 per cent or more of the population, especially in districts such as Saharanpur, Moradabad and Bijnor—Muslims refused to be drawn into conversation on politics. Except mentioning a common line against political parties, saying nobody has done anything for them.

'Uttar Pradesh has just finished its first phase of Lok Sabha elections and several recent reports have shown that Muslims have observed a "tactical silence" in this election.'[2]

'*SP, Congress, aur BSP ke hitaishi kahlaane ke bavjood Muslim sangathanon, tanzeemon ne chupi sadh rakhi thi* [Despite being sympathetic towards SP, Congress and BSP, Muslim organisations kept quiet].'[3]

Silence, silence and more silence. The 2024 election is the story of the silence of the marginalised—of Dalits, who have been silenced for centuries without any hope of ever regaining their voice; and of Muslims, who are the latest victims of the Hindutva ideology that has tried, with the help of the state, to muffle the voice of the entire community. In an election where Bharatiya Janata Party (BJP), led by Narendra Modi, played the Muslim card to polarise Hindu voters so they could consolidate its social base to win elections, Muslims countered by arming themselves with silence. Strategically, the Muslims did not react to the vitriol and venom unleashed by the prime minister and his party. In my memory, I have not witnessed an election in which the ruling party was so brazen and blatant with its communal agenda. However, Muslims saw through the design and they responded by not speaking, not reacting, not voicing and by not doing anything which might appear as a retaliation, neither in their words, nor in their deeds. It was this retaliation by silence that stumped BJP in UP. Throughout the seven phases, the party found itself helpless and restless when it realised that the silence of the Muslims was proving to be more potent than an outpouring of venomous words and fury.

Every reporter and every media platform that went to talk to the Muslim community in UP, to find out their views about the election, or their preference for the candidate or the party, or elicit a reaction about inflammatory statements made during elections, was met with silence. Even on being provoked and cajoled by the reporters, the Muslim community did not fall into the trap. They just kept quiet, and even when they spoke, they did not indulge in provocation and retaliation. Neither the ordinary Muslims nor their leaders spoke on the subject. Even their religious leaders were seen observing silence. These are leaders who, in the past, had spoken in hyperboles and aggression. But not this time. This silence was BJP's undoing in the state.

The silence was dangerous for BJP, as by the end of February, the euphoria about the consecration of the Ram Mandir had faded and that made BJP vulnerable. Since the beginning of March 2024, I could sense in private conversations that BJP leaders were not confident about the outcome of the elections, although most of them were very vocal about their party's massive victory in TV debates and on-record conversations. Many of them said that price rise and unemployment were huge issues and people seemed upset. But they still insisted that since Modi was there, they would manage.

On 5 April 2024, the day of the release of the Congress manifesto, in a primetime TV debate where I was one of the participants, I found it bizarre when a BJP spokesperson compared the Congress manifesto with Muslim League's manifesto of 1935. I assumed it to be his individual reaction and laughed at his assertion.

But I was bitterly surprised when I heard the prime minister using the same language the next day. In a rally in Saharanpur, the seat that BJP lost in the 2019 elections, and where the polling was to be held on 19 April, the prime minister said, 'Congress issued a bundle of lies in its manifesto ... every page reeks of attempts to tear India apart. It reflects the thoughts the Muslim League had before independence.'[4]

The prime minister was responding to the alleged promise of removing reservation limit of 50 per cent in its manifesto. However, Congress had not mentioned reservations on religious basis anywhere in its manifesto. In fact, even the word 'Muslim' was nowhere to be found in it. Evidently, BJP had decided to compare the Congress manifesto with that of Muslim League, to paint Congress as pro-Muslim and remind voters of how Congress's politics had led to the partition of the country. It was a diabolical, polarising strategy. Bharatiya Janata Party president J.P. Nadda confirmed my suspicions when he repeated the Muslim League jibe. He said, 'The Muslim League talked about reservation on basis of religion in 1929 ... Congress is repeating the same thing. The way there is talk of reservation on the basis of religion and premise of reservation beyond 50 per cent ... who is to be benefitted, Congress should make it clear.'[5]

Congress responded forcefully, with party general secretary Jairam Ramesh saying, 'The prime minister does not know his history as it was, in fact, none other than [Syama Prasad] Mookerjee, the president of the Hindu Mahasabha then, who was himself part of the coalition government in Bengal with the Muslim League ... It is the BJP, not the Congress, that believes in and practice the politics of divisiveness.'[6]

Despite this pushback, the Muslim League jibe was followed by an incessant carpet bombing of anti-Muslim narrative. The main focus of BJP was UP, as the state had 80 seats, and reports after the first phase of polling in western UP were not encouraging for the party. The prime minister made outrageous statements in UP like: 'If the SP and Congress come to power, they will send Ram Lalla back to the tent and bulldoze the [Ram] temple',[7] 'Today, the SP, Congress and INDI people want to make the majority community in India second-class citizens',[8] 'First they [opposition] will change the Constitution so that reservation can be given based on religion. Second, they will end reservations for SCs, STs, and OBCs. Third, they will distribute the entire reservation basket among Muslims'.[9] Amit Shah and Yogi Adityanath also followed in Modi's footsteps. Shah said that Samajwadi Party ensured 'power supply was uninterrupted during Ramzan but not on Janmashtami'[10] Yogi Adityanath was more brazen. He said that Muslim quota was part of Congress agenda to push country towards 'Islamisation and division'[11] and worse, 'Will not allow Taliban rule to be implemented in India.'[12]

Yogi Adityanath went to the extent of saying that if a Congress government was formed, then it would bring Sharia law in the country. He is the chief minister of UP, the state with the largest population in the country, approximately 2,400 million. Muslims constitute around 19.26 per cent of the population. Hindus comprise 79.71 per cent, according to the 2011 Census. That means every fifth person in UP is a Muslim. Out of seventy-five districts, Muslims constitute more than 40 per cent of the population in six districts: in Rampur 50.57 per cent, in Moradabad 47.12 per cent, in Bijnor 43.04 per cent, in Saharanpur 41.95 per cent, in Muzaffarnagar 41.30 per cent and in Amroha 40.78 per cent. In five districts, the percentage of Muslims is between 30 per cent and 40 per cent: in Balrampur 37.51 per cent, in Bareilly 34.55 per cent, in Meerut 34.43 per cent, in Bahraich 33.53 per cent and in Shravasti 30.79 per cent. In three districts, Muslims constitute less than 30 per cent but more than 20 per cent of the population: in Siddharthnagar 29.23 per cent, in Baghpat 27.98 per cent and in Ghaziabad 25.35 per cent.

According to a 2019 estimate, 20.4 crore Muslims live in India, which is approximately 14.2 per cent of the country's population. In proportion to their population, their presence in the Parliament should be 75 members, but that has never been the case. A maximum of 49 Muslim members of parliament were elected to the Lok Sabha in 1980. Since then, their number has declined consistently. In 2014, the number shrunk to an all-time low of 22. In 2019, it marginally increased to 25. And in the present Lok Sabha, their strength is 24.

In order to neutralise BJP's campaign of painting the opposition pro-Muslim and anti-Hindu, the Samajwadi Party (SP)–Congress alliance strategically decided not to nominate too many Muslims. Samajwadi Party gave only four tickets to Muslims and Congress chose two. All four from SP won and one of the two Congress candidates won. In order to polarise Hindu voters, BJP accused SP of indulging in vote bank politics, sheltering Muslim criminals and mafia, harbouring local Muslim gang lords, being soft on Muslim terrorists and only promoting Muslim interests at the cost of Hindus. 'Since west UP has a high population of Muslims, the BJP has over the years weaponised this demographic factor to communalise politics as well as elections to polarise Hindus against the minority community. Much of this has been communicated through the coded language of better law and order and dog-whistle tactics demonising Muslims.'[13]

Since Yogi has become the chief minister, he has deliberately and selectively targeted Muslim mafia men, like Atiq Ahmed, who was shot dead in front of live TV cameras, Mukhtar Ahmad Ansari, who died in jail and whose family members accused the administration of slow poisoning him, and former minister and powerful SP leader Azam Khan, on whom more than seventy cases were foisted by the BJP government. Yogi is also accused of taking great pride in his 'thoko niti', wherein fake encounters are allegedly conducted to eliminate and maim Muslim anti-social elements.

Under his regime, the 'bulldozer model' has also been promoted with much fanfare. His police have specialised in demolishing houses of alleged anti-social elements, even though they have not been convicted in a court of law. The majority of houses demolished are those of Muslims. His bulldozer model is so successful that even a seasoned chief minister like Shivraj Singh Chauhan introduced it in Madhya Pradesh. Ever since he became the chief minister in 2017, Yogi Adityanath has deliberately built an image of himself as a saviour of Hindus from the menace of Muslims.

While travelling through western UP to capture the mood of the voters, Omar Rashid found big endorsements amongst a large section of Hindu voters for the Yogi brand of governance. After the second phase of polling in UP, he wrote, 'While human rights activists have regularly criticized the Yogi Adityanath government for using extra-judicial means to tackle crime, suspected criminals and punish political opponents, especially Muslims, his policy epitomized by use of bulldozers and "encounter" killings was a big draw among a section of Hindus. ... They feel the BJP has put Muslims in their places through a more stringent implementation of law and order.'[14]

Muslim voters in UP are no different from the rest of the country. Modi has been pursuing majoritarian politics since he became the prime minister, which has created fear in the minority community. As Snigdhendu Bhattacharya says, 'The Hindu nationalists' aggressive majoritarianism made minorities feel insecure, a fact widely reported—due to incidents ranging from cow vigilantism to the spread of Islamophobia and vandalism of churches in Delhi, Maharashtra, and Chhattisgarh.'[15] Modi's politics of majoritarianism is the logical extension of the rise of Hindutva since the mid-1980s. Advani's Rath Yatra and the demolition of Babri Majid in Ayodhya turned the tide in Indian politics and gave Hindutva the legitimacy that RSS had been searching for since the assassination of Gandhi in 1948. Ghazala Wahab, in her award-winning book *Born a Muslim,* wrote how India changed post 1992. 'I realised that 6 December 1992 has been a turning point not just for my family, but for most Indian Muslims. We may ignore politics and turn our backs on it, but politics does not ignore anyone. And so, we too were caught up in the whirlpool that became the Indian political milieu after 1992. Civility was the first casualty. It was replaced by communal prejudice, which was no longer considered an individual predilection, but an assertion of facts. While earlier, one would not voice anti-Muslim views for fear of being judged as intolerant, now the public expression of such opinion was seen as the mark of an assertive Hindu.'[16]

Wahab also noticed changes in the Muslim community. She wrote, 'Suddenly, demonstrative religion was all around us. As the benign "Ram-Ram" was replaced by the militant "Jai Shri Ram", people started huddling with their own kind. A lot of business class Muslims who had stepped out of the mohallas and built swanky houses in mixed localities returned to the smothering comfort of narrow lanes and closed minds.'[17] Wahab underlined that with assertive Hindu-ness arrived an identity crisis amongst Muslims. 'I had grown up believing we were Muslims not because of our devoutness, but simply because we believed we were Muslims. Intolerance had crept into our family of liberal religious values and there was now a clear divide. Only my immediate family stood with me. The party broke up.'[18]

There is no denying the fact that Muslims in India today feel marginalised in their own country. The community had the option of moving to Pakistan in 1947 at the time of partition, but chose to stay here. Nothing could be more painful than their loyalty to the country being questioned and them being made to feel as 'other' in their own country. The onslaught of violent Hindutva, that paints Muslims as anti-nationals, has further accentuated the Muslims' sense of historical siege and persecution. Rakhshanda Jalil poured out her heart while underlining the irony of the whole community. She wrote, 'Indian Muslims have been labouring under the sense of siege, of being persecuted and punished for the sins of their fathers, of being wrongly accused of sins of omission and of being at the receiving end of all sorts of indignities, humiliations and violations.'[19]

The curse of the partition is still chasing them. Muslims of present-day India are being accused of a crime that they have not committed. Jalil writes, 'In the years after Partition, accused of being traitors whose rightful place was on the other side of the border, a border that their forefathers had helped create, they were reduced to pawns in a game of electoral politics. The elections of 2014 held up a mirror to the Indian Muslims; the results proved more effectively than any rhetoric how marginalized they have become and how ineffectual in the larger scheme.'[20] The stark reality today, to quote Jalil, is that 'The Indian Muslim is scared and silent, cowed down by the scale and strength of the violence all around him.'[21]

No other state showcases this reality better than UP. To map the sense of siege and persecution, the feminist writer and senior journalist Sheeba Aslam Fahmi talked to five Muslims in UP after the 2024 elections, and tried to examine their emotional world. She wrote a long report on my request:

> The very first respondent is a businessman from the construction industry in Kanpur. We call them 'builders' in UP. He said that our work requires many certifications, NOCs, and clearances which has become near impossible

in this government, so we have taken on Hindu 'partners' who become the face of the company and negotiate everything at the official level. It is our majboori [helplessness] now, otherwise we will not be able to do business. But the flip side is that the partners soon abandon us after getting the field experience and start their own company and become a competitor. This has also happened in the leather export business of Kanpur and in other similar trades, etc. ... Leather industry, handloom industry, bangle industry, metalworks where Muslims are employed are in poor shape. Many well-off business are shut down in Kanpur, Mirzapur, Moradabad, Firozabad, etc. ... Many businessmen are reduced to shopkeepers after their factory, tannery shut down.

A techie respondent from Ghaziabad said that the communal divide is overt and present in every walk of life. He, being a bearded person, has to face discrimination in day to day life. Vendors, hawker-level people show disdain publicly. The auto rickshawwalas, the vegetable vendors are openly insulting us now. He informed that housing is becoming a problem for Muslims everywhere, including the NCR. Not only rented accommodations are difficult, but to buy a flat in middle-class societies too is not possible in areas next to Delhi in Ghaziabad. He has been told by the builders that the other owners of the flats have put this condition that no Muslims should be allowed to reside here. It is an open ghettoisation of the community in urban space.

One of the respondents said that the community is facing serious challenges on the front of livelihood. 'On the question of livelihood ... the community has significantly deteriorated because the small businesses

> like eateries, hotels, meat shops, all are under attack from the goons of the right wing as well as from BJP politicians, administration and media that work in tandem with Bajrang Dal, etc. The police stations in this government are terrorising people instead of being protectors. To get an FIR done on simple issues has become quite a task for us.'

According to Sheeba's report, alienation of UP's Muslims has increased since Yogi was anointed as chief minister. The report reads, 'The fear of fake encounter and custodial death is commonly voiced. The community is suffering alienation as they can't voice their feelings, can't speak against atrocities, can't protest, and have been pushed against the wall through bulldozer-justice, love jihad narratives and extra judicial killings in custody, etc. As far as the perception of the government goes, the community feels that they are being openly persecuted to please the majority community. Unlike the majority community who demand food, healthcare, employment, etc., Muslims are worried for their lives. … We have lost our voices in the regime. There is nowhere we can go and discuss, demand on issues of law and order, police inaction, etc.'

Sheeba's report clearly establishes that Muslims have been rendered second-class citizens in UP, despite Modi's promise of 'Sabka Sath, Sabka Vikas'. If there has been a selective use of bulldozers to terrorise an entire community into submitting to the mercy of Hindus in UP, then elections have been used to make 19.26 per cent of the population irrelevant and invisible—as if they don't exist and don't matter. The party has no qualms in privately admitting that it doesn't need every fifth voter in UP. Ashok Singhal, one of the architects of the Ram Janmabhoomi movement and former leader of the Vishva Hindu Parishad, was ecstatic after the results of the 2014 general elections. He told a media entrepreneur with BJP links, 'You have ties with Muslims also. Tell them that 2014 has shown that elections can be won without Muslim support. It is time for them to understand that and respect Hindu sentiments.'[22]

Before Modi's rise, every political party, with the exception of BJP, was running pillar to post for Muslim support during elections. Congress lost its ground in UP as Muslims deserted them after the demolition of the Babri Masjid. Muslims moved towards SP led by Mulayam Singh Yadav who, as chief minster, had ordered police firing at karsevaks in 1990, in Ayodhya. In the firing, six karsevaks were killed, and BJP/RSS started calling him 'Maulana Mulayam'. Bahujan Samaj Party too tried to court them. It was believed that the Muslim vote would decide who would win and form the government in Lucknow and in Delhi. But BJP broke that myth. 'For too long, Muslims have thought they have a veto on the nation. But this has also consolidated the Hindus. Today, the Hindus have come together. After 700 years, a proud Hindu is ruling Delhi. And Muslims have become irrelevant. This is a setback to them. The table has turned,'[23] Singhal said this before his death in 2015.

Unlike Singhal, BJP leaders are not very vocal on this issue, but privately they boast that they don't need the Muslim vote and that their party does not campaign in Muslim-dominated areas. Instead, BJP strategically uses the presence of Muslims to 'counter-polarise Hindus'. Prashant Jha, in his book *How the BJP Wins: Inside India's Greatest Election Machine,* quoted a BJP strategist as saying, 'We told the Hindus—they will unite, we will always remain divided? Trump in the US showed that it is not Blacks and Hispanics and Muslims who will decide who becomes US president. It is Whites. Here too, it is not Muslims who will decide who rules UP. It is other Hindus. They want to defeat us. We want to defeat them and their parties. It is a battle.'[24]

Mark the use of the words 'it is a battle', 'they want to defeat us' and 'it is not Muslims who will decide who rules UP'. Though spoken by a political strategist, these words are an articulation of an ideology that is anti-Islamic in its nature, one that believes that Hindus have been at war with Muslims—and Christians—for the last 1,200 years. It is no coincidence that the language above has striking similarities to what RSS chief Mohan Bhagwat said in his speech in Ahmedabad on the platform of Bhartiya Vichar Manch. He said, 'Hindu society is under attack and in trouble. Its revival is vital. It must retaliate. Retaliation may take different forms. But Hindu society must rise and emerge victorious against all these assaults. Victory for Hindu society will mean victory for humanity. Hindus do not have the privilege to either turn back or concede defeat. Unless we emerge victorious, the current situation is going to prevail. Hindu society will remain, and so will the forces assaulting. And hence, we must emerge victorious. This situation will continue until we win. That is why the struggle has continued for the last 1,200 years. Only this war has gone on for such a long period of time. Therefore, we must win this war.'[25]

Bhagwat's statement is a reflection of the fact that for BJP, election is not simply gaining power, forming governments, making cabinets, formulating policies and defending the sovereignty of the country, as is the case with other political parties. For BJP, election is a 'different form' of war. Bhagwat did not specify who the enemy is, and also claimed in his speech that 'Hindutva is not opposed to Muslims and Christians', but he hinted that they [Muslims and Christians] have to accept the fact that 'they are Hindus'. Later in the speech, he underlined that Hindus were to 'eliminate' 'internal weaknesses'. He said,

'It is clear that our internal weaknesses are the main culprits. Therefore, we will have to eliminate such weaknesses.' Is it a mere coincidence that Bhagwat's theory of 'internal weaknesses' echoes Adolf Hitler's theory of 'internal enemies'? 'Even in those days when the destinies of the nation were in the balance, the internal enemy was not recognised; therefore all efforts to resist the external enemy were bound to be in vain.'[26]

To execute this theory of the elimination of internal weaknesses, BJP, since its rise in 1991, has been working on a twin strategy. One, they hardly give tickets to Muslims. Second, they employ the tool of 'Hindu Counter Mobilisation'. In 1991 and 1996, the party did not nominate any Muslims in parliamentary elections in UP. In 1998 and 1999, they gave one ticket, and in 2004 they offered tickets to two Muslims. In 2009 and 2014, they gave a ticket to one Muslim and in 2019 and 2024, no Muslim candidates were fielded by the party in UP. This is striking as UP has the highest number of seats (80) in the country, and Muslims constitute almost 20 per cent of the state's population.

As for the second strategy, Nalin Mehta has provided an interesting detail about BJP's 'Hindu Counter Mobilisation'. According to Mehta, there are 13 significant seats in UP where Muslims account for more than 30 per cent of the population. In these seats, BJP's opponents put Muslim candidates to consolidate Muslim votes, but BJP has always fielded Hindu candidates. 'It [BJP] benefited from a consolidation of Hindu voters in response to a perceived Muslim political mobilisation, which had the potential to override other issues of differences among them.'[27] Bharatiya Janata Party won all 13 seats in 2014, and in 2019, it won 5 seats despite garnering more votes than 2014.

Paradoxically, during BJP's national executive meet in Hyderabad in July 2022, Modi asked party people to reach out to

Pasmanda Muslims ('Pasmanda' is a Persian word which means 'ones left behind'). Pasmanda Muslims constitute approximately 85 per cent of the community. This word was popularised by former Rajya Sabha member Ali Anwar Ansari who belongs to Bihar and was once a close associate of Nitish Kumar. Ansari had launched a movement in 1998 to demand caste-based reservation within the Muslim community for Dalits and most backward castes. However, he contests that the Pasmanda movement is not Muslim-specific, and claims that it includes Dalits and untouchables of Hindu and Christian communities too. 'Modi also asked the partymen to reach out to Pasmanda Muslims (Dalit Muslims) as they have been left out of fruits of development. Party leader said Modi twice referred to Pasmanda Muslims in two days of BJP meeting. This was the first time that the prime minister may have referred to this section of the minority community within the party forum.'[28] It was debated that Modi's change of heart was because of his party's victory in assembly and Lok Sabha by-elections, in Muslim significant seats in Rampur and Azamgarh, a few months prior. The party leaders believed that BJP owed its victory to the Pasmanda votes. To send a message across to the Pasmanda Muslims, the party made Danish Ansari, a Pasmanda, a minister in Yogi's cabinet. It also took out Sneh Yatra to reach out to Pasmanda Muslims in UP, as suggested by the prime minister. Moreover, RSS chief Mohan Bhagwat too met Muslim intellectuals, led by Najeeb Jung and S.Y. Quraishi.

Bearing in mind BJP's rule since 2014, it is difficult to believe that the party is serious about its Muslim outreach programme. It is more of an image fine-tuning exercise. Muslims, including Pasmandas, never had any doubts about BJP's politico-social agenda. It is no wonder that despite Modi's Pasmanda tactics, Muslims as a political entity were not enticed to vote for BJP.

Rather, the ploy failed catastrophically. The post-poll survey conducted by the Centre for the Study of Developing Societies (CSDS) underlined this fact in detail. According to the post-poll survey of 2019, 6.7 per cent Muslims had opted for BJP and its alliance partners, whereas 68.1 per cent Muslims preferred the SP–BSP alliance. Only 13.4 per cent voters had chosen Congress. But in 2024, BJP's vote share nosedived. Only 2 per cent Muslims voted for BJP and its allies in UP. An astronomically high 92 per cent Muslims chose SP–Congress, which was part of the INDIA bloc.

Sheeba Aslam Fahmi cites the reason for the miserable failure of the prime minister's Pasmanda tactics in UP. She wrote, 'Even the Pasmanda ranting of PM Narendra Modi did not take off as those who are lynched, killed, harassed, molested are invariably from Pasmanda background only. The caste-based professions like meat business, non-veg eateries, hide and leather industry and petty workshops of metals, automobiles, chemical, refrigeration, carpentry, etc. belong to these groups and are severely affected by the right-wing politics.' As for BJPs aggressive Hindutva agenda, Muslims have realised that it is not a specific kind of Muslim who is targeted by Hindutvavadis, but Muslims as an entity are demonised, threatened and intimidated. Those who are targeted in the streets are essentially Muslims; it does not matter whether they are Shia or Sunni. It is this realisation that has led to an unprecedented unity among them to fight a common enemy. Sheeba says that a new phenomenon has emerged in the community. The old divide among Muslims due to religious sectarian reasons has vanished and instead a sense of unity has enveloped them. She writes, 'Among Muslims, the sectarian hatred of Shia, Sunni, Barelvi, Deobandi has considerably diminished. No Maulana is seen active on these lines anymore.'

Hilal Ahmed writes, 'The demonisation of Muslim identity in UP has been completely normalised. It has become a part of Muslim everyday existence.'[29] He quotes the Pew Research survey and says, 'Around 35 per cent of Muslims in north India claim that they have faced religious discrimination in the last one year.'[30] For a country like India that boasts of a great tradition of tolerance, Around 35 per cent is a huge number. This shows how much the country has changed for minorities in the last few years. Ahmed further says, 'Violent anti-Muslim Hindutva politics is a north-centric phenomenon ... the Babri Masjid dispute, the Shah Bano episode, the love jihad campaign, and the aggressive cow protection movement provide the contextual specificity to violent Hindutva in the north.'[31]

It is this normalisation of the demonisation of Muslims in UP that guided the voting behaviour of Muslims. Muslims worked on a well-defined strategy. This strategy had five pillars. One, identification of the party that could defeat BJP. Two, rejection of the party that was helping BJP win in the garb of secularism. Three, no division of Muslim votes at any cost. Four, no overt exhibition of their frustration with BJP and Hindutva, and no excitement even after extreme provocation during the campaign. Five, no demonstration of their identity on polling day; to avoid wearing identity markers and to avoid voting in bulk. Unlike earlier elections, this time, Muslims took a long-term perspective on elections and were more far-sighted. The creation of the INDIA gave them the confidence that BJP could be defeated, and for that, nationally, the INDIA should be their choice for voting. Accordingly, in every state, the INDIA partners were identified. West Bengal is a classic example. Despite the presence of Congress in the state, Muslims voted for Trinamool Congress in bulk and ignored Congress totally.

Similarly, in UP, SP–Congress alliance was their only choice and the community outright rejected Mayawati and her party, BSP. According to the CSDS survey, BSP got only 5 per cent Muslim votes in 2024. Sensing the mood of the Muslims, All India Majlis-e-Ittehadul Muslimeen (AIMIM) did not dare to put up candidates in UP as Owaisi has been doing earlier. Saba Naqvi, who has experience covering elections for more than three decades, told me, 'SP–Congress was the only alternative to BJP in the state. Smart ticket distribution by SP, although numbers of Muslim candidates were reduced, worked for the alliance.' Saba hints that nationally, Congress was the preferred choice of Muslims, and since Congress was an integral part of the alliance, the stock of INDIA rose and the alliance partners too benefited. She told me, 'Congress has been elevated in Muslim eyes as Rahul Gandhi is now a hugely popular leader among them since Bharat Jodo Yatra. The party may lack in structures, but there is huge goodwill among Muslims for Congress, suddenly, so alliance worked really well at this point.'

Sheeba's report also supports Saba's argument. 'All the respondents agree that INDIA alliance is the best thing that happened in the general elections as SP was facing disillusionment from the community but Congress joining hands arrested this trend. Congress has gained ground.' About Mayawati, Sheeba wrote, 'BSP is seen as Trojan horse of the BJP.'

But the weaponisation of their silence was the most potent ammunition in their armoury to fight the forces of Hindutva. This is not the first time the Muslim community harnessed this power in UP. During the 2017 assembly elections and the 2019 general elections, the parties opposed to BJP were kept guessing as to whom the Muslims would vote for. The prominent Hindi newspaper *Amar Ujala* had published a report about Noida and the adjoining areas during the 2017 assembly elections.

'Candidates are focusing on castes but the silence of Muslim voters is worrying everyone.'[32] In 2019 general elections in UP, Muslims were upset that none of the secular parties were ready to raise their voice for the rights of Muslims, as they were scared that BJP might brand them pro-Muslim and polarise Hindu votes. *Mint* had reported then, 'Muslims are realizing that there is barely any condemnation of blatant violence like lynching and fake encounters, let alone subtle forms of harassment like banning congregational Friday prayers. This lack of leadership and realization of being political orphans is among the reasons why Muslims have decided it is better to be silent spectators.'[33]

But the 2024 election was different. This time the silence of the Muslims was more organised and well-planned, and was executed till the very last mile. There was a consensus that Muslims would not do anything to let BJP exploit Hindu sentiments for the purpose of election.

Chetan Chauhan reported for the *Hindustan Times*,

> Prominent Muslim community leaders such as Yusuf [a lawyer at Uttarakhand's Haldwani lower court, and a member of Jamiat-Ulema-Hind, a national organisation of Muslims] said a decision has been taken not to protest but to vote silently. . . . This message has been delivered to the community through mosques and community leaders.
>
> 'The attempt is not to help the BJP to polarise the polls,' said a prominent Muslim leader of western UP. A community leader in western UP aware of the discussions and developments within the community said families have been advised to vote in batches so that long queues of Muslims are not visible at polling stations; people have been told to avoid wearing dresses which can identify them as Muslims at polling booths. The idea is not to give

> an impression that Muslims are voting in large numbers, the leader said, as it could polarise voting. … It appears that the silence of Muslim voters is real and strategic aimed at targeting the ruling Bharatiya Janata Party.'[34]

This strategy seems to have worked in UP. Bharatiya Janata Party has lost its sheen in its own bastion. It has been reduced to 33 seats while SP–Congress has 43. Silence has proved lethal. Those who think that the language of 'retaliation' is only to scream and shout have been proven wrong.

These are undoubtedly tough times for Muslims. They are fighting their own battle. Once again, it has been proven that the Gandhian method is unparalleled when the fight is with the macho state and war is waged by immoral means. Who says silence is not heard and non-violence is the armour of the weak?

But the last word has to be Ziya Us Salam's. He says, 'Being a Muslim amidst the ever-unfolding chapters of Islamophobia is not easy. India will have to speak up.'[35]

10
Internal Conflicts, External Ramifications

Pappu Pal, an auto driver taking me home from the metro station, was a very talkative person. He was from Kannauj in UP, which happens to be Akhilesh Yadav's Lok Sabha constituency. 'Yogi Adityanath is a good chief minister. Since he became chief minister, I feel safe and can roam around even late at night and nobody tries to harm me,' he said to me.

Pal came to Noida six years ago to drive an auto to support his parents and four siblings, who live in a village in Kannauj. He earns roughly ₹1,500 a day, and after paying rent for the tempo and CNG, he saves ₹600 to ₹700 per day. He works from 8 a.m. to 8 p.m.

When I asked him if he voted for Samajwadi Party (SP) or Bharatiya Janata Party (BJP), he confidently told me that he voted for BJP. When I asked him the reason, he said, '*Akhilesh ke zamane me bahut gundagardi thi. Yogi ji ne sabko theek kar diya.* [There was a lot of lawlessness during Akhilesh's government. Yogi has sorted things out.]'

Pal belongs to an OBC caste in UP. In the local language, they are called Gadaria, which is the herding caste that breeds sheep. The Pal community has traditionally supported BJP. Pappu Pal had no qualms in saying that Yogi is a strong leader and he has put an end to mafia members like Atiq Ahmed and Mukhtar Ansari. When I asked if it was okay that they were killed in front of the camera, he replied, 'See, sir, people like him had made life hell in UP. Whatever happened was good. Good riddance.' When I contested that there was so much price rise and unemployment, his reply was interesting. 'Sir, for a person like me, security is important. It will not make any difference even if Akhilesh is the chief minister, for even then I will be driving an auto.'

What emerges from the conversation is simple. It is that in the past seven years, Yogi has successfully projected himself as a leader who has frightened the mafia and broken their backs. He is the new 'Dabang' (strong man) in Indian politics. Sadly, despite such an image, Yogi could not save BJP in UP and the party had to face humiliation in the elections.

In 2017, when BJP stunned everybody by appointing Yogi Adityanath as the chief minister of UP, it was said that the party had committed a blunder and that Yogi might prove to be a disaster. Though he had been an MP five times from Gorakhpur, he was seen as a divisive figure. He had his own army, the Hindu Yuva Vahini, that was a law unto itself. He was seen as a leader with criminal intent, a rabble-rouser who had murder cases against him and had been to jail. In fact, he had cried in the Lok Sabha, while complaining to the Lok Sabha speaker that he feared for his life.

But today, Yogi is seen as Modi's successor. He is the second most popular leader in BJP. He is not only a star campaigner in UP but, after Modi, the most sought-after leader for electioneering in other states as well. If luck favours him, he can end up as the prime minister.

Although, at the time of writing this book, it was uncertain whether he would even survive as a chief minister. The knives were out for him. It was being hotly speculated in the corridors of power that Yogi was facing the Modi moment—when, in 2002, leaders had assembled in Goa to decide Modi's fate as the then prime minister Atal Bihari Vajpayee had wanted him to be sacked for the Gujarat riots. But Vajpayee could not have his way and Modi went on to become the prime minister. Modi was lucky that he had a mentor like L.K. Advani who stood by him like a rock and saved him from humiliation. The same thing cannot be said about Yogi today. There is no Advani in BJP today who can defend him and stand by him. Yogi is without a mentor in the party. He can find solace in the fact that RSS finds in him traces of a future leader who can be the torchbearer of Hindutva after Modi is gone. But it remains to be seen whether RSS will stand by him the way Advani stood by Modi, the reason for this being that BJP today is a vastly different party. Unlike the BJP of Atal–Advani, the party today is ruthless to the core and nothing but power defines the relationships within the organisation. There is serious struggle amongst the big leaders to position themselves to emerge as the supreme commander of the party in the post-Modi BJP. After the electoral debacle in UP, serious questions have been raised and a lot of conspiracy theories have been floated by Yogi's opponents in the party. Apparently, a section within the party has been conspiring to remove him and finish his political career.

Four theories were being circulated about Yogi Adityanath and BJP's defeat in UP, three of which were propagated by those wanting to oust Yogi, and one by his supporters.

Theory one: Yogi deliberately did not work hard to show Amit Shah his place, to fail him and to prove that every Chanakya needs a Chandragupta to win battles and build an empire.

Theory two: Yogi was seeking revenge for the conspiracy hatched before UP assembly elections in 2022 to replace him as chief minister.

Theory three: Yogi wanted to weaken Modi; to ensure that Modi would not get a majority in the Lok Sabha, as a third-time powerful prime minister would not hesitate to sack him, as Modi had done with Shivraj Singh Chauhan and Vasundhara Raje Scindia.

Theory four: Yogi is Rajput, a powerful caste in UP. The Rajputs were angry for two reasons—one, they were very upset with the rumour that Yogi would be replaced after the Parliament elections; two, they were upset with Gujarat's BJP leader Parshottam Rupala's insulting remarks about Rajputs.

Ever since Modi became the prime minister, he placed Amit Shah as his confidant, as his man Friday, an unchallengeable number two. Modi is the decision-maker and Shah the ruthless executor. I never believed the argument that the Modi–Shah jugalbandi is like Atal–Advani. It is true that Advani was drafted in Vajpayee's team to help him in his parliamentary work. Advani wrote, 'It was in early 1957 that Deendayal ji asked me to shift base from Rajasthan to Delhi to assist Atal ji and the other newly elected Jana Sangh MPs in their parliamentary work.'[1]

Advani has confessed that he was in awe of Vajpayee throughout his life. While defining his relationship with Vajpayee, Advani wrote, 'The relationship between Atal ji and me was never competitive, much less combative … From the very early stages of our association, I always used to submit to whatever Atal ji decided with regard to organisational and political matters.'[2] But Advani was a maverick. In later years, he carved a space for himself in the party, and once the Ram Janmabhoomi movement began, he undoubtedly emerged as the poster boy of Hindutva politics. It was his Rath Yatra that turned the tide in Indian politics and made BJP a serious contender for power at the Centre. There was a time, from the late 1980s to 1996, when Advani had eclipsed Vajpayee and nothing moved in the party without his nod.

Advani was one of the rare leaders who commanded the respect and unquestioned affection of his colleagues and juniors. If Vajpayee was the leader and the statesman, then Advani was the ideologue and the strategist. In the modern BJP, Modi is both the leader and the strategist. He is less of an ideologue, more of an 'action hero'. Shah cannot even imagine assuming parity with Modi, as Advani had with Vajpayee in later years. Because the nature of the relationship between Modi and Shah is not one of equals but of mentor and mentee. Vajpayee was not Advani's guardian, he did not shape Advani's career. But Modi picked Shah and nurtured him to be his second-in-command. As Vinay Sitapati writes, 'It is hard to imagine Narendra Modi one day serving under Amit Shah—the way Vajpayee and Advani were able to swap roles not once but twice.'[3] Shah is powerful because Modi wants him to be powerful. If Modi detaches himself from Shah, Shah will be reduced to just another leader in the party. Yogi knows this and that is why he resents Amit Shah's authority.

If Amit Shah fancies himself as the second-in-command and thinks that his writs should run the way Modi's words are taken in the party, then he cannot be blamed for that. He brought in fundamental changes in the party and created a mammoth election machine, which was once considered to be unbeatable. He had a special liking for UP. During the 2014 elections, when Shah was an unknown commodity in national politics, he was given the charge of UP to win the maximum number of seats for Modi. And he did not disappoint. It was because of his planning that BJP surprised everyone by winning 71 out of 80 seats. Once he was made the party president, Shah tried to transform the party's social profile by engaging in social engineering to make inroads into OBC and Dalit voters. Before Shah's experiments, BJP was called a Baniya–Brahmin party. 'To his shock, in 2014, he [Amit Shah] discovered that among party office-bearers across the state—from Lucknow down to the district level—only 7 per cent were OBCs and 3 per cent were Dalits. This meant that groups which together constituted almost 70 per cent of the population in the state had 10 per cent space in the BJP's organisation. The structure was dominated by Brahmans, Thakurs and Banias.' In two years because of Amit Shah's efforts, out of 75 districts, in UP, BJP had OBC presidents in 34 and in three districts, Dalit presidents and in the party structure share of Dalit and OBCs office bearers increased to 30 per cent. Prashant Jha writes, 'The BJP had engineered a silent, almost invisible disruption. And the genius of it lay in the fact that it happened without an outright rebellion of the existing leadership.'[4]

Amit Shah who was then the party president should also be given credit for BJP's stupendous success in the 2017 assembly elections. It was because of the social engineering carried out during his term as the party president and his astute election planning that BJP won 312 out of 403 seats. During the campaign, Yogi Adityanath was only one of the star campaigners and nowhere in the picture in the race for being the chief minister. But after the results he was catapulted to the top job in the state, leaving behind both Keshav Prasad Maurya, who was the state BJP president then, and Manoj Sinha, who was minister of state in Modi's cabinet.

There are two sets of beliefs about Yogi becoming the chief minister. According to the first, Yogi was Modi–Shah's choice and endorsed by RSS, while according to the other, RSS pushed Yogi's name because of his reputation as an aggressive Hindutva leader, and Modi–Shahi agreed. The second argument carries more weight. Now it is almost certain that Yogi was chosen by RSS, and he was chosen with a purpose. He was seen as a long-term investment for Hindutva. Vijay Trivedi, an expert on RSS, says, 'I was told by an RSS leader that senior leader of RSS Krishna Gopal was in favour of Yogi from the beginning. He was of the opinion that a person like Yogi was needed to expand the footprint of Hindutva and spread the RSS agenda. He passed on this message to another senior leader of RSS Bhaiya Ji Joshi [who was the second in command in the RSS then]. Then it was discussed with Mohan Bhagwat, RSS chief. After this message was sent to Amit Shah [who was then the party president] that Yogi would be the most suitable candidate but you have to decide.'[5]

Yogi was an unexpected choice for the post of chief minister of the biggest state in the country. Nobody had an inkling about it till his name was announced. I, too, was completely taken aback. My first reaction was that BJP had lost the plot and had committed a mistake. How could a mature political party like BJP choose someone who was not even considered a serious politician at the time? He had a disastrously negative image; he was seen as a Muslim hater, and someone who spewed venom against minorities. Ironically, he was doing this despite being the Peethadhishwar of Gorakhnath temple, which is known for Hindu–Muslim unity and harmony between different faiths. What shocked the media, particularly the global media, was that a religious head had been anointed as chief minister. Pratap Bhanu Mehta wrote, 'It is an odious choice because the BJP has picked someone who is widely regarded as the single most divisive, abusive, polarising figure in UP politics.'[6] *The New York Times*, in its editorial, reacted sharply: 'The move is a shocking rebuke to religious minorities. ... The appointment shows that Mr Modi sees no contradiction between economic development and a muscular Hindu nationalism that feeds on stoking anti-Muslim passions.'[7] Even the right-wing writers were sceptical. R. Jagannathan wrote, 'The election of Yogi Adityanath as the Bharatiya Janata Party's (BJP) choice to head Uttar Pradesh may be a risky one, given his firebrand Hindutva credentials.'[8] Swapan Dasgupta's sarcasm summed up the mood of secular India. He wrote, 'The past few days have witnessed an explosion of stupefied bewilderment in India. ... This decision has proved too much for the forces of intellectual enlightenment to stomach. The prevailing image of the Mahant of the Gorakhnath temple as one of India's foremost "communal" monsters, one who went a hundred steps beyond dog whistle polarisation, produced unequivocal outrage.'[9]

I don't know if BJP has realised this, but Yogi's was an extraordinary selection, one that triggered a major shift in Indian politics. In the past, several religious gurus and sadhvis had been elected to the Parliament and legislative assemblies and become MPs and MLAs. A few of them were also inducted into the cabinet in the state and at the Centre, but this was the first time a religious head of a major place of worship was made the political head of a state. Though the Indian Constitution does not restrict religious heads from becoming chief ministers or prime minister, this breaches the basic ethos of a secular Constitution. The concept of the modern state is based on the separation of religion and politics; it is based on the premise that spiritual and temporal heads should be two different entities. The Indian Constitution too has imbibed this ethos. It also advocates that the state should not align with one particular religion, as the chief minister or the prime minister, in a multi-religious society, does not belong to one particular religion. They represent everyone, they are the leader of the followers of all religions.

Yogi can always claim that as a chief minister, he has not favoured any particular religion, nor discriminated between the upholders of different religions, but he cannot wish away scrutiny from the followers of other faiths. The Nehruvian argument that a secular state should not align with a particular religion; that the prime minister, or the chief minister, does not belong to one particular religion, irrespective of their faith, has been shredded a thousand times over since Modi became the prime minister. Modi never loses an opportunity to present himself as a Hindu leader. Unlike Modi, Yogi is an actual religious head. The least he could have done to preserve the sanctity of the Constitution, before being sworn in as chief minister, was to abdicate from the position of the Peethadhishwar of Gorakhnath temple. That would have, at least notionally, separated religion and politics as is required by the constitutional morality; but he did no such thing.

The appointment of Yogi has literally erased the line between religion and politics, and unfortunately, this blurring of boundaries between religion and politics, instead of becoming Yogi's handicap, has become his USP. At a time when politics is defined by Hindutva, a religious marker, a saffron-robed chief minister automatically becomes the living embodiment of Hindutva. Yogi does not have to prove his Hindutva. He *is* Hindutva.

It is interesting to know that when he was chosen as chief minister, not many experts thought that Yogi would last long in the saddle. In a conversation, Sharat Pradhan, the co-author (along with Atul Chandra) of a biography of Yogi Adityanath, told me, 'Nobody was ready to give him a full term as it was widely believed that it was just a stopgap arrangement in the wake of the Sangh's opposition to Manoj Sinha, whom Narendra Modi had clearly tipped for the coveted job. But ambition in the determined saffron-clad monk led him to not only cross several hurdles but also establish himself as a larger-than-life Hindutva icon. So much that he even began to pose a threat to the mighty Modi's potential successor, Amit Shah.'

After becoming the chief minister, Yogi very cleverly began to consolidate his image of a Hindutva leader. Within days of his appointment, he targeted the Muslim community by closing down illegal slaughter houses. He created anti-Romeo squads in the name of ensuring safety and security of girls against sexual harassment. His government launched an aggressive campaign against 'love jihad', which was nothing more than an attempt to end interfaith marriages between Muslims and Hindus. Showering flower petals over kanwariyas was another innovative idea of his government. His crackdown on the Muslim mafia provided more sheen to his image as a saviour of Hindus. To quote Sharat Pradhan, '... Yogi left no stone unturned to reinforce his image as a Hindu hardliner—which he did by blatantly projecting himself more as "anti-Muslim". And his bulldozer policy was systematically used to manifest this image. Evidently, his bulldozer ran indiscriminately and menacingly over shanties, hutments, petty shops and even richer commercial establishments belonging to Muslims.' This fortification of his image as a Hindu icon, in Sharat's words, 'even began to pose threat to the mighty Modi's potential successor, Amit Shah.'

Amit Shah was, and is, widely speculated to be next in line to succeed Modi as the leader of BJP. Shah's biggest failure is his inability to catapult himself as a Hindutva leader. He enjoys enormous power due to his proximity to the prime minister. He is considered to be a modern-day Chanakya, a master strategist. He is a great organiser and a good orator, but he pales before

Yogi when compared on the Hindutva scale. Vijay Trivedi, who has written Yogi's biography in Hindi, told me, 'In the last seven years, the model which he developed to run the administration in UP has made him the biggest face of Hindutva in Sangh Parivar. He has emerged as a leader, who has eclipsed all other leaders except Narendra Modi.' Unhesitatingly, Trivedi added, 'Yogi's emergence as a Hindutva leader and his popularity is not sitting well with leaders who want to be number one leader in the post Modi age.'

The internal contradiction within BJP further intensified in 2022 when Yogi won a second term for himself. The man who was not supposed to last a full term was now deeply entrenched in Hindutva politics. And this was happening without Modi–Shah's blessings. Amit Shah, aware of Yogi's popularity, got to work to diminish his area of influence during the general elections. It is widely believed that Shah claimed that Yogi, despite being the chief minister, could not have a say in the selection of candidates. Coomi Kapoor, a senior and well-informed journalist, wrote in her column in *The Indian Express*, 'But the genesis of the UP defeat needs more introspection. The investigation should have started with the BJP's central election committee meeting on February 29, when the names of some 50 of the 80 UP seats were cleared. The committee members, including Adityanath, waited for over two hours since Narendra Modi, Amit Shah and J.P. Nadda first met informally at Lok Kalyan Marg, where a short list of 50 BJP Lok Sabha candidates was drawn up. At the official meeting, general secretary (organisation) B.L. Santosh read out the names and few interjected. The common refrain was "whatever the party thinks appropriate". The names from UP were cleared in barely 20 minutes and some 65% were sitting MPs, since the party seemed confident that UP's formidable "double engine ki sarkar" would ensure their victory. Adityanath's reported suggestion to change the names of 35 sitting MPs was ignored. Eventually, 27 BJP incumbents lost the polls.'[10] Coomi Kapoor's report was supported by Ratan Mani Lal, who wrote, 'There are also indications that names of many candidates suggested by Yogi Adityanath were not accepted, and the results in these constituencies have been unfavourable for the party.'[11] Rajesh Kumar Singh said in the *Hindustan Times*, 'A BJP leader said Adityanath's role was limited in the selection of candidates, suggesting that this could have played a part in the party's poor showing in the state.'[12] Sanjay Pandey wrote in the *Deccan Herald*, 'Another BJP leader ... said that Adityanath could not be held responsible for the party's dismal performance as he was not directly involved in the selection of candidates.'[13] *The Telegraph* reported, 'Privately, many leaders who have lost accused the "top leadership" in UP of not accepting their candidature wholeheartedly, which played a role in their defeat.'[14]

The story goes that Yogi was greatly hurt by being slighted in his own state and did not go out of his way to ensure the victory of the candidates who had Amit Shah's approval. Since Shah chose them, he should ensure their victory; consequently, why should Yogi take the blame for their loss? One BJP leader told me that Yogi wanted to convey that if Shah wished to win without Yogi, then so be it. It seems Yogi has successfully conveyed his message—there is no Chanakya without Chandragupta.

Not everybody buys this argument. A few political analysts believe differently. For them, Yogi has failed to deliver as his aggressive Hindutva has its limitations. Utkarsh Sinha, a veteran journalist, originally belongs to Gorakhpur, Yogi's hometown. He is now based in Lucknow, UP. He has seen Yogi's career from the very first day. He is of the opinion that Yogi's biggest undoing is his stubbornness and uncompromising attitude. He told me, 'Though Yogi supporters blame ignoring him in the ticket distribution as the main reason for the party's debacle, but his detractors are of the opinion that Yogi's over-the-top style of functioning and corruption of his unrestrained bureaucrats damaged BJP. Up to a certain extent, both the arguments are valid.' He concluded that 'politics is changing and Yogi's extra aggressive Hindutva has failed to attract many.'

There is another reason for Yogi to hold a grudge against Amit Shah. A source told me long back that Yogi firmly believed that before the 2022 assembly elections, a serious coup was being engineered to replace him with a pliable chief minister. This has been corroborated by senior journalist Shyam Lal Yadav who, in his recent book on chief ministers of UP, has given an account of that episode. Yadav writes,

> It was a year [2021] when difference between the BJP and Yogi had come to a boil and his removal was being discussed both within the party and outside. The alienation of the Brahmin community [Yogi is a Rajput] and the tussle with deputy CM Keshav Prasad Maurya were some of the major factors that caused ripples in Lucknow and Delhi. He was eventually retained with the prime minister Narendra Modi having to step in....
>
> The news of the unrest had reached Delhi. Many meetings were organised in Lucknow and Delhi in May and June 2021 at different levels. At one point, it seemed certain that Yogi Adityanath was going to be replaced. The central leadership was concerned about the assembly polls, which were nine months away. Amid his ongoing tussle with Deputy CM Maurya, Yogi Adityanath made a surprise visit to Maurya's residence on 22 June 2021 in an attempt to mend fences. Before Yogi Adityanath could be

> convinced about the change of leadership, the BJP leadership, assessing the situation, realised that if he was removed, the party would suffer. ... This put to rest all the rumours and made it clear that the party could not afford to replace Yogi Adityanath. He moved ahead and the 2022 assembly polls were contested with him as the face of the BJP in UP.[15]

The buzz about Yogi being removed started with Arvind Kumar Sharma, a close confidant of the prime minister, a 1988 batch IAS officer of the Gujarat cadre who took retirement before his superannuation in July 2022, reaching Lucknow. It was speculated that he had been sent by the top leadership to take over the UP administration in some capacity, either as a senior adviser or as the second-in-command, inducted into the Yogi cabinet, to effectively run the government. With this began the rumour that the Modi–Shah duo was not happy with Yogi's style of governance. The reason handed out was his handling of the COVID-19 pandemic, when the lack of oxygen tanks created an unprecedented humanitarian crisis in the state, and hundreds of dead bodies were seen floating in the river Ganga and openly buried in the sand on the riverbank. It was also believed that Shah wanted his man, Keshav Prasad Maurya, as the next chief minister. Yogi stunned the BJP leadership by refusing to acknowledge Sharma's presence in Lucknow. He did not meet him, although Sharma kept waiting in expectation. It was Yogi's way of communicating to Modi–Shah that he was no pushover and he would not succumb to their pressure tactics. Many people in the know told me then that Yogi had made up his mind that he would rebel if he was removed. Modi and Shah were not used to this kind of defiance within the party. Finally, RSS's second-in-command Dattatreya Hosabole flew down to Lucknow to intervene. He took feedback from the local functionaries of RSS and BJP. It was decided that removing Yogi would damage the party more than his continuance. And finally, Yogi Adityanath visited Keshav Prasad Maurya's home, which he had not done since becoming the chief minister. A picture was released of the meeting. 'The lunch at Maurya's house was also attended by RSS General Secretary Dattatreya Hosabole, Joint General Secretary Krishna Gopal and Deputy CM Dinesh Sharma.'[16]

Arvind Kumar Sharma was made vice president of BJP and a member of the legislative council. After winning handsomely in 2022, he was made a minister in Yogi's cabinet. A senior journalist, who doesn't want to be named, told me that 'Yogi had not forgotten that episode of 2021 and in the 2024 elections he replied with a vengeance. If Shah had then wanted him to be replaced, then in these elections, Yogi wanted to teach him a lesson in politics. *Hisaab Baraabar*.'

The peace which was brokered by Hosabole and Krishna Gopal was temporary. It was the declaration of a ceasefire, not the end of the war. That senior RSS leaders had to intervene shows that this was no ordinary battle.

The Yogi camp in Lucknow was apprehensive that if Modi were to form the government for the third time with more than three hundred seats, then Yogi would be removed ruthlessly. Even before the elections were announced, it was a hotly debated topic in media circles in Lucknow and Delhi as to when and how he would be removed after the election; would it happen immediately after the results or before December 2024? Or would the operation be enacted once the assembly elections in Maharashtra, Haryana and Jharkhand were over? Arvind Kejriwal shrewdly grabbed the opportunity. A day after he was out of Tihar jail, he made a statement in this regard. He said,

'They [Modi–Shah] ended the politics of Lal Krishna Advani, Murli Manohar Joshi, Shivraj Singh, Vasundhara Raje, [M.L.] Khattar, Raman Singh ... I can give in writing that they will change the UP chief minister within two months if they win the Lok Sabha polls. They will finish Yogi Adityanath politically.'[17] He alleged that this would be done to pave the way for Amit Shah as prime minister, because Modi would turn seventy-five in 2025, and as per law, he would have to step down. On the same day, Amit Shah rebutted Kejriwal's claim. He said, 'I will like to tell Arvind Kejriwal and company and the whole INDI Alliance, that there is no need for you to feel happy when Modi turns 75 ... Modi will complete the term and will continue to lead the country till 2029. There is no confusion in the BJP on this.'[18] Surprisingly, Shah maintained silence on the issue of Yogi's removal. The party too did not respond on that count till a day before the last phase of polling when J.P. Nadda said that Yogi enjoyed the unwavering trust of the party, and his removal from the office was unthinkable.[19]

Kejriwal, no doubt, was trying to create a wedge within BJP. Almost all top BJP leaders and chief ministers have either been neutralised by the Modi–Shah duo, or have been shunted to the margins. A few have reconciled to the fact that as long as Modi Shah are at the helm, they have no chance. Leaders like Shivraj Singh Chauhan, who was once touted as a prime ministerial candidate, has also reconciled with the fact and made way for Mohan Yadav as chief minister in Madhya Pradesh. Vasundhara Raje Scindia, who was defiant till the last minute, was shown the door. A political greenhorn/non-entity, Bhajan Lal Sharma replaced her as chief minister of Rajasthan. Today she is wandering in the political wilderness. Similarly, in Karnataka, B.S. Yediyurappa, the man who is credited with BJP's rise in the state, was replaced by a weak Basavaraj

Bommai. In Gujarat, all the senior leaders were sidelined, and first-time MLA Bhupendra Patel was given the command of the state. In Uttarakhand, Pushkar Dhami became the chief minister. Yogi is the only exception. He is the only who has not succumbed to the diktats of Modi and Shah. He is the last man standing. But nobody knows for how long.

After the general elections, knives were out once again. Leaders considered to be close to Shah attacked Yogi. An attempt was made to weave a narrative that Yogi had failed, and because of him, the party could not get the majority in Lok Sabha. Shah's protege Keshav Prasad Maurya said, 'No leader was bigger than the organisation.' Sharat Pradhan wrote to me, 'UP deputy chief minister Keshav Prasad Maurya, whose proximity to Shah was an open secret, came out in the open against the chief minister, while using the party's debacle at the LS poll as a tool. Maurya's confidence rose from the obvious fillip he got from the ultimate powers that be in Delhi.' Both Maurya and Brajesh Pathak did not attend several meetings called by the chief minister. They weren't the only ones; BJP allies like Apna Dal president Anupriya Patel and cabinet minister Sanjay Nishad also targeted Yogi. In a letter to Yogi, Patel said that candidates from OBC/SC/ST categories were often declared 'not found suitable' for the posts reserved for them. The posts are then declared unreserved.[20]

Sanjay Nishad questioned the USP of the Yogi Adityanath government—his bulldozer policy. He said, 'Uproot the poor, and they uproot us in politics.'[21]

It did not stop here. Moti Singh, BJP MLA and former minister, alleged, 'I have no hesitation in saying that in 42 years of my political life, I could not imagine or see such kind of corruption at the tehsil level and police station level, which is unimaginable.'[22]

As Sharat Pradhan observed, 'So his [Maurya] supporters went to town proclaiming that he would soon replace the monk, who would be given a slot in the Modi cabinet.' Yogi is astute enough to know that being chief minister is better than being a cabinet minister under Modi. He also knows that the whole exercise was an attempt to uproot him from his power base so that he does not pose any challenge for Shah in the future.

Sensing the mood, Yogi counter-attacked. He said that the party lost due to 'overconfidence'.[23] He was hinting at the '400 paar' slogan, which was coined by the prime minister himself. When I asked Vijay Trivedi the reason for the fierce fight in UP, he said, 'After the Lok Sabha results, the internal fight which has intensified in the BJP is basically the fight for who after Modi; it was less about Lucknow. Modi is running his third innings and after Modi, Amit Shah is the second most powerful leader, like once Advani was after Atal. Every leader who was a claimant after Modi has been sidelined, only Yogi Adityanath is left. His popularity unsettles those who want to emerge as the number one leader once Modi is gone.'

Besides the conspiracy theories, it is also true that the Rajputs, who are immensely powerful in a semi-feudal and caste-ridden society like UP, were angry with BJP. One of the major reasons were the whispers doing the rounds in UP even before the election process started—that Yogi would be replaced. The Rajputs got more infuriated when they heard Parshottam Rupala's insulting remark about the community 'at a Dalit event that the erstwhile "maharajas" broke bread with the British and also married off their daughters to them.'[24]

The statement was made in Gujarat but it triggered anger amongst the Rajput community across north India. In UP, it was further aggravated when a Rajput leader, the former army chief and a minister, V.K. Singh was denied a ticket from Ghaziabad.

It was also hotly discussed how another Rajput leader, Rajnath Singh, was sidelined in Delhi. 'The alleged sidelining of Rajnath Singh over the past 10 years is also something the Rajput base has been irked about. The perceived attack on Rajput cultural icons like Raja Bhoj and finally, a perception that Delhi BJP's top leaders want to clip the wings of Uttar Pradesh chief minister Adityanath appear to have goaded the Thakurs into coming out in open rebellion. Adityanath supporters taking cues from Rajasthan, Madhya Pradesh and Chhattisgarh say they fear that if Modi is re-elected and emerges as strengthened after June 4, Adityanath will be removed from office and replaced with a faceless loyalist.'[25]

Apparently, the Rajput anger was deliberately fuelled by Yogi and his supporters, and despite BJP high command's instructions, Yogi did not make any efforts to pacify his community. But whether Rajput anger really damaged BJP's chances in the election is debatable. According to CSDS post poll survey, '... 79% upper caste—especially Brahmins and Thakurs—largely favoured the BJP while only 16% of them backed the INDIA bloc. Compared to this, 77.2% upper caste voters preferred the BJP in 2019. The numbers are even more staggering when it comes to Thakurs' support to the BJP. ... A closer look reveals that close to 9 of every 10 Thakur (Rajput) voters (89%) favoured the BJP.'[26] The CSDS data smashes to smithereens the theory of Rajput anger and deliberate fanning of their anger by Yogi causing damage to BJP in the elections.

The reason for BJP's defeat in UP is much deeper; it is beyond conspiracy theories. If the party wants to win the 2027 assembly elections, then it has to do some serious course correction. Bharatiya Janata Party and RSS can find the road ahead only after solving the riddle of Indian social reality, especially in UP, which is a conundrum of caste structure and caste loyalties, and the internal civilisational war that has been intensified by the constitutional consciousness. On the one side of this war is Hindutva, which represents the desire to continue with thousands of years of hegemony of the upper caste, which incidentally reflects in the CSDS data that shows how almost 80 per cent upper-caste voters solidly supports BJP; on the other side of the war are the voiceless, the mooknayaks who have been suppressed and tortured throughout history, who demand equality, liberty, an equitable society and, fraternity and dignity of life, which manifests itself as the politics of social justice. In 2014 and 2019, BJP and RSS succeeded in appropriating a section of the voiceless—the Dalits and OBCs—by creating a division amongst them; but when these communities were faced with the perceived threat of the abrogation of the Constitution, they realised their folly, and decided not to vote for BJP. This process is irreversible. The party has failed to realise that for the majority of Hindus, the fight for social justice is a fight for their existence; it is a fight for their social identity; it is a fight for dignity, a dignity that has been denied to them for thousands of years.

The opposition has succeeded in conveying the message that BJP is ideologically averse to the very liberation of the majority of Hindus. That is why it is so opposed to the Caste Census and looks for new ground to neutralise the effects of reservation. The 'Save Constitution' movement during the elections and its continuance after the elections is the Brahmastra to demolish the Hindutva castle. The problem with Hindutva is that it wants to retain the caste structure which facilitates the control of the minority within Hindus over the majority of Hindus. Unless this division is mitigated, unless everyone is treated equally irrespective of caste, the war between social justice and Hindutva will continue. Bharatiya Janata Party and RSS have to decide which route they want to take from here onwards. If they decide to take the rigid Hindutva route then Yogi will be the obvious choice to lead the army of Hindutva soldiers. If they are ready to tweak Hindutva, to make adjustments for mooknayaks, to accommodate eternal desires for social justice, then a new leader will have to be chosen. This decision will influence the trajectory of Hindutva in the future. The final call will be taken by RSS and not BJP.

Let's not forget, BJP is only a political wing of RSS. It is a part of RSS, not the whole of RSS. Mohan Bhagwat could not have been more right when he said, '[But] politics is not everything. It is not prime importance; it's not at the centre of the scheme, but it is secondary and complementary.'[27]

Modi, Shah and Yogi are only instruments with which Bhagwat plays for the larger goal. They should not imagine that they are the kings who decide. Decisions are made elsewhere; they only play their part.

Epilogue

THE PEOPLE'S VERDICT IN THE 2024 PARLIAMENTARY ELECTIONS has led to the question: has India—or Bharat—been reclaimed? In the run-up to the elections, there was fear that if BJP, along with its allies, managed to get more than 400 seats, changes were likely to be introduced in the Constitution of India. The fear had its roots in the policies pursued by the Modi government and the way the Indian State collaborated with non-State actors in the last ten years. Since 2014, minorities have been deliberately targeted, and especially Muslims have found themselves brutally traumatised and helpless in their own motherland. The spirit of tolerance and democracy had made way for majoritarianism and one ideology rule, and those who did not subscribe to their way of understanding have been marginalised irrespective of their faith. There was major chest-thumping that Modi was the first Hindu ruler, and that he was taking India on the path of becoming a Hindu Rashtra.

It is a matter of common knowledge that Rashtriya Swayamsevak Sangh (RSS) and followers of Hindutva had not been enthusiastic about the Constitution of India that had been crafted under the leadership of B.R. Ambedkar. In their understanding, there was nothing Indian in it; it did not imbibe the spirit of Hindu civilisation. In fact, advocates of Hindu Rashtra wanted Manusmriti to guide national life after Independence. Fortunately, they were in no position to dictate terms. The framers of the Constitution were broad-minded and far-sighted, and they created an all-inclusive Constitution that imbibed the best of both worlds—the East and the West. Despite all the infirmities of Indian society, the Constitution of India has survived for 75 years. Except from 1975 to 1977, when Indira Gandhi imposed the Emergency, its viability was never questioned. Even during the Emergency, there was no attempt to abrogate the Constitution and impose a new one. The Emergency had been imposed through constitutional means and it was withdrawn through constitutional means as well.

Even during the Emergency, which remains a black spot in the history of India, there was no threat to Indian society, especially the Hindu–Muslim unity. No attempt was made to polarise society and/or politics on religious lines. The state was definitely repressive vis-à-vis the political class, but for the public at large, it was not discriminatory in its functioning. Minority communities did not feel orphaned; there was no attempt to 'other' them. The Emergency was the product of a fight between the two ruling classes. On one side of the spectrum was the Congress system, which was challenged by the rest of the political class led by J.P. Narayan. There was not much of an ideological difference between the two blocks. The government and the opposition both had a consensus on the Nehruvian ideology and had great faith in the Constitution of India, which was the derivative of the collective wisdom of our freedom fighters, inspired by thousands of years of civilisational values.

Rashtriya Swayamsevak Sangh and Jan Sangh were indeed part of the JP movement, which was launched to unseat Indira Gandhi. Then a marginal force struggling for survival, RSS was desperately looking for legitimacy in the eyes of the people. When JP proposed that all parties fighting Congress then should merge and form one political party, RSS asked its political wing Jan Sangh to do the same. Jan Sangh merged into the Janata Party. Opposition leaders, including JP, were aware of RSS's ideology and its opposition to the Constitution. Jan Sangh and later BJP happily participated in the democratic process despite their stated position vis-à-vis the Constitution. This was the time when, as a political force, they were too small to challenge the Nehruvian consensus. But after the Ram Mandir movement, the situation slowly but surely changed.

By 2014 the landscape of Indian politics transformed dramatically. The ideology that had opposed the Constitution of India emerged as a dominant force. Bharatiya Janata Party replaced the Congress system. This was the first time in independent India that a change of government resulted in a change in the nature of the state. This was due to the fact that BJP's ideology marked a departure from the secular values that had steered India thus far.

All this changed in 2014, and ever since then, serious attempts have been made to undermine the Indian Constitution, Hindu majoritarianism has been openly pursued, and the Hindu religion has 'informally' become the theology of the state. Discrimination in the name of religion has become rampant, the 'othering' of Muslims has been openly pursued, and the government has been complicit in this project. Though the government of the day and BJP/RSS still swear by the Constitution of India, and it has all been done within the framework of Babasaheb

Ambedkar's Constitution, the tension is palpable. The social fabric is tarred, and institutions have surrendered to the dictates of the government. All this led to the conjecture that if BJP were to get more than two-thirds majority in the lower house of Parliament in the 2024 elections, then the party would introduce changes in the Constitution of India.

It is also true that RSS has been always open about its desire to make India a Hindu Rashtra. And when BJP came to power with an absolute majority in 2014, RSS moved several steps in that direction. From 2014 to 2019, the Modi government, with the help of its organisational machine, created a framework to convince a large section of Hindus that Hindu Rashtra was essential to reclaim Bharat's 'Param Vaibhav', to become 'Vishwa Guru', as it was in the past. Once it manufactured the consent of a large section of Hindus, it took the next but more definitive step in its second term between 2019 and 2024. It started the process of making structural changes in the country's body politics. The abrogation of Article 370 was a step in that direction. The Supreme Court verdict on the issue of the Babri Masjid dispute helped the cause of Hindutva immensely. The Citizenship Amendment Act (CAA) and the National Register of Citizens (NRC), both blatant anti-minority laws, were promulgated. Law on Triple Talaq was also brought in. Prime Minister Modi, his cabinet colleagues and BJP chief ministers have had absolutely no qualms in aligning themselves with the Hindu religion.

This whole exercise had a single objective. As Sunil Ambekar, an RSS leader, puts it, 'RSS has only one goal—making India great.'[1] In its quest to make India great again, RSS has to make India—or Bharat—a Hindu Rashtra, and Hindutva is the vehicle that will make it a reality. Rashtriya Swayamsevak Sangh believes that it is because Hindus as a nation have moved away from the Hindu way of life that they had to suffer the humiliation of being ruled first by Islam and later by Christianity for almost a thousand years. And so, if Bharat had to rise again and reclaim its past glory, then the spirit of Hindu-ness has to be inculcated and regenerated in the psyche of Hindus. Without mincing words, Mohan Bhagwat says, 'The greatest challenge to our movement is to make everybody accept the fact they are Hindus and to create such a united force that would force any aggressor to think before trying to hurt Hindus. You will be heard only if you have a good standing in the world.'[2]

Rashtriya Swayamsevak Sangh's call to make India great again by transforming the country into a Hindu Rashtra is surprisingly akin to what Mussolini said in his 1922 speech in Naples. 'We have created our myth. The myth is a faith, a passion. It is not necessary for it to be reality .... Our myth is the nation, our myth is the greatness of the nation!'[3] Therefore, one can say that the 'harnessing the emotion of nostalgia' that Jason Stanley mentions in his book and its reclamation are integral parts of the same project. Rashtriya Swayamsevak Sangh has used the art of myth-making about the past and its retrieval in the present as the most potent emotional weapon to exploit the sentiment of the people for its political agenda, which is a hallmark of fascist politics. Stanley very succinctly describes this. He says, 'Fascist leaders appeal to history to replace the actual historical record with glorious mythic replacement that, in its specifics, can serve their political ends.'[4]

Strangely, the concept of Hindu Rashtra has not been defined in a structured manner. It is basically a stray thought, a collection of ideas. A vague answer is given when asked what Hindu Rashtra is. Sunil Ambekar says, 'Hindu nation [Rashtra] is a result of thousands of years of experiential living and history. It is not an ism propelled by any political or economic motivation. It is a comprehensive conception of civilisation developed through the observance of certain values and cultural way of life.'[5] A high-ranking official of RSS, H.V. Seshadri, says, 'It [Hindu Rashtra] is the supreme fact of this soil, and what the advocates of Hindu Rashtra are trying to do is just make our people realise this inmost reality of our national life and live in tune with it.'[6] Another RSS leader, Saji Narayanan, writes, 'The Hindu nation is a continuous organic personality, a complete being, and a living being, and a living unity that is ever evolving and ever progressing.'[7] Mohan Bhagwat creates more confusion when he says, 'There is no need to define Hindutva in any manner. Trying to define such things fuels confusion.'[8]

Paradoxically, despite M.S. Golwalkar's stated position that Muslims have to live in India with the benevolence of Hindus, like second-class citizens and will not have even civil rights,[9] RSS leaders claim that no discrimination will be observed in Hindu Rashtra on the basis of religion. Seshadri claims, 'No protagonist of the Hindu Rashtra even said that Hindus would receive preferential treatment and Muslims would be reduced to second-grade citizens in free Bharat. They all clearly affirmed that Bharat would be ruled under the democratic system of "one man, one vote, irrespective of one's faith." So, there was no question of any discrimination involved in the concept of Hindu Rashtra against Muslims that warranted separate protection for them as against the Hindus.'[10]

But the opposite has been true under Modi's regime. In the name of reclaiming Bharat, not only were Muslims targeted, but efforts were also made to erase the history of the medieval period and signs related to Muslim rulers. Similar to Babri Masjid, claims were made about several mosques having been constructed after demolishing Hindu temples. Besides the Gyanvapi mosque in Varanasi and Eidgah in Mathura, there were claims of several other Muslim places of worship having been Hindu at some point in history. Even courts ordered surveys at such places despite the Places of Worship Acts, 1991. Renaming of cities and other places that had been named after Muslim rulers was initiated at a massive scale. In the eyes of RSS, this was done to reclaim the lost history. Sunil Ambekar says, 'Renaming is an important part of the reclamation project. There are tangible cultural products flowing from this reclamation project, like the Ramayana Express, trains on the Ramayana route and restoration of Nalanda University.'[11]

This project is huge. It is being done at an industrial level. Sunil Ambekar further writes, 'Renaming is only one part; the reclamation projects demands massive research output. Our universities and students must rise to this task of rediscovering and reclaiming India. Popular genre formats of short films, plays, documentaries, cinema and songs should also help in spreading this awareness. ... The boards of study of different universities need to review their syllabi. Unhistorical representations and narrations have to be expunged. This is not the work of any one individual or organisation. There has to be societal involvement in identifying and examining issues.'[12]

For the RSS, the past is expandable. The reclamation project did not stop only with medieval history. Since 2014, it has expanded beyond that. In the guise of decolonisation of Hindu minds, the process of rewriting the history of freedom struggle and of independent India is also on. Rashtriya Swayamsevak Sangh believes that the English-educated elite of the country has done a great disservice to the nation, as they have contempt for the Hindu civilisation and are scared to call themselves Hindus. They are of the opinion that the British deliberately promoted the thought that Hindu civilisation was inferior and English rule was a civilising project to make inhabitants of India members of a civilised world. Dattopant Thengadi, one of the tall leaders of RSS, writes, 'Macauley's policy of education, the endeavour to mislead Indians, push them into self-forgetfulness, and make them a self-abnegating race had erroneous translation as one of its important organs ... what was surprising and shameful is that English educated Indian scholars and academics became the willing progeny of Macaulay and blindly adopted every act of his including the deliberate distortion's in translation his educational policy envisaged and engineered.'[13]

It is frightening to see how much contempt and disrespect RSS and its followers have for the English-educated elite or for those who do not subscribe to their thought process. Thengadi writes, 'Most members of this new tribe of intellectuals are cunning people. Their interest does not lie in the actual truth. Because they are cunning by nature and disposition, they realise quite quickly that it is only by producing and publicising those theories and conclusions that align with the vested interests of the owners of the means of communication, i.e., the media, that their own vested interests will be served. Such insincere intellectuals know very well which side of the bread is buttered and decide well beforehand what theory, idea, or conclusion can peddle. The only question that remains, therefore, is how to dress up the available facts so that only desired and favourable conclusions can emerge. These present-day 'thinkers' have become highly proficient in this particular art. In fact, this art is not only their profession but also their sole means of livelihood and the basis of their fame and acclaim. Such a manner of thinking is termed as "hypocritical" in English.'[14] One can easily trace RSS's contempt for the Constitution from Thengadi's conclusions when he says, 'The modern-day progeny of Macaulay carries the proclivity to accept the opinions and conclusions of Western thinkers in toto. This opinionated habit of blind acceptance of the master's opinion, whether Western or Eastern, as authority was not acceptable to Sri Guruji.'[15]

The adherence to the Constitution has always been a contentious issue for RSS and its political wing, Jan Sangh and BJP. In the 2024 general election, BJP's commitment to the Constitution became a big issue. It was also a major reason for the BJP not getting 272 seats, which was needed for the majority mark in the Lok Sabha. The 'Save the Constitution' campaign by the opposition unsettled a large section of Dalits and other backward communities. For BJP and its mother organisation, RSS, the past came back to haunt them. Despite several public declarations by the prime minister and home minister that BJP has no plans to ever change the Constitution, Dalits and followers of Ambedkar were not convinced.

Bharatiya Janata Party has always been aware of its electoral vulnerabilities in these social groups. However, for the Hindu unity project, RSS needed to mask its problematic ideological content. Thus began the process of appropriating Babasaheb Ambedkar and Mahatma Gandhi. This exercise was part of a deception game but helped them gain legitimacy for their reclamation project to a certain extent.

This was an audacious attempt as both the stalwarts of Indian history have been bitter critics of Hindutva, Hindu Rashtra and RSS's visceral hatred for the Muslims. In fact, Ambedkar had gone to the extent of saying, 'If Hindu Raj does become a fact, it will, no doubt, be the greatest calamity for this country. No matter what the Hindus say, Hinduism is a menace to liberty, equality and fraternity. On that account, it is incompatible with democracy. Hindu Raj must be prevented at any cost.'[16]

Despite calling himself a Sanatani Hindu, even Gandhi did not trust RSS and Golwalkar and never subscribed to their concept of Hindutva. The bitter truth is that the politics of

Hindutva and its translation on the ground under the Modi regime is diametrically opposite to Gandhi's idea of Hinduism. Gandhi has said, 'India's good lay in the unity of heart between Hindus and Muslims .... Three-fourths of India can never enjoy freedom if they remain hostile to the remaining one-fourth. The extermination of seven crore Muslims is equally impossible.... I, therefore, advise every Hindu to place full trust in his Muslim brethren. Man by nature is pure in his heart, and Muslims are no exception to this law.'[17] If RSS's Hindutva, by its own admission, has been engaged in 1,200 years of war with Islam, then Gandhi, on the other hand, says that 'the essence of Hinduism is truth and non-violence . . . The active manifestation of non-violence is love—the absence of ill will.'[18] Since 2014, India has witnessed State-sponsored unprecedented ill will and hostility towards Muslims.

Gandhi and Ambedkar have been equally critical of Muslim politics in their own ways. Ambedkar was scathing when he talked about it. He said, 'Muslim politicians do not recognise secular categories of life as the basis of their politics because to them it means weakening of the community in its fight against the Hindus.'[19] He further writes, 'If the Muslims in other countries have undertaken the task of reforming their society and Muslims of India refused to do so, it is because the former are free from communal and political clashes with rival communities, while the latter are not.'[20] Gandhi says, 'Though, in my opinion, non-violence has a predominant place in the Koran, the thirteen hundred years of imperialistic expansion has made the Mussalmans fighters as a body. They are, therefore, aggressive. Bullying is the natural excrescence of an aggressive spirit.'[21]

Gandhi and Ambedkar differed with each other on a range of issues but agreed on one principle that in India, every religion should have equality of space and there should be no discrimination on the basis of religion; both were opposed to spreading venom against any religion including Islam as is done by RSS and their affiliate organisations. Gandhi was a devout Hindu, but he said, 'Hinduism tells everyone to worship God according to his own faith or dharma, and so it lives at peace with all the religions.'[22]

Ambedkar was a bitter critic of Gandhi but it was Gandhi who proposed Ambedkar's name for the chairmanship of the drafting committee of the Constitution of India. The Constitution drafted under the leadership of Ambedkar laid the foundation of a modern, secular and democratic republic that espouses equality, liberty and fraternity and insists on the creation of a society with a scientific temper. Jawaharlal Nehru and Sardar Patel were committed to making India a secular country based on the Constitution. They were aware of the poison of Hindu communalism, and both, as members of the cabinet, fought this menace with full force. When asked which one is more dangerous, communism or communalism, Nehru categorically stated, 'The danger to India, mark you, is not communism. It is Hindu right-wing communalism.'[23] Nehru had no confusion about RSS. In his letter to Patel dated 27 October 1948, he wrote, 'The R.S.S. have a definite ideology which is entirely opposed to that of the Government and the Congress. They oppose definitely the idea of a secular state. In fact, their ideology strikes at the root of our Constitution, present and future.'[24]

There is no doubt that Patel had a soft corner for RSS, but he also had no confusion in his mind. In 1949 in Chennai (then Madras), he said, 'The government is dealing with the movement of RSS. They forcefully want to make this country Hindu Rashtra or want to impose Hindu culture. No government will tolerate this.'[25] In the same speech, he said, 'I have given them an open offer: change your plans, leave secrecy, leave the communal fight, respect Indian constitution, prove your loyalty to tricolour and make us believe that we can trust you. Say something and do something; this game we won't let you play.'[26]

The reclamation project of RSS/BJP is an attempt to annihilate the India of the dreams of Gandhi, Nehru, Ambedkar, Subhas Chandra Bose, Abul Kalam Azad and Patel. This exercise has been going on full steam over the last ten years. The brute reality is that India lost much ground to RSS's reclamation project under the Modi regime. This is not the India we grew up in, reading about its great civilisational values of truth, non-violence, compassion and tolerance, which define what Hindu is and what it is to be a Hindu. Since 2014, hate-mongering and spreading Islamophobia, killing the best traditions of the Constitution, and mauling the democratic spirit have been done in the name of uniting Hindus and decolonising Indian minds. The 2024 election was a fight to stall this project and reclaim India, that is, Bharat, in the true sense — the country which takes great pride in its multiculturalism, celebrates diversity, swears by its Constitution and breathes democracy; the country that does not spread venom against any religion, community or race and honestly believes in Vasudhaiva Kutumbakam (the whole world is a family). As Gandhi said, 'India is the home of Muslims no less than of Hindus.'[27]

The 2024 elections did partly help to reclaim the 'Idea of India' which was so dear to our freedom fighters and the real essence of our civilisation. It's a marginal victory. It is only a jolt. In the post-2024 elections scenario, BJP's position has weakened, and the Modi government's survival depends on its allies, many of which swear by secularism. The opposition today is much stronger, and under the leadership of Rahul Gandhi, the INDIA has not left any stone unturned to expose the government's follies. Prime Minister Modi is more subdued, and RSS too has realised that the time has come to stop, reflect, and take stock of gains and losses.

The 2024 elections have definitely shaken RSS and its followers. They are forced to question why, despite Modi's charisma, organisational leviathan and immense resources, BJP failed to touch the majority mark in the lower house of the Parliament. Why did Modi's victory margin shrink massively in Varanasi? Why did BJP lose in Faizabad—and that too at a time when the Ram Mandir consecration was still fresh in the minds of the people? Why did BJP have to face humiliation in UP despite their firebrand Hindutva icon and potentially future leader Yogi Adityanath? Why did Maharashtra slip out of its hands in the parliamentary election, and why did it fail to break new ground in south India? And why did BJP's vote share shrink in comparison to the 2019 elections?

The entire RSS family is undergoing internal turmoil. It is going through an ideological churning that can potentially create a wedge among its core leadership. It is faced with three serious issues that the 2024 election has posed before it. One, personality-based politics has its limitations. Modi has lost his sheen, and unlike in the past, he alone can't win elections—though within its ideological framework, RSS/BJP discourage individualism and believe in collectivism; for them, organisation is supreme and the individual is secondary, but with the rise of Modi, RSS/BJP made way for charisma and compromised with Modi's whims. Rashtriya Swayamsevak Sangh has realised that in the last ten years, organisations, despite phenomenal growth, have suffered a lot, which in the long run will damage both BJP and RSS. No wonder that, in subsequent assembly elections in Haryana, Maharashtra, Jammu and Kashmir, Jharkhand and Delhi, Modi took a back seat, and RSS as an organisation took charge of the steering. In the future, too, better coordination will be seen at two levels—between the leader and the organisation, and between BJP and RSS.

Second, unidimensional Hindutva has taken BJP this far, but if Hindutva is to become a pan-India phenomenon, then it has to be multidimensional; only spreading hatred against Muslims and other minorities will not fetch them new votes. In 2014, BJP, led by Modi, succeeded because Modi's packaging was attractive, presenting him as the leader of Hindutva Plus. He was seen as a Hindu leader who had the capacity to take India on a developmental path and could 'make India great again'. In 2019, voters thought Modi should be given another chance to prove that the Gujarat model was not a chimaera. But by 2024, that image proved to be hollow. Modi failed to address the important issues of price rise and unemployment. Instead, Modi and BJP heavily banked on Ram Mandir's consecration. When this approach did not click with Hindu voters, the whole party was left with no choice but to resort to Muslim bashing. In the end, anti-incumbency took its toll in the 2024 elections. Going forward, if BJP has to remain a hegemonic power, then it must rediscover that mojo of Hindutva Plus.

Third, Hindutva has to reform itself if it wants to broaden its area of influence among Hindus. One of BJP's biggest failures in this election was that it failed to conclusively answer questions raised by Dalits and a large section of OBCs. The issue of Caste Census and the 'Save Constitution' campaign became huge; it established a direct connection with the marginalised sections of the society, particularly with Dalits. Despite repeated clarifications by BJP that the Constitution would not be tampered with, Dalits and Ambedkarites did not believe it and organised themselves to stop the march of Hindu Rashtra. The party and its parent organisation RSS have to work seriously to erase the perception that Hindutva as an ideology is opposed to the Constitution and that it caters to the interests of the upper caste, especially Brahmins; it has to erase the impression that if Hindu Rashtra were to become a reality then Dalits and all those who are lower in the caste hierarchy will once again be pushed into the medieval age and treated less than a human.

I do not know if Modi and his deputy Amit Shah have seized on the matter, but RSS chief Mohan Bhagwat is definitely aware of the situation. In fact, he has been trying to make changes in the ideology since long before the 2024 elections. In 2018, he shocked his followers when he said that without Muslims, Hindutva is incomplete.[28]

This was a radical departure because RSS was born out of hatred towards Muslims. Bhagwat claimed that everyone's DNA is the same.[29]

This means anyone who lives in India, irrespective of their faith, shares similar DNA. Paradoxically, RSS believes that Islam is a foreign religion, and initially, its followers came from outside India as aggressors. When it became fashionable to claim that every mosque in India has been made over the debris of a temple, Bhagwat said, 'Why look for a "Shivling" in every Masjid?'[30]

In the context of reservation and the Dalit movement, he said, 'Dalits have been treated less than an animal for two thousand years, and now one should be prepared to give them reservation for 200 years.'[31]

His statements are testimony to the fact that long before the 2024 verdict, he realised the limits of Hindutva, and he wanted the RSS to change its ideological track if it wanted to become a pan-India phenomenon. Even after the elections, he took the risk of inviting the wrath of Modi's followers by directly attacking his style of campaigning in the election. Without mentioning

Modi by name, he called him arrogant,[32] someone who thinks of himself as 'God'.[33]

There are two problems with Bhagwat. One, he and RSS have been riding a ferocious tiger, and now he wants to tame the tiger, preach to him to tone down his roar. But in the last hundred years since its inception, RSS has created many generations of Hindus who have been born and brought up with Muslim hate. To ask them to embrace Muslims is asking his followers to disown their own identity, their own being. This is fraught with danger. This can enrage the tiger, and the tiger can turn its fury towards Bhagwat and RSS. Of late, the RSS chief, who is revered as Param Pujniya, whose opinion is the last word, is being severely criticised and abused by Hindutvavadis on social media. Second, why should one assume that Bhagwat is not playing a deception game? His utterances could be a smoke screen while they simultaneously played the good cop and the bad cop. As mentioned earlier, even leaders like Sardar Patel have said that RSS indulges in deception; they say something and do something else.

I am willing to give Bhagwat the benefit of doubt. I am ready to accept that he genuinely wants to change the path that Hindutva has taken in the last hundred years. My friends in RSS have told me that Bhagwat is a worried man today. He is worried as he has realised that if the march of Hindutva is not moderated or does not change its gear, then, like radical Islam, Hindutva would also become discredited, an abuse, not only in India but globally. The severe but almost universal criticism of the Modi regime on the issue of Hindutva in global media, especially in the Western world, has really shaken Bhagwat. Many senior RSS leaders share his opinion, as do a few in BJP. As they see it, if Hindutva doesn't tone down its rhetoric, then the whole purpose of the Hindu unity project is in serious jeopardy, and RSS can't afford to let that happen. In their understanding, Modi and BJP can be driven by their ambition to form a government; RSS is under no such compulsion. For them, politics is secondary; of primary import is reclaiming the past glory of Hindus, which can't be gained if Hindutva and Hindus, per se, turn into a cuss word, which is identified with violence, intolerance and hate. That will be civilisational suicide for RSS.

The results of the 2024 elections are a warning signal. Rashtriya Swayamsevak Sangh's leadership has received the sign too. No wonder that, on the issue of Caste Census, for the sake of Hindu unity, RSS has conceded that it can be—not for politics, rather for welfare purposes. But the rhetoric of '*Batenge toh katenge* (Divided we will be finished) and '*Ek hain toh safe hain* (United we are safe)' used during the Maharashtra and Jharkhand assembly elections soon after the parliamentary elections is also indicative of the fact that there is a war within RSS. Rashtriya Swayamsevak Sangh is known for its conflict resolution mechanism, which is why, in its history, there has been no split in the organisation ever. But then, it has never tasted such enormous power in the past, and ability has its own dynamics. Power has the power to make or break any empire, and RSS is no exception.

In the end, one can safely say that the INDIA led by Congress has a huge role to play. It has succeeded to a large extent in taming the tiger; it has reclaimed a lot of ground in this election. It has managed to weaken the forces of Hindutva. After defeating BJP conclusively in UP and Maharashtra in the Lok Sabha election, it has rekindled the hope that Hindutva is not invincible, and that the march of Hindu Rashtra can be stopped; the India of Gandhi, Nehru, Patel, Bose, Azad and Ambedkar can be reclaimed, provided it is united despite its several contradictions and clash of ambitions.

Notes

Introduction

1 Rakesh Sinha, *Adhunik Bharat ke Nirmata: Dr Keshav Baliram Hedgewar* (Prakashan Vibhag, Information and Broadcasting Ministry, Government of India, 2022), p. 179.
2 Devendra Swarup (ed.), *Deen Dayal Upadhyay's Integral Humanism* (Deen Dayal Research Institute, 1992), p. 46.
3 Swarup (ed.), *Deen Dayal Upadhyay's Integral Humanism*, p. 48.
4 A.G. Noorani, *The RSS: A Menace to India* (Left Word, 2019), p. 41.
5 Noorani, *The RSS*, p. 260.
6 Jason Stanley, *How Fascism Work: The Politics of US and Them* (Random House, 2020), pp. 30–31.
7 Francis Fukuyama, *Identity: The Demand for Dignity and the Politics of Resentment* (Picador, 2019), p. xvi.

1: Indian Politics and the Hindu Right

1 The legend goes that Ganga is a celestial river which landed on this planet, and the force of it would have caused damage to the world so Shiva took it on his head and let it flow through his hair gently down the Himalayan slopes.

2 '"Varanasi Is Like Mother … Maa Ganga Has Adopted Me": PM Modi', *The Economic Times*, 6 May 2024, https://economictimes.indiatimes.com/news/elections/lok-sabha/uttar-pradesh/varanasi-is-like-mother-maa-ganga-has-adopted-me-pm-modi/articleshow/109893295.cms?from=mdr.

3 '"Varanasi Is Like Mother … Maa Ganga Has Adopted Me": PM Modi'.

4 'Nehru's Will: Let My Ashes Scatter Over Fields and Mingle with the Dust and Soil of India', *National Herald*, 27 May 2020, https://www.nationalheraldindia.com/india/nehrus-will-let-my-ashes-scatter-over-fields-and-mingle-with-the-dust-and-soil-of-india.

5 'Nehru's Will: Let My Ashes Scatter Over Fields and Mingle with the Dust and Soil of India'.

6 Raj Chengappa, 'Mood of the Nation Poll | PM Modi and the BJP: Heading for a Hat-trick', *India Today*, 19 February 2024, https://www.indiatoday.in/magazine/cover-story/story/20240219-mood-of-the-nation-poll-pm-modi-and-the-bjp-heading-for-a-hat-trick-2499624-2024-02-09.

7 Chengappa, 'Mood of the Nation Poll | PM Modi and the BJP: Heading for a Hat-trick'.

8 Chengappa, 'Mood of the Nation Poll | PM Modi and the BJP: Heading for a Hat-trick'.

9 Chengappa, 'Mood of the Nation Poll | PM Modi and the BJP: Heading for a Hat-trick'.

10 'Unemployment Rate Rises to 45-Year High of 6.1% in FY18: Official Data', *Mint*, 31 May 2019, https://www.livemint.com/news/india/unemployment-rate-rises-to-45-year-high-of-6-1-in-fy18-official-data-1559306879836.html.

11 Assembly Elections Results 2023 | BJP Sweeps Madhya Pradesh, Rajasthan, Chhattisgarh; Congress to Bag Telangana', *The Hindu*, 3 December 2023, https://www.thehindu.com/elections/assembly-elections-2023-results-updates/article67600459.ece.

12 Sanjay Kumar, 'Pro-BJP Wave, Not Anti-Congress, Powered 2023 Assembly Election Results', *Frontline*, 13 December 2023, https://frontline.thehindu.com/politics/bjp-wave-welfare-schemes-modi-popularity-women-voters-2023-assembly-election-results-analysis/article67618017.ece.

13 Swapan Dasgupta, 'Ayodhya: Congress Boycott Sends Clear Message', *The Times of India*, 13 January 2024, https://timesofindia.indiatimes.com/india/ayodhya-congress-boycott-sends-clear-message/articleshow/106816919.cms.

14 Prithvijit Mitra, B.S. Anilkumar and A. Ragu Raman, 'As Temple Comes Up in North, Ram Finds More Worshippers in South, East', *The Times of India*, 21 January 2024, https://timesofindia.indiatimes.com/india/as-temple-comes-up-in-north-ram-finds-more-worshippers-in-south-east/articleshow/107025461.cms.

15 Mitra, Anilkumar and Raman, 'As Temple Comes Up in North, Ram Finds More Worshippers in South, East'.

16 Mitra, Anilkumar and Raman, 'As Temple Comes Up in North, Ram Finds More Worshippers in South, East'.

17 Gary Grestle, *The Rise and Fall of the Neo Liberal Order: America and the world in the Market Era* (Oxford University Press, 2023), p. 3.

18 Grestle, *The Rise and Fall of the Neo Liberal Order*.

19 Grestle, *The Rise and Fall of the Neo Liberal Order*.

20 R. Jagannathan, 'The Ayodhya Moment', *The Times of India*, 23 January 2024, https://timesofindia.indiatimes.com/blogs/toi-editorials/the-ayodhya-moment/.

21 R. Jagannathan, 'The Ayodhya Moment'.

22 R. Jagannathan, 'The Ayodhya Moment'.

23 'From Dev to Desh, Ram to Rashtra: PM Modi', *The Times of India*, 23 January 2024, https://timesofindia.indiatimes.com/india/pm-modi-speech-devotion-for-lord-ram-and-nationbuilding/articleshow/107064182.cms.

24 'From Dev to Desh, Ram to Rashtra: PM Modi'.

25 'From Dev to Desh, Ram to Rashtra: PM Modi'.

26 Nilanjan Mukhopadhyay, 'After Ayodhya: Will Modi's New Era End Old Conflicts?', *The Asian Age*, 1 February 2024, https://www.asianage.com/opinion/columnists/310124/after-ayodhya-will-modis-new-era-end-old-conflicts.html.

27 Mukhopadhyay, 'After Ayodhya: Will Modi's New Era End Old Conflicts?'

28 Mukhopadhyay, 'After Ayodhya: Will Modi's New Era End Old Conflicts?'

29 https://timesofindia.indiatimes.com/blogs/toi-editorials/after-consecration/

30 Aniruddha Dhar, 'Will Ayodhya Ram Mandir Help Realise PM Modi, BJP's 400 Lok Sabha Seats Dream?', *Hindustan Times*, 22 January 2024, https://www.hindustantimes.com/india-news/will-ayodhya-ram-mandir-pran-pratishtha-ceremony-change-poll-fortunes-for-pm-modi-bjp-101705920876411.html.

31 Hilal Ahmed, 'Mandir Mathematics', *The Times of India*, 22 January 2024, https://timesofindia.indiatimes.com/blogs/toi-edit-page/mandir-mathematics/.
32 Nalin Verma, 'Why Nitish Kumar Dumped BJP and What It Means for Opposition Parties', *The Wire*, 9 August 2022, https://thewire.in/politics/nitish-kumar-nda-exit-opposition-parties.
33 Verma, 'Why Nitish Kumar Dumped BJP and What It Means for Opposition Parties'.
34 Rajdeep Sardesai, 'As Nitish Kumar Breaks Up with BJP Yet Again, What Next for Bihar Politics? Key Takeaways', *India Today*, 9 August 2022, https://www.indiatoday.in/india/story/nitish-kumar-break-up-jdu-bjp-bihar-politics-key-takeaways-1985726-2022-08-09.
35 Nalin Verma, '16 Parties Vow to Unitedly Fight the BJP, Hark Back to Patna's Historic Role in Opposition Unity', *The Wire*, 23 June 2023, https://thewire.in/politics/patna-amidst-aap-congress-sparring-16-opposition-parties-vow-to-unitedly-fight-the-bjp.
36 'NDA Meeting in Delhi Updates: NDA's Vote Share in the 2024 Elections Will Be Over 50 per cent, says PM', *Mint*, 19 July 2023, https://www.livemint.com/news/india/nda-meeting-live-updates-bjp-pm-modi-amit-shah-chirag-paswan-ajit-pawar-meeting-in-delhi-nda-38-vs-opposition-26-11689649746366-page-2.html.
37 Ashutosh, 'Why Is Modi Scared of INDIA?', *The Diplomat*, 1 August 2023, https://thediplomat.com/2023/08/why-is-modi-scared-of-india/.
38 Ashutosh, 'Why Is Modi Scared of INDIA?'.
39 'Express View of INDIA's Mumbai meeting: Plus and Minus', *The Indian Express*, 4 September 2023, https://indianexpress.com/article/opinion/editorials/express-view-on-indias-mumbai-meeting-plus-and-minus-8922861/.
40 'Doubt Congress Will Get "Even 40 Seats" in Lok Sabha Polls: Mamata Banerjee', *The Economic Times*, 3 February 2024, https://economictimes.indiatimes.com/news/elections/lok-sabha/india/doubt-congress-will-get-even-40-seats-in-lok-sabha-polls-mamata-banerjee/articleshow/107368759.cms?from=mdr
41 'Why Nitish Kumar Left INDIA Bloc to Rejoin BJP-led NDA', *Mint*, 28 January 2024, https://www.livemint.com/politics/why-nitish-kumar-left-india-bloc-to-join-bjp-led-nda-bihar-politics-jdu-rjd-alliance-11706435699140.html.

2: The Constitution Debate

1 Quoted in Ramachandra Guha, 'Dangers of Hero Worship: Reading Ambedkar in the Time of Modi', *The Telegraph Online*, 3 May 2014, https://www.telegraphindia.com/opinion/dangers-of-hero-worship-reading-ambedkar-in-the-time-of-modi/cid/186946.

2 Quoted in Praveen Davar, 'Reacknowledging Ambedkar's Role as the Architect of India's Constitution', *The Wire*, 6 December 2023, https://thewire.in/history/reacknowledging-role-ambedkar-architect-india-constitution.

3 Ashutosh, 'Do the Election Results Indicate that the Nation Is Saved?', *The Free Press Journal*, 17 June 2024, https://www.freepressjournal.in/analysis/do-the-election-results-indicate-that-the-nation-is-saved.

4 Pratap Bhanu Mehta, 'Pratap Bhanu Mehta on 2024 Lok Sabha Election Results: Suffocating Shadow Has Lifted, Balance Restored', *The Indian Express*, 5 June 2024, https://indianexpress.com/article/opinion/columns/2024-lok-sabha-election-results-narendra-modi-9371534/.

5 Ashutosh Varshney, 'In the Results of 2024 Elections, Rebirth of the "Idea of India"', *The Indian Express*, 6 June 2024, https://indianexpress.com/article/opinion/columns/in-the-results-of-2024-elections-rebirth-of-the-idea-of-india-9374591/.

6 Swapan Dasgupta, 'Western Media's Already Out to Undermine Legitimacy of a Modi Win', *The Times of India*, 20 April 2024, https://timesofindia.indiatimes.com/india/western-medias-already-out-to-undermine-legitimacy-of-a-modi-win/articleshow/109462233.cms.

7 Dasgupta, 'Western Media's Already Out to Undermine Legitimacy of a Modi Win'.

8 Dasgupta, 'Western Media's Already Out to Undermine Legitimacy of a Modi Win'.

9 Abhishek Kumar Singh, 'This Time, BJP Will Get 370+ and NDA Over 400 Seats, Asserts PM', *The Times of India*, 9 February 2024, https://timesofindia.indiatimes.com/india/this-time-bjp-will-get-370-and-nda-over-400-seats-asserts-pm/articleshow/107438477.cms.

10 Singh, 'This Time, BJP Will Get 370+ and NDA Over 400 Seats, Asserts PM'.

11 Singh, 'This Time, BJP Will Get 370+ and NDA Over 400 Seats, Asserts PM'.
12 'People Will Bless BJP with 370 LS Seats as It Abrogated Article 370; NDA to Get Over 400 Seats: Shah', *The Print*, 10 February 2024, https://theprint.in/india/people-will-bless-bjp-with-370-ls-seats-as-it-abrogated-article-370-nda-to-get-over-400-seats-shah/1961693/.
13 'NDA Will Win More Than 400 Seats in LS Polls, and All 80 in UP: CM Yogi Adityanath', *The Times of India*, 1 March 2024, https://timesofindia.indiatimes.com/city/lucknow/nda-will-win-more-than-400-seats-in-ls-polls-and-all-80-in-up-cm-yogi/articleshow/108120901.cms.
14 Anastasia Piliavsky and Vikramaditya Thakur, 'Samvidhan: Sita of the Election Epic', *The Times of India*, 27 May 2024, https://timesofindia.indiatimes.com/india/samvidhan-sita-of-the-election-epic/articleshow/110471750.cms.
15 Sanchari Ghosh, 'Constitution Should Be Changed to Save Hinduism…: BJP's Anant Hegde on How This Can Happen After Lok Sabha Polls 2024', *Mint*, 10 March 2024, https://www.livemint.com/politics/news/Constitution-should-be-changed-to-save-hinduism-karnataka-bjp-mp-on-how-this-can-happen-after-lok-sabha-elections-2024-11710055104748.html.
16 Ghosh, 'Constitution Should Be Changed to Save Hinduism…: BJP's Anant Hegde on How This Can Happen After Lok Sabha Polls 2024'.
17 Hamza Khan, 'Another BJP Candidate's Remarks on "Amending Constitution" Give Ammo to Congress', *The Indian Express*, 4 April 2024, https://indianexpress.com/article/india/bjp-candidates-remarks-on-amending-constitution-give-ammo-to-congress-9247529/.
18 Khan, 'Another BJP Candidate's Remarks on "Amending Constitution" Give Ammo to Congress'.
19 Shashi Tharoor (@ShashiTharoor), 'After Anant Hegde let the cat out of …', X, 2 April 2024, https://x.com/ShashiTharoor/status/1775049739630960708.
20 Arshad Afzaal Khan, 'BJP MP Lands in Row for Remark on "Constitution"', *The Times of India*, 15 April 2024, https://timesofindia.indiatimes.com/city/lucknow/bjp-mp-lands-in-row-for-remark-on-Constitution/articleshow/109298708.cms.
21 Khan, 'BJP MP Lands in Row for Remark on "Constitution"'.
22 Khan, 'BJP MP Lands in Row for Remark on "Constitution"'.

23 Amit Bhelari, 'Dalits and Poor Will Gouge Out Eyes of Those Trying to Change the Constitution, Says Lalu', *The Hindu*, 16 April 2024, https://www.thehindu.com/elections/lok-sabha/dalits-and-poor-will-gouge-out-eyes-of-those-trying-to-change-the-Constitution-says-lalu/article68067928.ece.

24 'BJP Wants to Win 400-Plus Seats to Change Constitution, Says Uddhav', *Business Standard*, 8 May 2024, https://www.business-standard.com/elections/lok-sabha-election/bjp-wants-to-win-400-plus-seats-to-change-Constitution-says-uddhav-124050800011_1.html.

25 Abhay Singh and Alok Kumar, 'PM Modi Counters Opposition: "I'm Indebted to Constitution, It's Article of Faith for Us"', *The Times of India*, 17 April 2024, https://timesofindia.indiatimes.com/india/pm-modi-counters-opposition-im-indebted-to-Constitution-its-article-of-faith-for-us/articleshow/109356230.cms.

26 Sahil Sinha, 'Babasaheb Ambedkar Himself Can't Abolish Constitution Now: PM Slams Opposition', *India Today*, 12 April 2024, https://www.indiatoday.in/elections/lok-sabha/story/modi-on-bjp-changing-constitution-babasaheb-ambedkar-congress-remark-rajasthan-2526514-2024-04-12.

27 Vijay Pinjarkar, 'Want 400+ Seats for Reforms, Not to End Reservation: Shah', *The Times of India*, 24 April 2024, https://timesofindia.indiatimes.com/india/want-400-seats-for-reforms-not-to-end-reservation-shah/articleshow/109542059.cms.

28 Diwakar, Akhilesh Singh, Sidhartha, '"India Does Not Become an Electoral Autocracy if Yuvraj Cannot Get Power": PM Modi', *The Times of India*, 29 April 2024, https://timesofindia.indiatimes.com/india/india-does-not-become-an-electoral-autocracy-if-yuvraj-cannot-get-power/articleshow/109674796.cms.

29 Piliavsky and Thakur, 'Samvidhan: Sita of the Election Epic'.

30 Ashutosh Varshney, 'In the Results of 2024 Elections, Rebirth of the "Idea of India"', *The Indian Express*, 6 June 2024, https://indianexpress.com/article/opinion/columns/in-the-results-of-2024-elections-rebirth-of-the-idea-of-india-9374591/.

31 Varshney, 'In the Results of 2024 Elections, Rebirth of the "Idea of India"'.

32 Piliavsky and Thakur, 'Samvidhan: Sita of the Election Epic'.

33 Piliavsky and Thakur, 'Samvidhan: Sita of the Election Epic'.

34 Sheetal P. Singh interviewed by the author.

35 Shailvee Sharda, 'Thakurs, Other Upper Castes Remained Loyal to BJP in Uttar Pradesh in LS Polls: Survey', *The Times of India*, 16

June 2024, https://timesofindia.indiatimes.com/city/lucknow/thakurs-and-other-upper-castes-remain-loyal-to-bjp-in-up-in-ls-polls-survey/articleshow/111029904.cms.

36 Sharda, 'Thakurs, Other Upper Castes Remained Loyal to BJP in Uttar Pradesh in LS Polls: Survey'.

37 Ashutosh, 'This General Election Could Bring Changes Like No Other in India', *The Diplomat*, 5 April 2024, https://thediplomat.com/2024/04/this-general-election-could-bring-changes-like-no-other-in-india/.

38 Ashutosh, 'This General Election Could Bring Changes Like No Other in India'.

39 Ashutosh, 'This General Election Could Bring Changes Like No Other in India'.

40 Bibek Debroy, 'There's a Case for "We the People" to Embrace a New Constitution', *Mint*, 14 August 2023, https://www.livemint.com/opinion/online-views/theres-a-case-for-we-the-people-to-embrace-a-new-Constitution-11692021963182.html.

41 Debroy, 'There's a Case for "We the People" to Embrace a New Constitution'.

42 Shamsul Islam, 'How RSS Denigrated the Constitution', *Sab Rang*, 26 November 2021, https://sabrangindia.in/how-rss-denigrated-Constitution/.

43 Islam, 'How RSS Denigrated the Constitution'.

44 Islam, 'How RSS Denigrated the Constitution'.

45 Laws of Manu taken from F. Max Muller, *Laws of Manu* (L P Publications, Delhi, 1996, first published in 1886), as quoted in Islam, 'How RSS Denigrated the Constitution'.

46 Laws of Manu taken from F. Max Muller, *Laws of Manu* (L P Publications, Delhi, 1996, first published in 1886), as quoted in Islam, 'How RSS Denigrated the Constitution'.

47 A.G. Noorani, 'Is Constitution Anti-Hindu or RSS Anti-Indian', *Deccan Chronicle*, 29 September 2019, https://www.deccanchronicle.com/opinion/columnists/290919/is-constitution-anti-hindu-or-the-rss-anti-indian.html.

48 Noorani, 'Is Constitution Anti-Hindu or RSS Anti-Indian'.

49 Kuldeep Kumar, 'RSS and the Constitution: Ram Bahadur Rai's Comments Come at An Inopportune Moment', *The Wire*, 9 June 2016, https://thewire.in/politics/rss-and-the-Constitution-ram-bahadur-rais-comments-come-at-an-inopportune-moment.

50 Noorani, 'Is Constitution Anti-Hindu or RSS Anti-Indian'.

51 A.G. Noorani, *The RSS: A Menace to India* (Left Word Books, 2019), p. 260.
52 Ashutosh, 'This General Election Could Bring Changes Like No Other in India'.
53 Ashutosh, 'Analysis: Why Changing the Constitution Is Cause for Alarm', *The Free Press Journal*, 8 April 2024, https://www.freepressjournal.in/analysis/analysis-why-changing-the-Constitution-is-cause-for-alarm.
54 Ashutosh, 'Analysis: Why Changing the Constitution Is Cause for Alarm'.
55 Ashutosh, 'Analysis: Why Changing the Constitution Is Cause for Alarm'.
56 Ashutosh, 'Analysis: Why Changing the Constitution Is Cause for Alarm'.
57 Ashutosh, 'Analysis: Why Changing the Constitution Is Cause for Alarm'.

3: The Divinity Factor

1 Original transcript: 'पिछली बार जब मैंने आपका इंटरव्यू लिया था और बहुत से लोग हैं जिन्होंने इस सवाल पर बहुत खिल्लियाँ उड़ाई हैं लेकिन वो सवाल मैंने इसलिये पूछा था कि खेत में गन्ना काट रही एक औरत ने मुझसे कहा था और आज फिर मैं वो सवाल आप से पूछूंगी । पाँच साल पहले मैंने आपसे कहा था कि आप थकते क्यों नहीं हैं । आज पाँच साल बीत जाने के बाद आप ज़्यादा मुझे एनर्जेटिक लग रहे हैं ज्यादा आपने रैलियाँ की हैं, ज़्यादा आप काम कर रहे हैं । आप वाकई थकते क्यों नहीं हैं ।'
2 Original transcript: 'पहले जब तक माँ ज़िंदा थी मुझे लगता था कि शायद biologically मुझे जन्म दिया गया है। माँ के जाने के बाद इन सारे अनुभवों को जोड़ कर मैं देखता हूँ तो मैं convince हो चुका हूँ, ग़लत हो सकता हूँ, लेफ़्टिस्ट लोग तो मेरी धज्जियाँ उड़ा देंगे, मेरे बाल नोच लेंगे, मैं convince हो चुका हूँ कि परमात्मा ने मुझे भेजा है । ये ऊर्जा biological शरीर से नहीं निकली है । ये ऊर्जा ईश्वर ने मुझसे कुछ काम लेना है, इसलिये मुझे विधा भी दी है, और काम करने का सामर्थ्य भी दिया है । इसलिये मुझे नेकदिली भी दी है, और प्रेरणा भी वही दे रहा है । और काम करने का सामर्थ्य भी वही दे रहा है । मैं कुछ नहीं हूँ । एक instrument हूँ । जो ईश्वर ने मेरे रूप में मुझसे लेना तय किया है और इसलिये मैं जब भी कुछ करता हूँ तो मैं मानता हूँ कि ईश्वर मुझसे कुछ करवाना चाहता है कि आपका नाम होगा, चिंता छोड़ो । दूसरा, मैं उस ईश्वर को देख नहीं सकता । मैं भी एक

पुजारी हूँ । मैं भी एक भक्त हूँ । तो मैंने 140 करोड़ देशवासियों को ईश्वर का रूप कर चलता हूँ, वही मेरे भगवान हैं ।'

3 Original transcript: 'आप भगवान के बीच में हैं । और भगवान आपके साथ हैं । माँ आपमें समाई हुई हैं । आपको ख़ूब सारी शुभकामनाएँ ।'

4 'The PM Interview LIVE | PM Modi LIVE Interview with Rubika | PM Modi LIVE | N18L | News18 LIVE', CNN-News18, 14 May 2024, https://www.youtube.com/live/93aGs1ah0So?si=pXM8AD8s88vH_PP1.

5 Sidharth Bhatia, 'Modi's Divine Complex: A Political Ploy or Genuine Self Belief?', *The Wire*, 24 May 2024, https://thewire.in/politics/modis-divine-complex-a-political-ploy-or-genuine-self-belief.

6 Bhatia, 'Modi's Divine Complex'.

7 Manoj Kumar, Aftab Ahmed, 'Low Turnout, Apathy in India Election a Worry for Modi's Campaign', *Reuters*, 2 May 2024, https://www.reuters.com/world/india/low-turnout-apathy-india-election-worry-modis-campaign-2024-05-02/.

8 Kumar and Ahmed, 'Low Turnout, Apathy in India Election a Worry for Modi's Campaign'.

9 'Congress Manifesto Has Muslim League Imprint: PM Modi', *The Times of India*, 7 April 2024, https://timesofindia.indiatimes.com/india/pm-cong-manifesto-has-muslim-league-imprint/articleshow/109095098.cms.

10 'Congress Plans to Redistribute Wealth to "Infiltrators": PM Modi', *The Times of* India, 22 April 2024, https://timesofindia.indiatimes.com/india/congress-plans-to-redistribute-wealth-to-infiltrators-pm-modi/articleshow/109482926.cms.

11 'Congress Plans to Redistribute Wealth to "Infiltrators": PM Modi'.

12 'Congress Plans to Redistribute Wealth to "Infiltrators": PM Modi'.

13 'Show Use of "Hindu", "Muslim" in Nyay Patra: Congress to PM Modi', *The Times of India*, 22 April 2024, https://timesofindia.indiatimes.com/india/show-use-of-hindu-muslim-in-nyay-patra-congress-to-pm-modi/articleshow/109482545.cms.

14 Subodh Ghidiyal, 'Congress Moves EC on PM Modi Speech; Calling a Spade a Spade: BJP', *The Times of India*, 23 April 2024, https://timesofindia.indiatimes.com/india/congress-moves-ec-on-pm-modi-speech-calling-a-spade-a-spade-bjp/articleshow/109511870.cms.

15 https://www.ndtv.com/india-news/bjp-defends-pm-modis-infiltrators-jibe-says-he-called-a-spade-a-spade-5496538
16 Hilal Ahmed, '4 Ideas Have Won the Election', *The Times of India*, 29 May 2024, https://timesofindia.indiatimes.com/blogs/toi-edit-page/4-ideas-have-won-the-election/.
17 'The PM Interview LIVE | PM Modi LIVE Interview with Rubika | PM Modi LIVE | N18L | News18 LIVE', CNN-News18, 14 May 2024, https://www.youtube.com/live/93aGs1ah0So?si=pXM8AD8s88vH_PP1.
18 Sheo Shankar Jaiswal, Gaurav Talwar, 'Congress Razed Rajasthan Temples, Rahul Gandhi Doubted Army's Valour: PM Narendra Modi', *The Times of India*, 12 April 2024, https://timesofindia.indiatimes.com/india/congress-razed-rajasthan-temples-rahul-gandhi-doubted-armys-valour-pm-narendra-modi/articleshow/109227473.cms.
19 The month in the Hindu calender when non vegetarian food is not supposed to be eaten.
20 'PM Modi: Flaunting Meat Videos in Sawan Shows Mughal Mindset', *The Times of India*, 13 April 2024, https://timesofindia.indiatimes.com/india/pm-modi-flaunting-meat-videos-in-sawan-shows-mughal-mindset/articleshow/109256508.cms.
21 'PM Modi: Flaunting Meat Videos in Sawan Shows Mughal Mindset'.
22 'PM Modi Targets Rahul Gandhi: "Congress Shehzada Will Flee from Wayanad Like He Did in Amethi"', *The Indian Express*, 20 April 2024, https://indianexpress.com/article/cities/mumbai/pm-modi-targets-rahul-gandhi-congress-shehzada-will-flee-from-wayanad-9281155/.
23 Hamza Khan, 'Congress Tried to Give Reservation to Muslims by Reducing SC/ST Quota: Modi in Rajasthan', *The Indian Express*, 24 April 2024, https://indianexpress.com/article/india/pm-modi-rajasthan-tonk-speech-congress-muslims-9285772/.
24 Khan, 'Congress Tried to Give Reservation to Muslims by Reducing SC/ST Quota: Modi in Rajasthan'.
25 Khan, 'Congress Tried to Give Reservation to Muslims by Reducing SC/ST Quota: Modi in Rajasthan'.
26 Kancha Ilaiah Shepherd, 'Foreword', in Ali Anwar, *Masawat ki Jung: The Battle for Equality* (Forward Press, 2023), p. xi.
27 Ali Anwar, *Masawat ki Jung: The Battle for Equality*, 2nd edition (Forward Press, 2023), p. 35.
28 Anwar, *Masawat ki Jung*, p. 36.

29 TNN, 'In 1994, Cong in Undivided AP Initiated Muslim Quota Move', *The Times of India*, 24 April 2024, https://timesofindia.indiatimes.com/city/hyderabad/in-1994-cong-in-undivided-ap-initiated-muslim-quota-move/articleshow/109543717.cms.

30 Sahil Sinha, 'BJP Ally Chandrababu Naidu Promises 4% Muslim Reservation in Andhra', *India Today*, 5 May 2024, https://www.indiatoday.in/elections/lok-sabha/story/lok-sabha-polls-chandrababu-naidu-assures-4-reservation-for-muslims-in-andhra-pradesh-2535475-2024-05-05.

31 Marya Shakil, '"Social Justice, Not Appeasement": Key BJP Ally on Reservation for Muslims', *NDTV*, 8 June 2024, https://www.ndtv.com/india-news/chandrababu-naidu-son-muslims-reservation-social-justice-not-appeasement-tdp-nara-lokesh-on-reservation-for-muslims-5838952.

32 'Why the Wind Changes in Rajasthan? | LOKSABHA ELECTION 2024 | SACHIN PILOT | BJP RAJASTHAN', *Satya Hindi*, 18 April 2024, https://youtu.be/ZXZm-Qb5DWY?si=jeHgN4iXe FYX_XGx.

33 'Why the Wind Changes in Rajasthan? | LOKSABHA ELECTION 2024 | SACHIN PILOT | BJP RAJASTHAN'.

34 Diwakar, Akhilesh Singh, Sidhartha, '"India Does Not Become an Electoral Autocracy if Yuvraj Cannot Get Power": PM Modi', *The Times of India*, 29 April 2024, https://timesofindia.indiatimes.com/india/india-does-not-become-an-electoral-autocracy-if-yuvraj-cannot-get-power/articleshow/109674796.cms.

35 Srinivas Rao Apparasu, 'BJP Will Raise SC, ST, OBC Quota, End It for Muslims: Shah in Telangana', *Hindustan Times*, 10 May 2024, https://www.hindustantimes.com/india-news/bjp-will-raise-sc-st-obc-quota-end-it-for-muslims-shah-in-telangana-101715281433012.html.

36 "'If BJP Wins, We Will Scrap Muslim Reservation and Give It to SC, ST, and OBC,' Says Amit Shah in Telangana," *The Times of India*, 9 May 2024, https://timesofindia.indiatimes.com/india/if-bjp-wins-we-will-scrap-muslim-reservation-and-give-it-to-sc-st-and-obc-says-amit-shah-in-telangana/articleshow/109979007.cms.

37 Subodh Ghildiyal, 'PM Modi Rattled by Congress Revolutionary Manifesto: Rahul Gandhi', *The Times of India*, 25 April 2024, https://timesofindia.indiatimes.com/india/pm-modi-rattled-by-congress-revolutionary-manifesto-rahul-gandhi/articleshow/109573181.cms.

38 Ghildiyal, 'PM Modi Rattled by Congress Revolutionary Manifesto: Rahul Gandhi'.

39 Abhijeet Patil, Govind Maad, Murari Shetye, 'It's Congress That Wants to Change the Constitution: PM Modi', *The Times of India*, 28 April 2024, https://timesofindia.indiatimes.com/india/its-congress-that-wants-to-change-Constitution-pm-modi/articleshow/109654630.cms.
40 Diwakar, Akhilesh Singh, Sidhartha, "'India Does Not Become an Electoral Autocracy if Yuvraj Cannot Get Power': PM Modi."
41 'Call for "Vote Jihad" Insult to Democracy, Constitution: PM Modi', *The Times of India*, 3 May 2024, https://timesofindia.indiatimes.com/india/call-for-vote-jihad-insult-to-democracy-Constitution-pm-modi/articleshow/109796189.cms.
42 'Congress Party Is a "Mureed" of Pakistan', *The Times of India*, 2 May 2024, https://timesofindia.indiatimes.com/india/congress-party-is-a-mureed-of-pakistan-pm-modi/articleshow/109779665.cms.
43 Jai Narain Pandey, 'Lalu Tried to Save Those Behind Godhra Train Arson: PM at Rally', *The Times of India*, 5 May 2024, https://timesofindia.indiatimes.com/city/patna/lalu-tried-to-save-those-behind-godhra-train-arson-pm-at-rally/articleshow/109850012.cms.
44 'PM Modi Warns OBCs of SP-Congress's Karnataka Quota Plan for UP', *The Times of India*, 6 May 2024, https://timesofindia.indiatimes.com/india/pm-warns-obcs-of-sp-congs-karnataka-quota-plan-for-up/articleshow/109864980.cms.
45 'Give BJP 400, Ensure Congress Can't Put Babri Lock on Temple: PM Narendra Modi', *The Times of India*, 8 May 2024, https://timesofindia.indiatimes.com/city/indore/give-bjp-400-ensure-congress-cant-put-babri-lock-on-temple-pm-modi/articleshow/109927854.cms.
46 'Give BJP 400, Ensure Congress Can't Put Babri Lock on Temple: PM Narendra Modi'.
47 Sribala Vadlapatla, '"Ram Is the Idea of India, Congress Can't See as It Uses Foreign Lens": PM Modi', *The Times of India*, 11 May 2024, https://timesofindia.indiatimes.com/india/ram-is-the-idea-of-india-congress-cant-see-as-it-uses-foreign-lens-pm-modi/articleshow/110019885.cms.
48 '"Will This Country Run on Sharia?" Union Home Minister Amit Shah Tears into Congress Manifesto', *The Economic Times*, 26 April 2024, https://economictimes.indiatimes.com/news/elections/lok-sabha/india/will-this-country-run-on-sharia-union-home

-minister-amit-shah-tears-into-congress-manifesto/articleshow/109617834.cms?from=mdr.

49 '"Will This Country Run on Sharia?" Union Home Minister Amit Shah Tears into Congress Manifesto'.

50 Asim Ali, 'It's V for Variety', *The Times of India*, 6 May 2024, https://timesofindia.indiatimes.com/india/its-v-for-variety/articleshow/109892241.cms.

51 Bharat Hun and Uday Chandra, 'Election's Caste of Characters', *The Times of India*, 24 May 2024, https://timesofindia.indiatimes.com/blogs/toi-edit-page/elections-caste-of-characters/.

52 Deeptiman Tiwary, 'God Has Chosen Me, Bless Me: Narendra Modi', *The Times of India*, 24 April 2014, https://timesofindia.indiatimes.com/news/god-has-chosen-me-bless-me-narendra-modi/articleshow/34126724.cms.

53 'Past Governments Didn't Build Memorial, God Chose Me for Noble Task, Says PM Modi', *The Indian Express*, 22 October 2018, https://indianexpress.com/article/india/past-governments-didnt-build-memorial-god-chose-me-for-noble-task-says-pm-modi-5411852/.

54 Neelam Pandey, '"God Has Chosen Me to Empower Women,' Says Modi as Govt Tables Women's Reservation Bill in LS," *The Print*, 19 September 2023, https://theprint.in/politics/god-has-chosen-me-to-empower-women-says-modi-as-govt-tables-womens-reservation-bill-in-ls/1768472/.

55 'God Has Chosen Me: PM Begins Religious Exercise', *Rediff.com*, 12 January 2024, https://news.rediff.com/commentary/2024/jan/12/god-has-chosen-me-pm-begins-religious-exercise/92e03ef1100ad2838149a6ff6d2708b0.

56 'Whatever I'm Doing Is Inspired by a Divine Power, God Has Sent Me to Do This Work: PM Modi', *News18*, https://www.news18.com/elections/whatever-im-doing-is-inspired-by-a-divine-power-god-has-sent-me-to-do-this-work-pm-modi-8870459.html.

57 'Oppn's Lies No Longer Work, Get Exposed Within Minutes: PM Modi', *The Times of India*, 23 May 2024, https://timesofindia.indiatimes.com/india/oppns-lies-no-longer-work-get-exposed-within-minutes-pm-modi/articleshow/110343292.cms.

58 Pradeep Gupta and Abhilash Botekar, 'Congress Wanted to Spend 15% of Budget on Muslims: PM Modi', *The Times of India*, 16 May 2024, https://timesofindia.indiatimes.com/india/congress-wanted-to-spend-15-of-budget-on-muslims-pm-modi/articleshow/110157229.cms.

59 'SP-Cong Govt Will Run Bulldozers Over Ram Temple: PM Modi', *The Times of India*, 18 May 2024, https://timesofindia.indiatimes.com/india/sp-cong-govt-will-run-bulldozers-over-ram-temple-pm-modi/articleshow/110221216.cms
60 'Congress Pushing Sharia in Name of Personal Law but BJP Will Bring UCC: PM Modi', *The Times of India*, 25 May 2024, https://timesofindia.indiatimes.com/india/congress-pushing-sharia-in-name-of-personal-law-but-bjp-will-bring-ucc-pm/articleshow/110407010.cms.
61 Nirmanyu Chouhan and Sanjeer Alam, 'CSDS-Lokniti 2024 Pre-poll Survey | Remarkable Support for Religious Pluralism', *The Hindu*, 12 April 2024, https://www.thehindu.com/elections/lok-sabha/csds-lokniti-2024-pre-poll-survey-remarkable-support-for-religious-pluralism/article68055497.ece.
62 Anand Soondas, 'Vocal Dalits, Silent Muslims', *The Times of India*, 19 May 2024, https://timesofindia.indiatimes.com/india/vocal-dalits-silent-muslims/articleshow/110253367.cms.
63 Raj Chengappa, 'India Today Mood of the Nation Poll | Modi All Set to Return', *India Today*, 4 September 2023, https://www.indiatoday.in/magazine/cover-story/story/20230904-india-today-mood-of-the-nation-poll-modi-all-set-to-return-2426489-2023-08-25.
64 Ashutosh, 'Why Did Modi's Usage of Divinity as a Political Instrument Not Succeed?', *The Diplomat*, 11 June 2024, https://thediplomat.com/2024/06/why-did-modis-usage-of-divinity-as-a-political-instrument-not-succeed/.

4: When the Referee Turns Rogue

1 Suhas Palshikar, 'After Lok Sabha Election Verdict 2024: INDIA's Challenge Has Just Begun', *The Indian Express*, 6 June 2024, https://indianexpress.com/article/opinion/columns/lok-sabha-election-results-2024-opposition-congress-9371843/.
2 'Taking Uttar Pradesh Lightly Cost Us Badly: Axis My India's Pradeep Gupta on Exit Polls Being Wrong', *The Hindu*, 22 June 2024, https://www.thehindu.com/elections/taking-up-lightly-cost-us-badly-axis-my-indias-pradeep-gupta-on-exit-polls-being-wrong/article68320126.ece.
3 'Taking Uttar Pradesh Lightly Cost Us Badly: Axis My India's Pradeep Gupta on Exit Polls Being Wrong'.

4 'Why Prashant Kishore Is Talking About BJP's Victory? Why PM Is Again Talking About 400 Seats?', *Satya Hindi*, 23 May 2024, https://youtu.be/SF6eHv73BBg?si=eBu20fhwBt6pR4q4.
5 Asad Rehman, 'INDIA Bloc Leaders Put Up Brave Face: People's Exit Poll Favours Us, Wait for June 4', *The Indian Express*, 3 June 2024, https://indianexpress.com/article/political-pulse/india-bloc-leaders-exit-poll-favours-9366295/.
6 Rehman, 'INDIA Bloc Leaders Put Up Brave Face: People's Exit Poll Favours Us, Wait for June 4'.
7 Bharti Jain, 'Pattern in Fake Narratives, We Failed to Stop Them: CEC', *The Times of India*, 4 June 2024, https://timesofindia.indiatimes.com/india/pattern-in-fake-narratives-we-failed-to-stop-them-cec/articleshow/110679347.cms.
8 'Mallikarjun Kharge Writes to INDIA Bloc Leaders over Alleged Discrepancies in Voter Turnout', *The Times of India*, 7 May 2024, https://timesofindia.indiatimes.com/india/mallikarjun-kharge-writes-to-india-bloc-leaders-over-alleged-discrepancies-in-voter-turnout/articleshow/109901335.cms.
9 'Mallikarjun Kharge Writes to INDIA Bloc Leaders over Alleged Discrepancies in Voter Turnout'.
10 Dipak K. Dash, 'Congress Chief Mallikarjun Kharge Could Create Anarchic Situation, Claims Baseless, Says EC; Party Hits Back', *The Times of India*, 11 May 2024, https://timesofindia.indiatimes.com/india/lok-sabha-elections-congress-chief-mallikarjun-kharge-could-create-anarchic-situation-claims-baseless-says-ec-party-hits-back/articleshow/110019866.cms.
11 Dash, 'Congress Chief Mallikarjun Kharge Could Create Anarchic Situation, Claims Baseless, Says EC; Party Hits Back'.
12 Dash, 'Congress Chief Mallikarjun Kharge Could Create Anarchic Situation, Claims Baseless, Says EC; Party Hits Back'.
13 Ambika Pandit, 'Lok Sabha Elections: EC's Response to Congress President Mallikarjun Kharge's Letter "Permanent Blot" on Institution', *The Times of India*, 11 May 2024, https://timesofindia.indiatimes.com/india/lok-sabha-elections-ecs-response-to-congress-president-mallikarjun-kharges-letter-permanent-blot-on-institution/articleshow/110019388.cms.
14 Suman K. Jha, 'Advani Has Doubts About EVM, Wants Ballot Papers Back', *The Indian Express*, 5 July 2009, https://indianexpress.com/article/news-archive/web/advani-has-doubts-about-evm-wants-ballot-papers-back/.

15 'SC Asks EC to Install VVPAT in Evms for 2014 Polls', *Business Standard*, 8 October 2013, https://www.business-standard.com/amp/article/current-affairs/sc-asks-ec-to-install-vvpat-in-evms-for-2014-polls-113100800259_1.html.
16 Amit Anand Choudhary, 'SC Rejects Return to Ballots, Says Distrust of EVMs "Blind"', *The Times of India*, 27 April 2024, https://timesofindia.indiatimes.com/india/sc-rejects-return-to-ballots-says-distrust-of-evms-blind/articleshow/109633831.cms
17 Bharti Jain, 'EC Gives Losing Candidates Choice on How They Want to Check EVMs', *The Times of India*, 17 July 2024, https://timesofindia.indiatimes.com/india/ec-gives-losing-candidates-choice-on-how-they-want-to-check-evms/articleshow/111795678.cms.
18 Amit Anand Choudhary, 'SC: Vested Interest Groups Undermining India Progress', *The Times of India*, 27 April 2024, https://timesofindia.indiatimes.com/india/sc-vested-interest-groups-undermining-india-progress/articleshow/109634085.cms.
19 Sandeep Shastri, 'CSDS-Lokniti 2024 Pre-poll Survey | Level and Intensity of Voter Trust in Select Institutions and Processes', *The Hindu*, 12 April 2024, https://www.thehindu.com/elections/csds-lokniti-2024-pre-poll-survey-level-and-intensity-of-voter-trust-in-select-institutions-and-processes/article68054233.ece.
20 Apurva Vishwanath, 'Supreme Court Verdict on ECI Appointments', *The Indian Express*, 3 March 2023, https://indianexpress.com/article/explained/explained-law/supreme-court-verdict-on-election-commission-of-india-appointments-8476545/.
21 Vishwanath, 'Supreme Court Verdict on ECI Appointments'.
22 Dipak K. Dash, 'EC Sends Notices to BJP, Cong Chiefs over Modi, Rahul Speeches', *The Times of India*, 26 April 2024, https://timesofindia.indiatimes.com/india/ec-sends-notices-to-bjp-cong-chiefs-over-modi-rahul-speeches/articleshow/109603556.cms.
23 Anurag Kundu, 'Why the 2024 General Election Is Unfair', *The Indian Express*, 10 May 2024, https://indianexpress.com/article/opinion/columns/why-the-2024-general-election-is-unfair-9320107/.
24 The Wire Analysis, "'A New Low, No Longer an Umpire': Political Scientists Decry Election Commission," *The Wire*, 11 May 2024, https://m.thewire.in/article/politics/a-new-low-no-longer-an-umpire-political-scientists-decry-election-commission/amp.

5: A Rigged Playing Field?

1 David Selbourne, *The Politics of Illusion: An Eye to India, the Unmasking of a Tyranny* (Penguin Books, 1977), p. 95. Selbourne quotes from: IG, to Rajya Sabha, 22 July 1975, qu. *PODS*, P.13; *PODS*, P.13; IG, qu. *Ind. Exp.*, 20.7.75; Kuldip Nayar, Ind. Exp., 15.1.76; Jaganath Mishra, Chief Minister of Bihar, qu. *Guardian*, 7.7.75; Brahmananda Reddy, Minister of Home Affairs, qu. *Econ. Times*, 6.4.76; IG, qu. Econ. Times, 4.3.76; S.S. Ray, qu. *Deccan Herald*, 30.12.75; G.P. Yadav, qu. *Hindu*, 8.1.76; J.P. Narayan, *The Times*, 5.6.76 (see chapter 1, n. 155); IG, to Institute of Democracy and Socialism, qu. *Econ*. Times, 24.3.76; cf. 'Opposition is undermining the democratic system: P.M.' (headline in *Times of India*, 11.12.75).

2 Abhishek Angad, 'What Is the 8.5-acre Land Case in Which Hemant Soren Was Arrested, What Is He Accused Of?', *The Indian Express*, 10 March 2024, https://indianexpress.com/article/explained/explained-politics/why-was-hemant-soren-arrested-explained-9147266/.

3 Amit Bhelari, 'Former Jharkhand CM Hemant Soren Gets Bail in Alleged Money Laundering Case, Walks Out of Jail', *The Hindu*, 28 June 2024, https://www.thehindu.com/news/national/former-jharkhand-chief-minister-hemant-soren-gets-bail/article68343525.ece.

4 'Arvind Kejriwal Arrested: Can a CM Run Govt from Jail? Can LG Seek President's Rule? Here Is What May Happen Next', *The Economic Times*, 22 March 2024, https://economictimes.indiatimes.com/news/politics-and-nation/arvind-kejriwal-arrested-can-a-cm-run-govt-from-jail-can-lg-seek-presidents-rule-here-is-what-may-happen-next-atishi-saurabh-bharadwaj-aap/articleshow/108696890.cms?from=mdr.

5 'Arvind Kejriwal Arrested: Can a CM Run Govt from Jail? Can LG Seek President's Rule? Here Is What May Happen Next'.

6 Amit Anand Choudhary, '"21 Days Will Not Make Any Difference": SC Grants CM Interim Bail Till June 1', *The Times of India*, 11 May 2024, https://timesofindia.indiatimes.com/india/21-days-will-not-make-any-difference-sc-grants-cm-interim-bail-till-june-1/articleshow/110019382.cms.

7 'Back Among His Supporters, Kejriwal Says 140 cr People Have to Fight Against Dictatorship', *Bhaskar Live*, 10 May 2024, https://

bhaskarlive.in/back-among-his-supporters-kejriwal-says-140-cr-people-have-to-fight-against-dictatorship/.

8 Soni Mishra, 'AAP Amends Its Constitution, Allows More Than One Person in a Family to Contest Polls', *The Week*, 28 January 2021, https://www.theweek.in/news/india/2021/01/28/aap-amends-its-Constitution-allows-more-than-one-person-in-a-family-to-contest-polls.amp.html.

9 Ambika Pandit, 'INDIA Bloc Demands Level Playing Field, Release of Arrested Leaders', *The Times of India*, 1 April 2024, https://timesofindia.indiatimes.com/india/india-bloc-demands-level-playing-field-release-of-arrested-leaders/articleshow/108926112.cms.

10 Utkarsh Mishra (ed.), 'Sunita Kejriwal Set to Replace Husband as Delhi CM?', *Rediff.com*, 2 April 2024, https://m.rediff.com/amp/news/report/sunit-kejriwal-set-to-replace-husband-as-delhi-cm/20240402.htm.

11 Ajmal Abbas, 'UN Reacts to Arvind Kejriwal's Arrest, Hopes "Everyone's Rights Are Protected"', *India Today*, 29 March 2024, https://www.indiatoday.in/amp/india/story/hope-everyones-rights-are-protected-un-united-nations-on-arvind-kejriwals-arrest-2520604-2024-03-29.

12 Chandrashekhar Srinivasan (ed.), "'Encourage Fair, Transparent Legal Process': US on Arvind Kejriwal Arrest," *NDTV*, 26 March 2024, https://www.ndtv.com/india-news/encourage-fair-transparent-legal-process-us-on-arvind-kejriwal-arrest-5313351.

13 Kallol Bhattacherjee, 'Arvind Kejriwal Entitled to Fair and Impartial Trial, says German Foreign Ministry', *The Hindu*, 22 March 2024, https://www.thehindu.com/news/national/arvind-kejriwal-entitled-to-fair-and-impartial-trial-says-german-foreign-ministry/article67981586.ece.

14 Khushi Mehrotra and Jaspreet Singh, "'INDIA Will Give Befitting Reply': Opposition Leaders Slam Kejriwal's Arrest," *The Quint*, 22 March 2024, https://www.thequint.com/amp/story/news/politics/delhi-cm-arvind-kejriwal-arrested-india-alliance-reacts-latest-news.

15 'Kejriwal Arrest Destroys Level Playing Field: INDIA Bloc to EC', *The Indian Express*, 23 March 2024, https://indianexpress.com/article/india/india-bloc-leaders-ec-door-misuse-central-agencies-9229254/.

16 'I-T Department Freezes Congress Bank Accounts Over 2018-19 Returns; Appellate Tribunal Provides Partial Relief', *The Hindu*, 16

February 2024, https://www.thehindu.com/news/national/bank-accounts-of-congress-youth-congress-frozen/article67852292.ece.

17 'Bank Account Freeze Case: Why Accounts of Congress Were Under I-T Dept's Scanner | Explained', *Mint*, 16 February 2024, https://www.livemint.com/politics/news/bank-account-freeze-case-why-accounts-of-congress-were-under-i-t-depts-scanner-explained-11708091086498.html.

18 'Bank Account Freeze Case: Why Accounts of Congress Were Under I-T Dept's Scanner | Explained'.

19 'How India's Grand Old Party Was Left with Bank Accounts Frozen', *The Economic Times*, 23 March 2024, https://economictimes.indiatimes.com/news/elections/lok-sabha/india/how-indias-grand-old-party-was-left-with-bank-accounts-frozen/articleshow/108715070.cms?from=mdr.

20 'Just 3-4 Of Congress' Bank Accounts Have Been Attached, "Not Frozen": BJP', *The Hindu*, 23 March 2024, https://www.thehindu.com/news/national/just-3-4-of-congress-bank-accounts-attached-not-frozen-bjp/article67984333.ece.

21 'Just 3-4 Of Congress' Bank Accounts Have Been Attached, "Not Frozen": BJP'.

22 Nandini Singh, "'BJP Engaging in Tax Terrorism': Congress on Rs 1,700 Crore I-T Notice," *Business Standard*, 29 March 2024, https://www.business-standard.com/politics/bjp-engaging-in-tax-terrorism-congress-on-rs-1-700-crore-i-t-notice-124032900293_1.html.

23 Singh, "'BJP Engaging in Tax Terrorism': Congress on Rs 1,700 Crore I-T Notice."

24 'Our Accounts Dept Staff Raided by Income Tax, Vendetta, Claims Congress', *The Indian Express*, 13 October 2019, https://indianexpress.com/article/india/congress-claims-accounts-department-raided-by-income-tax-officials-6066457/.

6: The Roadblock to Hindutva's Juggernaut

1 Sharat Pradhan and Atul Chandra, *Yogi Adityanath: Religion, Politics and Power: The Untold Story* (Penguin Books, 2021), p. 101.

2 Pradhan and Chandra, *Yogi Adityanath*, p. 111.

3 Pradhan and Chandra, *Yogi Adityanath*, p. 122.

4 Swapan Dasgupta, *Awakening Bharat Mata: The Political Beliefs of the Indian Right* (Penguin Viking, 2019), p. 331.
5 Nilanjan Mukhopadhyay, *The Demolition and the Verdict: Ayodhya and Rage Project to Reconfigure India* (Speaking Tiger, 2021), p. xvi.
6 Mukhopadhyay, *The Demolition and the Verdict*, pp. ix–x.
7 Vaibhav Tiwari, 'Kamal Nath Says "Chhodo Akhilesh Vakhilesh" as SP Vs Congress Intensifies', *Hindustan Times*, 20 October 2023, https://www.hindustantimes.com/india-news/kamal-nath-says-chhodo-akhilesh-vakhilesh-as-sp-vs-congress-intensifies-101697795489685-amp.html.
8 Tiwari, 'Kamal Nath Says "Chhodo Akhilesh Vakhilesh" as SP Vs Congress Intensifies'.
9 Pankaj Shah, 'Jats Punch Above Weight, Turn Power Players in West UP Poll Arena', *The Times of India*, 12 April 2024, https://timesofindia.indiatimes.com/city/lucknow/jats-punch-above-weight-turn-power-players-in-west-up-poll-arena/articleshow/109230288.cms.
10 Uday Chandra and Shikoh Zaidi, 'Battle of Yamuna Doab', *The Times of India*, 12 April 2024, https://timesofindia.indiatimes.com/blogs/toi-editorials/battle-of-the-yamuna-doab/.
11 Shyamlal Yadav, 'Bharat Ratna for Chaudhary Charan Singh: Why This Is Significant', *The Indian Express*, 9 February 2024, https://indianexpress.com/article/explained/explained-history/bharat-ratna-chaudhary-charan-singh-9152952/.
12 Yadav, 'Bharat Ratna for Chaudhary Charan Singh: Why This Is Significant'.
13 Arun Kumar, 'Akhilesh Yadav and Rahul Gandhi's Strategy — Promise of Caste Census and More Reservation', *The Indian Express*, 30 May 2024, https://indianexpress.com/article/opinion/columns/akhilesh-yadav-and-rahul-gandhis-strategy-promise-of-caste-census-and-more-reservation-9356524/.
14 Biswajeet Banerjee, 'SP's Strategic Shift: From MY Formula to Inclusive Politics', *Money Control*, 12 May 2024, https://www.moneycontrol.com/elections/lok-sabha-election/uttar-pradesh/samajwadi-partys-strategic-revolution-from-m-y-to-inclusive-politics-article-12720171.html/amp.
15 Prabhu Chawla, 'Akhilesh Redefines and Reinvents Himself', *The New Indian Express*, 28 July 2024, https://www.newindianexpress.com/opinions/2024/Jul/27/akhilesh-redefines-and-reinvents-himself.

16 Biswajeet Banerjee, 'SP's Strategic Shift: From MY Formula to Inclusive Politics'.

17 Rajiv Kumar, 'The UP Caste Calculus: What the State's Poll History Tells Us about Who Stands Where', *News18*, 4 October 2021, https://www.news18.com/amp/news/opinion/the-up-caste-calculus-what-the-states-poll-history-tells-us-about-who-stands-where-4283663.html.

18 Amitabh Tiwari, 'Opinion: UP Poll Debacle Report: Why BJP Lost Non-Yadav OBC and Non-Jatav Support', *India Today*, 19 July 2024, https://www.indiatoday.in/opinion/story/up-poll-debacle-report-why-bjp-lost-non-yadav-obc-and-non-jatav-support-opinion-2569269-2024-07-19.

19 Tiwari, 'Opinion: UP Poll Debacle Report: Why BJP Lost Non-Yadav OBC and Non-Jatav Support'.

20 B.R. Ambedkar, *Annihilation of Caste*, p. 353.

21 Brijesh Shukla, 'कहानी मायावती और BSP की ... कभी UP की राजनीति में मुलायम और BJP दोनों को दी टक्कर, अब अपना वोट मिलना भी हो गया मुश्किल', *Money Control Hindi*, 7 June 2024, https://hindi.moneycontrol.com/news/lok-sabha-election/mayawati-bsp-gave-fight-to-both-mulayam-and-bjp-in-up-politics-now-it-has-become-difficult-to-even-get-one-s-vote-1905856.html, translated by the author.

22 Vivek Kumar, *Rise and Fall of Bahujan Samaj Party: Limitations of Caste Mobilisation*.

23 Supriya Sharma, 'Constitution, Cows, Rations: Why Dalits in UP Want to Vote Out the BJP', *Scroll.in*, 17 May 2024, https://scroll.in/article/1067962/constitution-cows-ration-why-dalits-in-up-want-to-vote-out-the-bjp.

24 Sanjay Kapoor, 'India Election: Why Did Modi's BJP Lose in Uttar Pradesh, Its Fortress?', *Al Jazeera*, 6 June 2024, https://www.aljazeera.com/news/2024/6/6/india-election-why-did-modis-bjp-lose-in-uttar-pradesh-its-fortress.

25 Kapoor, 'India Election: Why Did Modi's BJP Lose in Uttar Pradesh, Its Fortress?'

26 Purva Chitnis, 'After Poll Drubbing That Saw Dalits "Shift to Congress", Prakash Ambedkar's VBA Has Tough Road Ahead', *The Print*, 15 June 2024, https://theprint.in/politics/after-poll-drubbing-that-saw-dalits-shift-to-congress-prakash-ambedkars-vba-has-tough-road-ahead/2132606/.

27 A.G. Noorani, 'Ambedkar's Warning', *The Hindu*, 5 July 2017, https://frontline.thehindu.com/cover-story/ambedkars-warning/article23595905.ece.

28 Gulam Jeelani, "'Paper Leaks' to 'Hasty' Ticket Distribution: 10 Key Reasons Listed by BJP for Its Lok Sabha Poll Debacle in UP," *Mint*, 10 July 2024, https://www.livemint.com/politics/news/paper-leak-to-hasty-ticket-distribution-10-key-reasons-listed-by-bjp-for-its-lok-sabha-debacle-in-uttar-pradesh/amp-11720609358739.html.

29 Statesman News Service, 'Keshav Prasad Maurya's Statement Sets Off Internal Bickering in UP BJP', *The Statesman*, July 2024, https://www.thestatesman.com/india/keshav-prasad-mauryas-statement-sets-off-internal-bickering-in-up-bjp-1503321588.html/amp.

30 "'Over-confidence Caused Harm in Elections; Everyone Will Have to Be Active Now': UP CM Yogi," *The Times of India*, 15 July 2024, https://timesofindia.indiatimes.com/india/over-confidence-caused-harm-in-elections-everyone-will-have-to-be-active-now-up-cm-yogi/amp_articleshow/111735545.cms.

7: Varanasi's (Un)Expected Verdict

1 "'Had Priyanka Contested, PM Modi Would Have Lost in Varanasi': Rahul Gandhi in Rae Bareli," *Business Today*, 11 June 2024, https://www.businesstoday.in/india/story/lok-sabha-elections-had-priyanka-contested-pm-modi-would-have-lost-in-varanasi-rahul-gandhi-in-rae-bareli-432971-2024-06-11.

2 Deeptiman Tiwary, 'Mohan Bhagwat: 'True Sevak Is Never Arrogant ... in Polls, Decorum Was Not Kept', *The Indian Express*, 11 June 2024, https://indianexpress.com/article/political-pulse/mohan-bhagwat-elections-decorum-sevakl-campaign-9384552/.

3 Manoj Bhadra, 'Varanasi: Winning No Challenge for PM, but Record Margin Could Be', *The Statesman*, June 2024, https://www.thestatesman.com/india/varanasi-winning-no-challenge-to-pm-but-record-margin-is-1503305268.html/amp.

4 Bhadra, 'Varanasi: Winning No Challenge for PM, but Record Margin Could Be'.

5 Bhupendra Pandey, 'As PM Modi Meditates, Amit Shah, Senior BJP Leaders Hold Fort in Varanasi: "Koi Fight Hi Nahi Hai"', *The Indian Express*, 31 May 2024, https://indianexpress.com/article

/political-pulse/pm-modi-away-amit-shah-senior-bjp-leaders-hold-fort-in-varanasi-9362803/.

6 Pandey, 'As PM Modi Meditates, Amit Shah, Senior BJP Leaders Hold Fort in Varanasi: "Koi Fight Hi Nahi Hai"'.

7 Pandey, 'As PM Modi Meditates, Amit Shah, Senior BJP Leaders Hold Fort in Varanasi: "Koi Fight Hi Nahi Hai"'.

8 Pandey, 'As PM Modi Meditates, Amit Shah, Senior BJP Leaders Hold Fort in Varanasi: "Koi Fight Hi Nahi Hai"'.

9 Kedarnath Singh, 'Benaras', translated by Nidhi Singh, World Literature Today, https://www.worldliteraturetoday.org/2019/summer/banaras-kedarnath-singh.

10 Anand K. Sahay, 'Ground Report: In UP, Narendra Modi's Name No Longer Ignites the Enthusiasm it Once Did', *The Wire*, 24 May 2024, https://thewire.in/politics/ground-report-in-up-narendra-modis-name-no-longer-ignites-the-enthusiasm-it-once-did.

11 Sanjay Kapoor, 'India Election: Why Did Modi's BJP Lose in Uttar Pradesh, Its Fortress?', *Al Jazeera*, 6 June 2024, https://www.aljazeera.com/news/2024/6/6/india-election-why-did-modis-bjp-lose-in-uttar-pradesh-its-fortress.

12 Sudhir Kumar, 'PM Modi Opens Kashi Vishwanath Corridor', *Hindustan Times*, 14 December 2021, https://www.hindustantimes.com/india-news/pm-modi-opens-kashi-vishwanath-corridor-101639420391917.html.

13 Kumar, 'PM Modi Opens Kashi Vishwanath Corridor'.

14 Ratan Sharda, 'Kashi Vishwanath Corridor: Corridor to Civilisational Resurgence', *Organiser*, 17 December 2021, https://organiser.org/2021/12/17/15570/bharat/kashi-vishwanath-corridor-corridor-to-civilisational-resurgence/.

15 'Kashi Vishwanath Corridor Project Explained in 10 Points', *Mint*, 13 December 2021, https://www.livemint.com/news/india/kashi-vishwanath-corridor-project-explained-in-10-points/amp-11639386843034.html.

16 Sumati Mehrishi, "'Mool Karyakarta Is Disheartened'; 'Modi's Gujarati Friends Have Cornered All Benefits': Murmurs and Stories Behind the Almost-Upset in Varanasi," *Swarajya*, 6 August 2024, https://swarajyamag.com/politics/mool-karyakarta-is-disheartened-modis-gujarati-friends-have-cornered-all-benefits-murmurs-and-stories-behind-the-almost-upset-in-varanasi.

17 Mehrishi, "'Mool Karyakarta Is Disheartened'; 'Modi's Gujarati Friends Have Cornered All Benefits': Murmurs and Stories Behind the Almost-Upset in Varanasi."

18 ET Online, 'Teesri Baar Modi Sarkar, or a Twist in the Tale? What Ground Reports from Varanasi Suggest', *The Economic Times*, 1 June 2024, https://economictimes.indiatimes.com/news/elections/lok-sabha/uttar-pradesh/modified-kashi-says-teesri-baar-modi-sarkar-guaranteed-focus-now-on-5-lakh-margin/articleshow/110585041.cms.
19 ET Online, 'Teesri Baar Modi Sarkar, or a Twist in the Tale? What Ground Reports from Varanasi Suggest'.
20 Mehrishi, "'Mool Karyakarta Is Disheartened'; 'Modi's Gujarati Friends Have Cornered All Benefits': Murmurs and Stories Behind the Almost-Upset in Varanasi."
21 Virendra Singh Rawat, 'Lok Sabha Polls: In Varanasi, Modi's Win Margin the Only Point of Interest', *Business Standard*, 31 May 31 2024, https://www.business-standard.com/elections/lok-sabha-election/lok-sabha-polls-in-varanasi-modi-s-win-margin-the-only-point-of-interest-124053100004_1.html.
22 Hannah Jose, 'Is Narendra Modi Losing His Sheen in His Own Seat? Here's What Indian Voters Had to Say', *ABC News*, 1 June 2024, https://www.abc.net.au/news/2024-06-01/is-narendra-modi-losing-his-sheen-in-his-own-seat-/103917394.
23 Sahay, 'Ground Report: In UP, Narendra Modi's Name No Longer Ignites the Enthusiasm it Once Did'.
24 Sahay, 'Ground Report: In UP, Narendra Modi's Name No Longer Ignites the Enthusiasm it Once Did'.
25 Ashutosh, *The Gladiator, the Crown Prince, and the Hope: Battle for Change* (HarperCollins *Publishers*, 2015), pp. 184–85.
26 Sahay, 'Ground Report: In UP, Narendra Modi's Name No Longer Ignites the Enthusiasm it Once Did'.
27 Rajeev Dikshit, 'PM Modi Margin Dips from 4.8 Lakh to 1.5 Lakh, Vote Share from 63.6% to 54.2%', *The Times of India*, 5 June 2024, https://timesofindia.indiatimes.com/city/varanasi/pm-modi-margin-dips-from-4-8-lakh-to-1-5-lakh-vote-share-from-63-6-to-54-2/articleshow/110721833.cms.

8: Ayodhya and the Politics of Arrogance

1 Waquar Hasan, 'Ayodhya Residents Face Hate After BJP's Defeat in Faizabad', *Clarion India*, June 2024, https://clarionindia.net/ayodhya-residents-face-hate-after-bjps-defeat-in-faizabad/?amp=1.
2 Hasan, 'Ayodhya Residents Face Hate After BJP's Defeat in Faizabad'.

3 Hasan, 'Ayodhya Residents Face Hate After BJP's Defeat in Faizabad'.
4 Hasan, 'Ayodhya Residents Face Hate After BJP's Defeat in Faizabad'.
5 Tanul Thakur, 'Ayodhya: How BJP Lost the Land of Ram Mandir', *Outlook*, 12 June 2024, https://www.outlookindia.com/national/ayodhya-why-bjp-lost-in-the-land-of-ram-mandir.
6 The Election Commission recognises Faizabad as the Lok Sabha Constituency, though the Uttar Pradesh Government of Yogi Adityanath has renamed Faizabad as Ayodhya. We will be using 'Ayodhya' to refer to Faizabad.
7 Omar Rashid, 'Abusing Ayodhya's Voters Is Like a Slur on Voting Rights, Constitution: Faizabad MP Awadhesh Prasad', *The Wire*, 12 June 2024, https://thewire.in/politics/abusing-ayodhyas-voters-is-like-a-slur-on-voting-rights-Constitution-faizabad-mp-awadhesh-prasad.
8 Rashid, 'Abusing Ayodhya's Voters Is Like a Slur on Voting Rights, Constitution: Faizabad MP Awadhesh Prasad'.
9 Rashid, 'Abusing Ayodhya's Voters is Like a Slur on Voting Rights, Constitution: Faizabad MP Awadhesh Prasad'.
10 Omar Rashid, 'Those Blaming People of Ayodhya for Election Result Showing "Foolishness": Ram Mandir Chief Priest', *The Wire*, 10 June 2024, https://thewire.in/politics/bjp-forgets-ram-after-up-debacle-supporters-vilify-hindus-of-ayodhya.
11 'जिन्होंने सरयू में खून बहाया, उनकी हुई अयोध्या में जीत... कारसेवक हार गए", मथुरा में बोले साक्षी महाराज', *Punjab Kesari*, 15 June 2024, https://m.up.punjabkesari.in/uttar-pradesh/news/those-who-shed-blood-in-saryu-1993594.
12 Ashish Mishra, 'फ़ैज़ाबाद : 'मथुरा न काशी, अबकी बार अवधेश पासी' के नारे ने कैसे हराया भाजपा को?', *India Today Hindi*, 6 June 2024, https://www.indiatodayhindi.com/amp/state/story/bjp-lost-ayodhya-seats-what-is-the-main-reason-behind-it-1022010-2024-06-05.
13 Bhoomi pooja is an exclusively Indian ritual conducted before a major construction is undertaken. It involves many rituals with Vedic chants honouring Mother Earth, which is being disturbed for construction. Bhoomi is earth, and pooja is worship.
14 Hemant Sharma, *Ram Fir Laute* (Prabhat Prakashan, 2024), p. 132.
15 Nilanjan Mukhopadhyay, *The Demolition and the Verdict: Ayodhya and the Project to Reconfigure India* (Speaking Tiger, 2021), p. 80.

16 Narasimha Rao, *Ayodhya: 6 December 1992* (Penguin Viking), p. 3.
17 'Introduction', in Gopal Sarvepalli (ed.), *Anatomy of a Confrontation: Ayodhya and the Rise of Communal Politics in India* (Viking Penguin, 1991), p. 16.
18 Rao, *Ayodhya: 6 December 1992*, p. 21.
19 Rao, *Ayodhya 6: December 1992*, p. 7.
20 Neeladri Bhattacharya, 'Myth, History and the Politics of Ramjanmabhumi', in Sarvepalli (ed.), *Anatomy of a Confrontation*, p. 125
21 H.V. Seshadri, 'Wiping Out the Blot of Foreign Slavery', *Organiser*, 5 January 1986, cited in Bhattacharya, 'Myth, History and the Politics of Ramjanmabhumi', p. 126
22 Bhattacharya, 'Myth, History and the Politics of Ramjanmabhumi', p. 131.
23 L.K. Advani, White paper on Ayodhya and the Ram Temple Movement, Bharatiya Janata Party, Delhi, 1993, pp. 1—4, cited in Swapan Dasgupta, *Awakening Bharat Mata, The Political Belief of The Indian Right* (Penguin Viking, 2019), p. 331.
24 Bhattacharya, 'Myth, History and the Politics of Ramjanmabhumi', p. 131.
25 Dasgupta, *Awakening Bharat Mata*, p. 331.
26 Bhattacharya, 'Myth, History and the Politics of Ramjanmabhumi', p. 131.
27 Tanul Thakur, 'Ayodhya: How BJP Lost the Land of Ram Mandir', *Outlook*, 12 June 2024, https://www.outlookindia.com/national/ayodhya-why-bjp-lost-in-the-land-of-ram-mandir.
28 Thakur, 'Ayodhya: How BJP Lost the Land of Ram Mandir'.
29 Thakur, 'Ayodhya: How BJP Lost the Land of Ram Mandir'.
30 Krishna Pratap Singh, 'For the BJP, Attempts to Review Ayodhya Loss Turning Out to Be an Embarrassment', *The Wire*, 21 June 2024, https://thewire.in/politics/for-the-bjp-attempts-to-review-ayodhya-loss-turning-out-to-be-an-embarrassment.
31 Swati Goel Sharma, 'Why BJP Lost in Ayodhya Despite Ram Janmabhoomi Temple', *Swarajya*, 10 June 2024, https://swarajyamag.com/politics/what-went-wrong-for-bjp-in-ayodhya.
32 Ram resides in the heart of those who don't harbour malice and arrogance. And of those who are not possessed by attachment, anger, arrogance and ego and also those who are above lust, indignation, passion and rancour.

9: The Tacit Retaliation of Muslims

1 Anand Soondas, 'Muslim Silence Speaks Amid Poll Noise in UP', *The* Times of India, 18 April 2024, https://timesofindia.indiatimes.com/india/muslim-silence-speaks-amid-poll-noise-in-up/articleshow/109386621.cms.

2 Fahad Zuberi, 'The Tacitly Silent Indian Muslim Voter', *Hindustan* Times, 23 April 2024, https://www.hindustantimes.com/opinion/the-tactically-silent-indian-muslim-voter-101713884497307.html.

3 News Desk, Krishna Bajpai (ed.), 'Lok Sabha Results … ', *Jansatta*, 5 June 2024, https://www.jansatta.com/national/lok-sabha-results-up-muslim-voters-silent-voters-bjp-bigget-lose-akhilesh-yadav-rahul-gandhi-duo-sp-congress-pda-alliance/3407540.

4 Aishwarya Jain, "'Its Best Friend ...': M Kharge Responds to BJP's 'Muslim League Imprint' Jab," *NDTV*, 8 April 2024, https://www.ndtv.com/india-news/congress-manifesto-lok-sabha-election-muslim-league-imprint-jibe-congress-files-complaint-after-bjp-calls-manifesto-muslim-league-imprint-5399532.

5 Aishwarya Jain, "'Its Best Friend ...': M Kharge Responds to BJP's 'Muslim League Imprint' Jab."

6 HT News Desk, 'PM Does Not Know History: Congress Counters Modi's "Muslim League Imprint" Jab', *Hindustan* Times, 6 April 2024, https://www.hindustantimes.com/india-news/pm-does-not-know-his-history-congress-counters-modis-muslim-league-imprint-jab-101712405801381.html.

7 Mayank Kumar, SP, Congress Will Run Bulldozer Over Ram Temple if Voted to Power, Says PM Modi in U.P.'s Barabanki', *The* Hindu, 18 May 2024, https://www.thehindu.com/elections/lok-sabha/sp-congress-will-run-bulldozer-over-ram-temple-if-voted-to-power-says-modi-in-up/article68187833.ece.

8 PTI, 'India Bloc Will Rewrite Constitution to Give Reservation on the Basis of Religion: PM Modi', *The* Times of India, 26 May 2024, https://timesofindia.indiatimes.com/india/india-bloc-will-rewrite-constitution-to-give-reservation-on-basis-of-religion-pm-modi/articleshow/110439456.cms.

9 Pankaj Shah and Shalabh, 'Opposition Wants to Turn Majority into 2nd-Class Citizens: PM Modi', *The Times of India*,27 May 2024, https://timesofindia.indiatimes.com/india /opposition-wants-to-turn-majority-into-2nd-class-citizens-pm-modi/articleshow/110445191.cms.

10 TNN, 'Samajwadi Party Made Ramzan Power Cut-free But Not Janmashtami: Amit Shah', *The* Times of India, 30 May 2024, https://timesofindia.indiatimes.com/india/samajwadi-party-made-ramzan-power-cut-free-but-not-janmashtami-amit-shah/articleshow/110543629.cms.

11 HT Correspondent, 'Muslim Quota Part of Agenda to Push Country Towards Islamisation: Yogi', *Hindustan Times*, 26 April 2024, https://www.hindustantimes.com/cities/lucknow-news/muslim-quota-part-of-agenda-to-push-country-towards-islamisation-yogi-101714074574750.html.

12 ET Online, '"Will Not Allow Taliban Rule in India': CM Yogi on Congress' Muslim Reservations Remarks', *The* Economic Times, 29 May 2024, https://economictimes.indiatimes.com/news/elections/lok-sabha/india/will-not-allow-taliban-rule-in-india-cm-yogi-on-congress-muslim-reservations-remarks/videoshow/110535250.cms?from=mdr.

13 Omar Rashid, 'Mistrust Towards Muslims Is Fuelling BJP's Prospects in Uttar Pradesh', *The Wire,* 28 April 2024, https://thewire.in/politics/mistrust-towards-muslims-is-fuelling-bjps-prospects-in-uttar-pradesh/?mid_related_new.

14 Rashid, 'Mistrust Towards Muslims Is Fuelling BJP's Prospects in Uttar Pradesh'.

15 Snigdhendu Bhattacharya, 'How Minorities Voted in the Indian General Election', *The Diplomat,* 10 June 2024, https://thediplomat.com/2024/06/how-minorities-voted-in-the-indian-general-election/.

16 Ghazala Wahab, *Born a Muslim:* Some Truths About Islam in India (Aleph, 2021), p. 32.

17 Wahab, *Born* a Muslim, p. 32.

18 Wahab, *Born* a Muslim, p. 34.

19 Rakshanda Jalil, *But You Don't look Like a Muslim* (HarperCollins *Publishers* India, 2019), p. xii.

20 Jalil, *But You Don't look Like a Muslim,* p. xii.

21 Jalil, *But You Don't look Like a Muslim,* p. xii.

22 Prashant Jha, *How the BJP Wins:* Inside India's Greatest Election Machine (Juggernaut, 2017), p. 172.

23 Jha, *How* the BJP Wins, p. 172.

24 Jha, *How* the BJP Wins, p. 174.

25 J. Nandkumar (ed), *Cultural* Contours of Hindu Rashtra (Indus Scrolls Press), p. xxi.

26 Adolf Hitler, *Mein* Kampf (ABC Publishing House, 1968), p. 276.

27 Nalin Mehta, *The New BJP:* Modi and the Making of the World's Largest Political Party (Westland Books, 2022), p. 88.
28 Pratul Sharma, 'PM Modi Asks BJP to Undertake a "Sneh Yatra"', *The Week*, 3 July 2022, https://www.theweek.in/news/india/2022/07/03/pm-modi-asks-bjp-workers-to-undertake-a-sneh-yatra.html.
29 Hilal Ahmed, *A Brief History of the Present: Muslims in New India* (Penguin Random House India, 2024), p. 122
30 Ahmed, *A Brief History of the Present*, p. 80.
31 Ahmed, *A Brief History of the Present*, p. 81.
32 S.S. Awasthi, Amar Ujala, 'ये है यूपी चुनाव का जातिगत समीकरण, जानिए क्यों चुप हैं मुस्लिम वोटर', *Amar Ujala*, 12 February 2017, https://www.amarujala.com/delhi-ncr/muslim-voters-are-silent-in-up-election.
33 Ashwaq Masoodi, 'Opinion | Why the Muslim Voter Decided to Be Silent Spectator in Elections 2019', *Mint*, 10 April 2019, https://www.livemint.com/elections/opinion/opinion-why-the-muslim-voter-decided-to-be-silent-spectator-in-elections-2019-1554914018839.html.
34 Chetan Chauhan, 'Ecostani | The Silence of the Muslim Voter Could Be Real and Strategic', *Hindustan Times*, 29 April 2024, https://www.hindustantimes.com/opinion/ecostani-the-silence-of-the-muslim-voter-could-be-real-and-strategic-101714387337829.html.
35 Ziya Us Salam, *Being Muslim in Hindu India* (HarperCollins *Publishers* India, 2023), p. xxx.

10: Internal Conflicts, External Ramifications

1 L.K. Advani, *My* Country, My Life (Rupa & Co, 2008), p. 101.
2 Advani, *My* Country, My Life, pp. 840–41.
3 Vinay Sitapati, *Jugalbandi: The BJP Before Modi* (Penguin Viking, 2020), p. 301.
4 Prashant Jha, *How the BJP Wins: India's Greatest Election Machine* (Juggernaut, 2017), pp. 106–7.
5 Vijay Trivedi, *Yada Yada hi Yogi: Satta ke Singhasan Par Sanyasi ka ek Sal* (Westland Publications, 2018), p. 23.
6 Pratap Bhanu Mehta, 'In the Moment of His Political Triumph, Modi Has Chosen to Defeat India', *The Indian Express*, 20 March 2017, https://indianexpress.com/article/opinion/columns/yogic-madness-yogi-adityanath-uttar-pradesh-bjp-narendra-modi-4576588/.

7 The Editorial Board, 'Mr. Modi's Perilous Embrace of Hindu Extremists', *The New York Times*, 23 March 2017, https://www.nytimes.com/2017/03/23/opinion/mr-modis-perilous-embrace-of-hindu-extremists.html.

8 R. Jagannathan, 'Yogi Adityanath May Be a Risky Choice for UP, but He Ticks Many of the Right Boxes for BJP', *Swarajya*, 18 March 2017, https://swarajyamag.com/politics/yogi-adityanath-may-be-a-risky-choice-for-up-but-he-ticks-many-of-the-right-boxes-for-bjp.

9 Swapan Dasgupta, 'Yogi Adityanath Has Cross-caste Support, Judge Him on Performance, Writes Swapan Dasgupta', *Hindustan Times*, 23 March 2017, https://www.hindustantimes.com/analysis/yogi-adityanath-has-cross-caste-support-judge-him-on-performance-not-his-past/story-KpIJuxZ3R6Xv6Eu2iMlL6J.html.

10 Coomi Kapoor, 'Inside Track by Coomi Kapoor: Genesis of BJP's UP Defeat Needs More Introspection', *The Indian Express*, 14 July 2024, https://indianexpress.com/article/opinion/columns/inside-track-incomplete-enquiry-9451823/.

11 Ratan Mani Lal, 'UP Results a Setback Not Just for the BJP, but for Yogi Adityanath too', *The New Indian Express*, 4 June 2024, https://www.newindianexpress.com/web-only/2024/Jun/04/up-results-a-setback-not-just-for-the-bjp-but-for-yogi-adityanath-too.

12 Rajesh Kumar Singh, 'BJP's Poor Showing in UP Puts Spotlight on CM Yogi', *Hindustan Times*, 5 June 2024, https://www.hindustantimes.com/india-news/bjps-poor-showing-in-up-puts-spotlight-on-cm-yogi-101717531533446.html.

13 Sanjay Pandey, 'Lok Sabha Elections 2024: "Brand Yogi" Severely Dented in Uttar Pradesh', *Deccan Herald*, 5 June 2024, https://www.deccanherald.com/elections/india/lok-sabha-elections-2024-brand-yogi-severely-dented-in-uttar-pradesh-3054364.

14 J.P. Yadav, 'BJP's "Disastrous" Performance in Uttar Pradesh: Yogi in Delhi Amid Concerns in Party About "Internal Sabotage"', *The Telegraph Online*, 7 June 2024, https://www.telegraphindia.com/elections/lok-sabha-election-2024/bjps-disastrous-performance-in-uttar-pradesh-yogi-adityanath-in-delhi-amid-concerns-in-party-about-internal-sabotage/cid/2025165.

15 Shyamlal Yadav, 'When Yogi Adityanath Almost Lost the Backing of BJP', *The* Times of India, 7 June 2024, https://timesofindia.

indiatimes.com/india/why-yogi-adityanath-almost-lost-the-backing-of-bjp/articleshow/110794137.cms.

16 'CM Adityanath Visits UP Dy CM Maurya, RSS Leaders Also Present', *The Quint*, 23 June 2021, https://www.thequint.com/news/india/yogi-adityanath-rss-leaders-meet-at-uttar-pradesh-deputy-chief-minister-mauryas-residence.

17 Atul Mathur, 'After Polls, BJP Will Remove Yogi Adityanath: Delhi CM Arvind Kejjriwal', *The* Times of India, 12 May 2024, https://timesofindia.indiatimes.com/city/delhi/bjp-will-remove-yogi-cm-after-polls/articleshow/110044229.cms.

18 Srinivasa Rao Apparasu, "'Modi Will Continue To Lead Nation': Shah Dismisses Kejriwal's Retirement Remark," *Hindustan Times*, 12 May 2024, https://www.hindustantimes.com/india-news/modi-will-continue-to-lead-nation-shah-dismisses-kejriwal-s-retirement-remark-101715454097377.html.

19 'Yogi Is the Most Capable CM, Says Nadda, Dismisses Kejriwal's Claim', *The* Times of India, 1 June 2024, https://timesofindia.indiatimes.com/city/lucknow/yogi-is-the-most-capable-cm-says-nadda-dismisses-kejriwals-claim/articleshow/110617276.cms.

20 Jatin Takkar, 'Reserved Vacancies in UP Sometimes Filled with General Candidates: Anupriya Patel to UP CM Yogi', *The Economic Times*, 28 June 2024, https://m.economictimes.com/news/india/reserved-vacancies-in-up-sometimes-filled-with-general-candidates-anupriya-patel-to-up-cm-yogi/amp_articleshow/111348815.cms.

21 Maulshree Seth, 'BJP Ally, UP Minister Hints Bulldozer "Misuse" Behind Poll Setback: "Uproot Poor, and They Will Uproot You"', *The Indian Express*, 17 July 2024, https://indianexpress.com/article/political-pulse/bjp-ally-uttar-pradesh-minister-bulldozer-misuse-lok-sabha-polls-setback-9457464/.

22 'Unimaginable Level of Corruption at Local Level: Ex-BJP Minister', *The Indian Express*, 13 July 2024, https://indianexpress.com/article/cities/lucknow/unimaginable-level-of-corruption-at-local-level-ex-bjp-minister-9450385/.

23 Mayank Kumar, 'Overconfidence Hurt BJP's Expectations in 2024 Polls, Says Yogi Adityanath in Key Party Meet', *The Hindu*, 14 July 2024, https://www.thehindu.com/news/national/uttar-pradesh/overconfidence-hurt-bjps-expectations-in-2024-polls-says-yogi-adityanath-in-key-party-meet/article68403803.ece.

24 Abhishek Anand, 'To Pacify Rajput Anger, BJP Sends Adityanath, Rajnath Singh to Western UP', *India Today*, 1 May 2024, https://

www.indiatoday.in/elections/lok-sabha/story/uttar-pradesh-kshatriya-rajputs-bjp-anger-fatehpur-sikri-agra-2533903-2024-05-01.

25 Indra Shekhar Singh, 'In UP, Is the BJP Pressuring Rajputs to Get Back into the Fold?', *The Wire*, 8 May 2024, https://thewire.in/politics/in-up-is-the-bjp-pressuring-rajputs-to-get-back-into-the-fold.

26 Shailvee Sharda, 'Thakurs, Other Upper Castes Remained Loyal to BJP in Uttar Pradesh in LS Polls: Survey', *The Times of India*, 16 June 2024, https://timesofindia.indiatimes.com/city/lucknow/thakurs-and-other-upper-castes-remain-loyal-to-bjp-in-up-in-ls-polls per cent20survey/amp_articleshow/111029904.cms.

27 J. Nandkumar (ed.), *Cultural Contours of Hindu Rashtra* (Indus Scroll Press, 2023), p. xxiii.

Epilogue

1 Sunil Ambekar, *The RSS Roadmaps for the 21st Century* (Rupa Publications, 2019), p. 27.

2 J. Nandkumar (ed.), *Cultural Contours of Hindus Rashtra* (Indus Scroll Press, 2023), p. xvi.

3 Jason Stanley, *How Fascism Works: The Politics of US and Them* (Random House, 2020), p. 5.

4 Stanley, *How Fascism Works*, p. 21.

5 Sunil Ambekar, *The RSS Roadmaps for the 21st Century*, p. 85.

6 Nandkumar (ed.), *Cultural Contours of Hindus Rashtra*, p. 90.

7 Nandkumar (ed.), *Cultural Contours of Hindus Rashtra*, p. 167.

8 Nandkumar (ed.), *Cultural Contours of Hindus Rashtra*, p. ix.

9 Dr Shamsul Islam, *Golwalkar's We or Our Nationhood Defined: A Critique* (Pharos Media, 2015). p. 183.

10 Nandkumar (ed.), *Cultural Contours of Hindus Rashtra*, pp. 85–6.

11 Ambedkar, *The RSS Roadmaps*, p. 76.

12 Sunil Ambedkar, *The RSS Roadmaps*, p. 76.

13 Nandkumar (ed.), *Cultural Contours of Hindus Rashtra*, p. 25.

14 Nandkumar (ed.), *Cultural Contours of Hindus Rashtra*, p. 27.

15 Nandkumar (ed.), *Cultural Contours of Hindus Rashtra*, p. 28.

16 Dr B.R. Ambedkar, *Pakistan or the Partition of India* (Infinite Words, Saket Prakashan, 2024), p. 415.

17 M.K. Gandhi, *Hindu Dharma* (Orient Paperbacks, 1991), pp. 53–4.

18 Gandhi, *Hindu Dharma*, p. 42.

19 Ambedkar, *Pakistan or the Partition of India*, p. 269.
20 Ambedkar, *Pakistan or the Partition of India*, p. 270.
21 Gandhi, *Hindu Dharma*, p. 50.
22 Gandhi, *Hindu Dharma*, p. 15.
23 Dhirendra K. Jha, *Golwalkar: The Myth Behind the Man and Man Behind the Machine* (Simon & Schuster, 2024), p. 303.
24 Jha, *Golwalkar*, p. 242.
25 S. Irfan Habib (ed.), *Bhartiya Rashtravad: Ek Anivarya Path* (Rajkamal, 2023), p. 207.
26 Habib (ed.), *Bhartiya Rashtravad*, p. 209.
27 Jha, *Golwalkar*, p. 206.
28 Smriti Kak Ramachandran, 'No Hindu Rashtra Without Muslims, Hindutva Based on Unity In Diversity: Mohan Bhagwat', *Hindustan Times*, 18 September 2018, https://www.hindustantimes.com/india-news/no-hindu-rashtra-without-muslims-hindutva-based-on-unity-in-diversity-mohan-bhagwat/story-DRFWYkKTNfSVyDPQMVFV1I_amp.html.
29 Special Correspondent, 'All Indians Share the Same DNA, Cannot Be Differentiated on Basis of Worship, Says RSS Chief', *The Hindu*, 4 July 2021, https://www.thehindu.com/news/national/all-indians-share-the-same-dna-cannot-be-differentiated-on-basis-of-worship-says-rss-chief/article35136818.ece.
30 Poulomi Saha and Yogesh Pandey, 'Why Look for "Shivling" in Every Mosque, Asks RSS Chief Mohan Bhagwat', *India Today*, 3 June 2022, https://www.indiatoday.in/india/story/shivling-in-mosque-rss-chief-mohan-bhagwat-1957718-2022-06-02.
31 Outlook Web Desk, '"Dalits Are Treated Worse Than Animals, Dogs, Snakes", *Outlook*, 5 February 2022, https://www.outlookindia.com/society/dalits-are-treated-worse-than-animals-dogs-snakes-news-217916.
32 Online Desk, "'Shed Arrogance, Practise Modesty': What Was the RSS Chief Aiming at with His Address?," *The New Indian Express*, 11 June 2024, https://www.newindianexpress.com/web-only/2024/Jun/11/shed-arrogance-practise-modesty-what-was-the-rss-chief-aiming-at-with-his-address.
33 J.P. Yadav, 'One Should Not Claim Himself to Be God, Let People Decide: RSS Chief Mohan Bhagat Ire at PM Modi', *The Telegraph Online*, 7 September 2024, https://www.telegraphindia.com/india/rss-chief-mohan-bhagat-ire-at-pm-modi-one-should-not-claim-himself-to-be-god-let-people-decide/cid/2046347.

Acknowledgements

LONG BACK, GEORGE ORWELL WROTE, 'ALL WRITERS ARE VAIN, selfish, and lazy, and at the very bottom of their motives, there lies a mystery. Writing a book is a horrible, exhausting struggle, like a long bout of some painful illness. One would never undertake such thing if one were not driven on by some demon whom one can neither resist nor understand.'

Yes, I was driven by a demon, but I was never vain or selfish. The idea of writing this book was an endeavour to understand the changing fabric of India's political landscape; it was a desire to catch the undercurrent that dented the phenomenon called Modi, driven and propelled by the idea called Hindutva, which had desired to change the basic texture of the country, create a Hindu Rashtra. It was an unfathomable mystery how Bharatiya Janata Party could lose a state where Ram Mandir had been consecrated with so much fanfare and pomp. It was a mystery to me why BJP lost a state that had two iconic figures driving the engine of Hindutva in their own ways; one was Modi, the other was Yogi Adityanath. It was a mystery to me why Uttar Pradesh did not respond positively to BJP despite being the abode of Ram Mandir, Kashi Vishwanath and Mathura Krishna Janmabhoomi, for whose liberation the party had been fighting. Demon did indeed catch me, and the result is this book, which traces the history of the 2024 parliamentary elections with a special focus on UP.

This book is an attempt to understand the Hindutva movement and its connect with the people. It is an attempt to understand why the Ram Mandir's consecration, the cult of Modi and the organisational election machine of BJP and Rashtriya Swayamsevak Sangh failed to get a majority mark in the lower house of the Parliament despite tall claims of winning more than 400 seats. This is also an attempt to understand the limits of the march of Hindutva and RSS's civilisational project of Hindu unity.

This book does not chronicle events. It tries to understand events. It dives into RSS's ideology, tries to connect it with the present and draws a picture of the future. Like my earlier book *Hindu Rashtra*, this further explores the ideological basis of the Modi government and BJP's expansion across the country.

I agree with Orwell that writing a book is an exhausting struggle, and it would not have been possible without the active support of my friends, family members and well-wishers. I am deeply indebted to Karthika V.K. and her brilliant team for creating this book, for their meticulous editing, and for making the prose more readable and beautiful. Thank you, Karthika, Sonia Madan, Abhirami Lal and the team at Westland.

I am extremely thankful to my digital channel, *Satya Hindi*, and its team of brilliant journalists for keeping me updated on developments during elections. Sheetal P. Singh and Dr Ravikant (Lucknow University), who strongly defended their views that BJP would lose in UP, should be complimented. They were probably the only ones who said publicly that BJP would not get more than 35 seats in UP. This was when the whole BJP ecosystem was overwhelmingly betting that BJP would get more than 70 seats like it did in 2014. Dr Laxman Yadav and Sheeba Aslam Fahmi explained to me, through their writings, the mood of Muslim and OBC voters in UP. Senior journalists Brajesh Shukla, Sharat Pradhan, Vinod Agnihotri and Sangeet Ragi were more than gracious in offering their expert comments on the political developments in UP, which immensely helped my understanding.

I am equally indebted to dozens of journalists who were in the field and were reporting for their channels and publications, with whom I chatted for hours to get a feel of the people's mood. It is not possible to write the names of all of them, but I owe them all my gratitude.

Professor Ashutosh Varshney took pains to read my introductory chapter and gave some valuable suggestions. In fact, once he okayed the draft of my first chapter, I was relieved and felt that I was on the right track. A big thanks to him.

I would not like to embarrass Maneesha, my friend and life partner, who is always my first editor and always comes up with good suggestions that help me fine-tune my thought process by saying thanks. Aman, Soumya, Suveesha, Chacha, Chachi, Amma, Babu and Purnima for always being there like pillars of strength. Last but not least, I want to mention Mogu, Tutu and Billo for their unconditional love. Mogu, I will miss you for the rest of my life. Thanks for being a part of our lives for eighteen and a half years.